Multicul
Competencies:

A Guidebook of Practices

Edited by

Gargi Roysircar
Daya Singh Sandhu
Victor E. Bibbins, Sr.

Multicultural Competencies:

A Guidebook of Practices

10 9 8 7 6 5 4 3 2 1

Association for Multicultural Counseling and Development
5999 Stevenson Avenue
Alexandria, VA 22304

Director of Publications • Carolyn C. Baker

Production Manager • Bonny E. Gaston

Copy Editor • Lucy Blanton
Cover Art • Cheryl Wilczak
Cover design • Martha Woolsey

Library of Congress Cataloging-in-Publication Data

Multicultural competencies : a guidebook of practices / edited by Gargi Roysircar, Daya Singh Sandhu, Victor E. Bibbins, Sr.
  p. cm.
Includes bibliographical references and index.
  ISBN 1-55620-198-2
  1. Cross-cultural counseling. I. Roysircar, Gargi, II. Sandhu, Daya Singh, 1943– III. Bibbins, Victor E.

BF637.C6 M836 2003
158'.3—dc21

2002151998

Dedication

This book is dedicated to all who devoted themselves selflessly and courageously, and continue to do so, in the search, rescue, recovery, counseling, outreach, volunteer, defense, research, and creative efforts as related to the aftermath of September 11, 2001.

Table of Contents

Foreword   *Jane Goodman*   *ix*
Prologue   *Victor E. Bibbins, Sr.*   *xv*
Acknowledgments   *xix*
About the Editors   *xxi*
About the Authors   *xxiii*

Part One
Counselor Multicultural Training

Chapter 1   Experiential Training in Multicultural
             Counseling: Implementation and
             Evaluation of Counselor Process   *3*
             Gargi Roysircar, together with
             David R. Webster, Juliann Germer,
             Jodi J. Palensky, Erica Lynne, Genelle
             R. Campbell, Yongwei Yang, Jie Liu,
             and Jason Blodgett-McDeavitt

Chapter 2   Multicultural Competency Intervent-
             ions for Building Positive Racial
             Identity in White Counselor Trainees   *17*
             Daya Singh Sandhu and Eugenie
             Joan Looby

Chapter 3   "Walking the Talk": Simulations in
             Multicultural Training   *29*
             Paul B. Pedersen

Chapter 4   Engaging Students in the Quest for
             Competence in Multiculturalism:
             An Expanded View of Mentoring   *39*
             Azara L. Santiago-Rivera and
             Marcia Moody

Table of Contents

Chapter 5   Cultural Considerations in Counselor
Training and Supervision   *51*
Marie Faubert and Don C. Locke

Part Two
Multicultural Interventions

Chapter 6   Women of Color and Substance Abuse:
A Counseling Model for an African
American Woman Client   *67*
*Octavia Madison-Colmore and
James L. Moore III*

Chapter 7   Multicultural Issues in Assessment:
Assessment Procedures With a Latina   *81*
Robert M. Davison Avilés

Chapter 8   The Power of Context: Counseling
South Asians Within a Family Context   *97*
Arpana G. Inman and Nita Tewari

Chapter 9   Deconstructing Black Gay Shame:
A Multicultural Perspective on the
Quest for a Healthy Ethnic and
Sexual Identity   *109*
Ron McLean

Chapter 10   Use of Narratives, Metaphor, and
Relationship in the Assessment and
Treatment of a Sexually Reactive
Native American Youth   *119*
Lisa L. Frey

Chapter 11   Multiculturalism and Immigrants   *129*
Jane Uchison

Part Three
Multicultural Practices Applied to Theory and Setting

Chapter 12   Multicultural Competencies and
              Group Work: A Collectivistic View   *141*
              Tarrell Awe Agabe Portman

Chapter 13   Culture-Centered Counseling From an
              Existential Perspective: What Does It
              Look Like and How Does It Work for
              an African American Woman Client?   *149*
              *Marcheta P. Evans and
              Albert A. Valadez*

Chapter 14   Including Spirituality in Multicultural
              Counseling: Overcoming Counselor
              Resistance   *161*
              Kathy M. Evans

Chapter 15   Applying Multicultural Competencies
              in the School Setting: Sexual Identity
              of an African American Adolescent   *173*
              Canary C. Hogan

Chapter 16   Culturally Diverse Clients in
              Employment Counseling: What Do
              Multiculturally Competent Counselors
              Need to Know to Be Effective?   *185*
              S. Craig Rooney and William M. Liu

Chapter 17   Multiculturalism in Cyberspace:
              Hypertext Hyperbole or a Bridge
              Between People?   *193*
              Michael D. Hawkins

Table of Contents

Part Four
Multicultural Organizational Development

Chapter 18   Against the Odds: Successfully
              Implementing Multicultural Counseling
              Competencies in a Counseling Center
              on a Predominantly White Campus   205
              *Mary A. Fukuyama and Edward A.
              Delgado-Romero*

Chapter 19   Transforming College Campuses:
              Implications of the Multicultural
              Competencies Guidelines   217
              *Kwong-Liem Karl Kwan and
              Deborah J. Taub*

Chapter 20   Applying Multicultural Competencies
              in Predominantly White Institutions of
              Higher Education   229
              Patricia Arredondo

Chapter 21   Multicultural Practices in Historically
              Black Institutions: The Case of Lincoln
              University   243
              Queen Dunlap Fowler

Chapter 22   Multiculturalism in the Military   255
              Jim Henderson

Afterword   The Competent Practice of
              Multicultural Counseling:
              Making It Happen   261
              Judy Lewis

Index   269

Foreword

I am particularly pleased to have the opportunity of writing the foreword to *Multicultural Competencies: A Guidebook of Practices (MCC Guidebook)* in the year of my presidency of the American Counseling Association (ACA) and ACA's 50th anniversary. My theme as 2001–2002 ACA president is "Unity Through Diversity." With this theme we have looked at ACA's diversity both organizationally and multiculturally. We have celebrated the multiplicity of structures that make up ACA and have celebrated the different views and perspectives represented by our members. This focus on diversity enables us to work toward ACA's mission, which is to enhance the quality of life in society by promoting the development of professional counselors, advancing the counseling profession, and using the profession and practice of counseling to promote respect for human dignity and diversity.

Delivery of effective multicultural counseling depends on many factors, such as self-awareness and understanding of the differences among people derived from their cultural history, personal cultural background, and current societal milieu. As is pointed out in chapter 1 by Roysircar, one of the editors of this book, and her colleagues, multicultural competency depends on the reflective process of cultural awareness and developing relationship-alliance skills through supervised work with linguistic minorities. This type of skill development requires changing negative counselor thoughts about the challenges of working with ethnically diverse adolescent school clients. As Roysircar says in discussing background and training in counseling courses, "I have come to understand that my trainees might additionally need training in a self-reflexive process of listening to and learning from the real stories of culturally different individuals. Multiculturalism recognizes the complexity of human stories, with multiple identifications and contexts, which makes one process and gain awareness into the relative nature of 'what makes sense,' as it relates to the differing stories and perspectives of counselor and client. Thus the crucial task set before the trainee is to understand the client's story and then affirm its meaning."

Good multicultural counselors have a strong commitment to and understanding of multicultural competencies and take advantage of opportunities to expand their knowledge base through intensive training and through reading books such as the *MCC Guidebook*. Many of its chapters suggest ways of both delivering and acquiring such knowledge. In the prologue, Bibbins, the second editor, traces the historical leadership of the Association of Multicultural Counseling and Development (AMCD) in the multicultural counseling competency movement, which has included the development of two previous AMCD documents (Arredondo et al., 1996; Sue, Arredondo, & McDavis, 1992) and now this one. Bibbins distinguishes multicultural counseling from diversity counseling, and also envisions collaborative exchanges between multiculturalism and related disciplines and other specializations across our counseling and development profession.

This book includes chapters by 43 members of AMCD that describe how they have successfully utilized multicultural perspectives and/or methods within their respective counseling specialties. Each delineates successful multicultural competencies, methods, tasks, or techniques. In chapter 2, Sandhu, the third editor, and Looby, his coauthor, argue, through a literature review, that the stronger the degree of counselor trainee White racial identity and racial self-awareness, the greater the trainee's multicultural competency. They present interventions based on the multicultural competencies, which trainees apply to their racial and ethnic contexts in order to work on personal biases and gain knowledge. Sandhu and Looby's training applications are based on select competencies from Domain 1: Counselor Awareness of Own Cultural Values and Biases (Arredondo et al., 1996), thus operationalizing the competencies as training interventions while also addressing process and outcome of interventions. Pedersen, in chapter 3, presents a simulation training model that increases the likelihood of multicultural training leading to behavior change. He also reminds us that "complexity is your friend" and that "attempts to find simple answers to complex questions are likely to fail and are dangerous."

In chapter 4, Santiago-Rivera and Moody describe a mentoring approach involving small group discussions, research teams, and cross-campus multicultural meetings for a cross-section of counseling psychology and counselor education students to provide "learning opportunities that extend beyond the traditional classroom environment." In chapter 5, Faubert and Locke concentrate specifically on multicultural considerations in the teaching and supervision of counseling students. They describe Paulo Freire's liberation or empowerment model of reciprocal pedagogy in which "all are teachers and all are learners."

Other chapters are designed to help practitioners better serve a diverse clientele. Madison-Colmore and Moore in chapter 6 describe a model for counselors working with African American women who abuse substances. They refer to the H.E.R.S. model, a humane and credible way of reaching the difficult substance abuse client population that includes addressing the client's history, empowerment, rapport, and spirituality. Avilés in chapter 7 illuminates specific multicultural aspects of assessment, integrating systematic assessment procedures (a model developed by Ridley, Hill, & Li, 1998, and Ridley, Li, & Hill, 1998) and the counselor–client contextual dyadic process in assessment (previously put forth by Roysircar-Sodowsky & Kuo, 2001) with a sensitive case study of a bilingual Puerto Rican client. He provides 12 recommendations for counselors, including seeking alternative explanations for assessment results, involving the client in the assessment process by seeking client feedback, and making a habit of thinking deliberately. He urges us to learn about as many cultures as possible, outside of what we may pick up in our communications with our clients. He points out that "the face of the future is colored with a multicultural palette; you may as well learn to paint."

In chapter 8, Inman and Tewari provide a family-systems analysis for understanding South Asian and U.S. South Asian families, focusing particularly on their ways of selective acculturation. While cautioning that there is great diversity within the South Asian population, Inman and Tewari highlight a number of common cultural factors and describe several areas in which these differ from the practices of the dominant culture. They describe culture-specific family-related interventions for a young depressed woman who still lives at home, has many differences from her traditional mother, and faces the possibility of a marriage arranged by her father with an unknown man in India. McLean in chapter 9 discusses the shame faced by Black gay men who experience several minority statuses because they are marginalized by racism, heterosexism, and their own ethnic group. He describes a process of deconstructing shame that includes Africentric spiritual values, social advocacy, a uniquely trusting relationship fostered by the counselor, and coalition-building with allies for larger humanitarian causes and policy change. Like McLean, Frey in chapter 10 presents child sexual abuse work from a cultural-relationship perspective. She says that although reading and educating herself "about Native American culture, their lives in reservations versus urban areas, and disenfranchisement and traumatization" is for her "an important part of being multiculturally competent in the relationship," she feels that it is equally important to be open to each client's "subjective cultural experience" and also "to acknowledge that talking about our differences [is] not only acceptable but essential."

Jane Uchison, in chapter 11, presents a case conceptualization of an ethnic European immigrant based on an interactional learning project that she completed in her doctoral diversity course under the supervision of Gargi Roysircar, one of the editors of this book. Uchison utilizes the multicultural counseling competencies framework to analyze her interviewing interventions; integrates this with an acculturation theoretical model that she uses as a qualitative tool to assess the issues of the immigrant woman; and provides a good learning model on how to integrate theory with practice.

Another group of chapters addresses counseling modalities or perspectives. In chapter 12, Portman describes an American Indian approach to group work that she says has been a part of Indian culture for many years, an approach that "permeates our lives, thoughts, and healing practices" and that includes her own present time orientation— the here and now of group work—and the concepts of harmony and balance. In chapter 13, Evans and Valadez make a compelling case for the use of an existential approach in multicultural counseling, in that this approach allows the counselor to focus on human issues such as death, love, and loss that transcend culture. Yet the African American woman client discussed in the chapter seeks an African American female counselor and speaks extensively, within a counseling relationship that facilitates cultural self-enhancement and self-worth, about her extended family and duties to her aging mother, which entailed relocation and a career change on the client's part. Evans and Valadez remind us that counseling thus "must not be a process of making the client fit the theory" but of the counselor molding "the theory to meet the needs of the individual client." In chapter 14 Kathy Evans exhorts us to add an understanding of spiritual identity development to our counseling repertoire, encouraging us particularly to explore clients' religious and spiritual backgrounds in the context of their culture.

Yet another group of chapters is setting-specific. Through an extensive case study in chapter 15, Hogan illustrates the role of a professional school counselor in helping a seventh grade African American youth who presents transgender identity behaviors. Her recommendations for increasing diversity support in the schools include systemwide policies, parent education, counselor self-education, and advocacy. In chapter 16, Rooney and Liu address multicultural considerations in the employment setting and focus on the practicalities of resume writing, interviewing skills, and "cultural presentations to potential employers." This last includes helping clients prepare how or how not to demonstrate or discuss their distinct cultures, such as their Latina ethnicity interface with a lesbian orientation, as well as how to research or inquire about the heterogeneity of a potential workplace. In chapter 17, Hawkins discusses the special setting of cyberspace, suggesting that the Internet is in itself a cultural setting wherein individuals can create themselves online, changing any aspect of their culture or identity they choose. This can create a community in which people "share values, attitudes, and beliefs with others they've never seen," or it can provide an opportunity for "false, predatory identities." Several chapters are devoted to the college/university environment. These include both implementing the competencies in the environment as a whole and using the competencies in counselor education. In chapter 18, Fukuyama and Delgado-Romero describe the process of infusing multicultural counseling competencies in the university counseling center of a predominantly White university with a politically conservative student body that is unfriendly toward affirmative action and equally unsympathetic to a substantial Latino student body. In chapter 19, Kwan and Taub focus on the competencies needed by both individuals, including faculty members, and the organization in order to transform college campuses, and call on student life professionals to lead the way. In chapter 20, Arredondo describes a consultation model for working with colleges and universities that points to the "necessity of a systemic approach to plan and implement organizational change driven by diversity considerations."

In chapter 21, Fowler describes the unique mission of Lincoln University, a historically Black college and university (HBCU) in Missouri, which has had the opportunity to be a higher education center in which multicultural issues can be brought to the forefront. Predominantly White institutions can learn from Lincoln University and other HBCUs how to bring a large group of diverse students together in a place where their needs are recognized and provide an education that pays attention to diverse backgrounds and contributions of culture.

In chapter 22 Henderson addresses a variety of multicultural issues in the military and provides a history of laws and administrative rulings as well as a reality check concerning their implementation. For example, the "don't ask, don't tell" policy regarding homosexuality has resulted in an 80% increase in discharges for gay and lesbian service men and women. He reminds us that although racial and ethnic diversity can be required by law in the military, people revert to their accustomed ways of segregation once they separate from the military.

It is my belief that readers will become more multiculturally competent counselors after reading *Multicultural Competencies: A Guidebook of Practices.*

Jane Goodman, PhD
President 2001–2002
American Counseling Association

References

Arredondo, P., Toporek, R., Brown, S. P., Jones, J., Locke, D. C., Sanchez, J., & Stadler, H. (1996). Operationalization of the multicultural counseling competencies. *Journal of Multicultural Counseling and Development, 24*, 42-78.

Ridley, C. R., Hill, C. L., & Li, L. C. (1998). Revisiting and refining the multicultural assessment procedure. *The Counseling Psychologist, 26*, 939-947.

Ridley, C. L., Li, L. C., & Hill, C. L. (1998). Multicultural assessment: Reexamination, reconceptualization, and practical application. *The Counseling Psychologist, 26*, 827-910.

Roysircar-Sodowsky, G., & Kuo, P. Y. (2001). Determining cultural validity of personality assessment. In D. B. Pope & H. L. K. Coleman (Eds.), *The intersection of class and gender in multicultural counseling* (pp. 213-239). Thousand Oaks, CA: Sage.

Sue, D. W., Arredondo, P., & McDavis, R. J. (1992). Multicultural counseling competencies and standards: A call to the profession. *Journal of Multicultural Counseling & Development, 20*, 477-486.

Prologue

Multicultural counseling emerged from a variety of content areas within disciplines of behavioral and social sciences. Precepts such as race relations, bias awareness, prejudice reduction, cultural value assumptions, acculturation, and intercultural and cross-cultural communication have shaped many of the principles of multicultural counseling competencies. Many theoreticians intimate that concepts such as race relations and ethnic cultural issues have their own disciplinary boundaries. However, in the actual practice of multiculturalism, there seems to be no substantial evidence for making the case that concepts like these are mutually exclusive. In fact, few deny that it has been works pertaining to race and ethnicity, and their cultural ramifications, that have fueled the proliferation of the counseling principles classified as multicultural competencies (MCC).

Although there is a growing body of research based on theoretical assumptions and ethical precepts explaining MCC, data have not documented how MCC have been successfully applied within the various specialties of professional counseling. This book, *Multicultural Competencies: A Guidebook of Practices (MCC Guidebook)*, discusses effective practices of what has been deemed the fourth force in counseling: multicultural counseling. The *MCC Guidebook* emphasizes issues of race, ethnicity, and culture, and presents qualitative self-reports of trainers, educators, counselors, outreach service providers, social justice advocates, and organizational change agents that illustrate successful and widespread utilization of MCC principles in various counseling specialties.

The idea for the development of the *MCC Guidebook* emanated from concerns arising from the current use of the term *multicultural counseling*. The applications of multicultural counseling often interface with the highly related issues of diversity counseling. Although diversity concerns and multiculturalism may often be similar and sometimes share competency principles, there is a primary distinction between the two. Notwithstanding, this distinction does not imply that multicultural issues in counseling are more or less important than the related issues of diversity, but it does mean that the integrity of multicultural counseling is predicated on, and is saliently recognizable by, the visibility of race, ethnicity, and their respective implications for racial and cultural dynamics. The philosophical positions of both W. E. B. Dubois and Cornel West are that race in our society holds preeminent importance in societal, cultural, and social realities (West, 1994). Thus the concerns for racial, ethnic, and cultural interactions that arise from such a societal context are predominant factors within multicultural counseling. Furthermore, these factors also influence greatly our profession's multicultural counseling competencies.

A succinct discernment of multicultural counseling reveals that it has its own extensive diversity. Individuals and populations of different racial and ethnic backgrounds are not only required to interface with culture, class, religion, spirituality, and ability status, as well as issues of the elderly, gender, and sexual orientation in the general course of living, but these individuals and populations must also address the complex diversity within their own race and ethnicity. Moreover, fundamental competencies for delivering effective multicultural counseling, including collaborative exchanges with related disciplines and the integration of related cross-cultural concepts, are tied to and begin with the awareness, knowledge, and skills of a counselor with regard to his or her own race, ethnicity, and culture as well as the worldviews of the clients he or she serves.

With a national movement in the counseling profession embracing multicultural studies as a part of the core curriculum for accrediting counseling and applied psychology programs in higher education, a wide spectrum of counselors and psychologists have begun systematically to seek more understanding of how multicultural competencies can be applied across their specialities. Likewise, with multicultural knowledge as a requirement for licensure as a professional counselor and as a psychologist in many states, interest has expanded in both multicultural and diversity issues at various levels: for individuals and organizations, in educational and political areas, among practitioners, academicians, and publishers.

When the Association for Multicultural Counseling and Development suggested joint publication of the *MCC Guidebook* with its parent body, the American Counseling Association , it was seen as a "golden idea laced in platinum timing" given the concurrent celebration in the year 2002 of AMCD's 30th anniversary and ACA's 50th anniversary. The *MCC Guidebook* has provided ideal opportunities for diverse counseling professionals to collaborate in addressing the competencies of multiculturalism.

A central part of AMCD's mission to the counseling profession is to provide professional leadership concerning the issues of race and ethnicity and their related cultural aspects. To advance this mission, the idea of the *MCC Guidebook* was conceived in year the 2000, during my presidency of AMCD, as a way of expressing the diversity of multicultural counseling in the upcoming 21st century. The *MCC Guidebook* is an illustration of how AMCD's members have successfully implemented multicultural competencies across the length and breadth of every ACA organizational division and affiliate.

One aim of the *MCC Guidebook* is to develop a qualitative database containing many multicultural voices speaking on effective practices of multicultural counseling competencies. Another is to provide opportunities for multicultural practitioners to ascertain whether, in fact, the multicultural counseling competencies discussed by Arredondo et al. in 1996 are consistent with the actual successful practices of multiculturalism conducted across varied specialties of counseling. Yet another aim for this *MCC Guidebook* is to serve as an easily readable general resource book or common reader on multiculturalism both at graduate and undergraduate levels for counselors in training as well as for students in education and other social and behavioral sciences interested in the helping professions.

Emphasized throughout the *MCC Guidebook* are (1) issues of race and ethnicity and their cultural aspects, and (2) instructional approaches for facilitating the best practices of multicultural counseling competencies within various counseling specialties. Whether these practices occur in cyberspace, predominantly White institutions, institutions predominantly of color, the corporate sector, public schools settings, the military, the employment security venue, or a clinical or therapeutic environment, the *MCC Guidebook* provides effective and successful models. One hypothesis for research consideration is that these practices, regardless of the counseling specialty in which they are implemented, substantiate the principles delineated in Arredondo et al. (1996) as well as earlier in Sue, Arredondo, and McDavis (1992). In summation, the *MCC Guidebook* will facilitate confluence in the theory and practice of multicultural counseling competencies. Ideally, the *MCC Guidebook* will also foster enhanced levels of reaffirmation, clarification, and refinement in implementing the diversity of multicultural counseling.

Victor E. Bibbins, Sr., PhD
AMCD President 2000–2001

References

Arredondo, P., Toporek, R., Brown, S. B., Jones, J., Locke, D. C., Sanchez, J., & Stadler, H. (1996). Operationalization of the multicultural counseling competencies. *Journal of Multicultural Counseling and Development, 24,* 42–78.

Sue, D. W., Arredondo, P., & McDavis, R. J. (1992). Multicultural counseling competencies and standards: A call to the profession. *Journal of Multicultural Counseling and Development, 20,* 477–486.

West, C. (1994) *Race matters.* New York: Vintage Books.

Acknowledgments

We acknowledge our clients, students, trainees, supervisees, colleagues, consultants, professors, and pioneers in multicultural psychology, counseling, and education, whose diverse influences on us are embodied in this book.

About the Editors

Gargi Roysircar, PhD, is the founding director of Antioch New England Multicultural Center for Research and Practice (www.multiculturalcenter.org) and professor of clinical psychology at Antioch New England Graduate School, Antioch University. She does research on the interface of acculturation and ethnic identity with the mental health of immigrants and ethnic minorities; worldview differences between and within cultural groups; multicultural competencies and training in professional psychology; and multicultural assessment and instrumentation. She was awarded the 2002 Extended Research Award of the American Counseling Association for having consistently furthered and broadened the counseling profession's understanding of diversity through research. She is a fellow of the American Psychological Association (APA) in Division 17 (Counseling Psychology) and Division 45 (Society of the Psychological Study of Ethnic Minority Issues). She has served as president of the Association for Multicultural Counseling and Development, as editor of APA's *Division 17 Counseling Psychology Newsletter*, and as editorial board member of several professional journals. Dr. Roysircar has approximately 130 journal articles, book chapters, and national paper presentations. She is the author or coeditor of three books: *Multicultural Assessment in Counseling and Clinical Psychology* (1997), *Multicultural Counseling Competencies 2003: Association for Multicultural Counseling and Development*, and *Multicultural Cases: Community Interventions* (in progress). At the Antioch Multicultural Center, she integrates research with clinical services, consultation, and education. She may be reached at Department of Clinical Psychology, Antioch New England Graduate School, 40 Avon Street, Keene, NH 03431-3516, or by telephone (603-357-3122, ext. 342) or e-mail (g_roysircar-sodowsky@antiochne.edu).

Daya Singh Sandhu, EdD, is professor and chair of the Department of Educational and Counseling Psychology at the University of Louisville, Kentucky. He has coauthored and coedited several books, such as *Counseling for Prejudice Prevention and Reduction* (1997); *Empowering Women for Equity: A Counseling Approach* (1999); *Asian and Pacific Islander Americans: Issues and Concerns for Counseling and Psy-*

chotherapy (1999); *Violence in American Schools: A Practical Guide for Counselors* (2000); *Faces of Violence: Psychological Correlates, Concepts, and Intervention Strategies* (2001); *Elementary School Counseling in the New Millennium* (2001); and *Counseling Employees: A Multifaceted Approach* (2002). Dr. Sandhu has several book chapters and more than 50 articles in refereed journals. He was honored as one of the 12 pioneers in multicultural counseling, with his autobiographical account appearing in the *Handbook of Multicultural Counseling* (2001, 2nd ed.), published by Sage. Dr. Sandhu was the recipient of the President's Distinguished Faculty Award at the University of Louisville, Alumnus of the Year Award (2001) at Mississippi State University, Multicultural Teaching Award at the University of Louisville (2000), and AMCD's Multicultural Research Award (2000). In 2001, Dr. Sandhu received a Fulbright Research Award for India to conduct cross-cultural studies on depression. Dr. Sandhu served as the chair of the Research and Knowledge Committee of the American Counseling Association 2000–2002. He may be reached at 320 Education Building, College of Education and Human Development, University of Louisville, KY 40292, or by e-mail (Dssand01@louisville.edu).

Victor E. Bibbins, Sr., PhD, received his doctorate in educational psychology from the University of Michigan. He has served as a teacher and counselor in public secondary schools and in the community college system in Detroit. His management experience includes service as director of employee counseling for the police department in Washington, DC, assistant vice chancellor for student affairs at Elizabeth City State University in Elizabeth City, North Carolina, and chief executive officer of his own educational consultant enterprise, Consolidated Counseling Associates. Dr. Bibbins currently serves as the dean for student development at the Manassas campus of Northern Virginia Community College. Dr. Bibbins served the Association for Multicultural Counseling and Development as its 27th president (2000–2001). He has also served as a member of the State of Maryland's Board of Examiners of Professional Counselors.

About the Authors

Patricia Arredondo, EdD, is an associate professor at Arizona State University, and is known for her contributions in the development of multicultural counseling competencies, her dedication to Latina/Latino issues, and her leadership in promoting organizational change through a focus on diversity. Dr. Arredondo has served as president of APA's Division 45, the Society for the Psychological Study of Ethnic Minority Issues, and the Association for Multicultural Counseling and Development. A licensed psychologist, Dr. Arredondo began her professional career as a teacher and high school counselor. She has facilitated psychoeducational groups for immigrant adolescents. In 1985, she established Empowerment Workshops, Inc., in Boston, an organizational consulting firm focusing on workforce diversity initiatives. Her major publications include three books: *Successful Diversity Management Initiatives; Key Words in Multicultural Interventions—A Dictionary* (coedited); and *Counseling Latinas/os and la Familia: A Practitioner's Guide* (coauthored). She is coauthor or lead author on several major multicultural competency documents through AMCD and APA. These include *Multicultural Counseling Competencies and Standards: A Call to the Profession* (1992); *Operationalization of the Multicultural Counseling Competencies* (1996); and *Guidelines for Multicultural Proficiency in Education and Training, Research, and Practice* (2002). Dr. Arredondo is a fellow of APA's Division 45.

Robert M. Davison Avilés, PhD, is Latino and bilingual, born in Nogales, AZ, to Mexican immigrant parents. His undergraduate degree in psychology is from the University of Arizona and his master's and doctorate in counseling psychology are from Lehigh University's APA-approved program. He specializes in multicultural/diversity issues in counseling, school counseling, higher education, and minority career development. He has experience in public school counseling, counseling in university settings, and agency and private practice counseling. Dr. Avilés is associate professor and coordinator of the school counseling program in the Department of Education Leadership and Human Development at Bradley University in Illinois. He is president elect of AMCD, on the ACA Human Rights Committee, and on the editorial board of the *Journal of Measurement and Evaluation in Counseling and Development*. His research interests include Latino/a career development and multicultural issues in assessment, counselor education, and supervision.

Jason Blodgett-McDeavitt, MA, received his master's degree in counseling psychology at the University of Nebraska–Lincoln. He is a mental health practitioner in community mental health settings in Lincoln.

Genelle R. Campbell, MA, received her master's degree in counseling psychology at the University of Nebraska–Lincoln. She is taking postgraduate coursework at Harvard University in Cambridge, Massachusetts.

Edward A. Delgado-Romero, PhD, is an assistant professor in the Department of Counseling and Educational Psychology at Indiana University. He was formerly assistant clinical professor and assistant director for clinical services at the University of Florida Counseling Center. His research focuses on multiculturalism in the university setting, with an emphasis on Hispanic/Latino/a issues. He may be reached at Wright Education Building, Room 4060, 201 North Rose Avenue, Indiana University, Bloomington, IN 47405-1006, or by telephone (812–856–8300) or e-mail (edelgado@indiana.edu).

Kathy M. Evans, PhD, is an associate professor of counselor education at the University of South Carolina. She received her doctorate from Pennsylvania State University and has been a counselor educator for 13 years. Dr. Evans has over 30 publications and has made over 100 national, regional, and local presentations. She is the senior editor of a recently released book, *Synthesizing Family, Career, and Culture: A Model for Counseling in the 21st Century.* Her research, writing, and teaching focus on multicultural, career, and women's issues and counselor training.

Marcheta P. Evans, PhD, LPC, NCC, is an assistant professor in counseling in the College of Education and Human Development of the University of Texas at San Antonio. She is the counseling program coordinator and the graduate advisor of record. Her BS, MA, and PhD are from the University of Alabama, and she also has a MEd from the University of Alabama in Birmingham. Dr. Evans's research interests are in multiculturalism and diversity initiatives, gender studies, leadership, job satisfaction, and organizational commitment. She may be reached at University of Texas, San

Antonio, CEPAHE, 501 West Durango Boulevard, San Antonio, TX 78207, or by telephone (210-458-2647) or e-mail (mevans@utsa.edu).

Marie Faubert, EdD, is director of the Counselor Education Program at the University of Saint Thomas, Houston, Texas. This program, which includes professional school counseling and agency counseling, has as its foundation a Freirian model of pedagogy and as its focus multiculturalism and diversity. She may be reached at the University of Saint Thomas, 3800 Montrose Boulevard, Houston, TX 77006, or by e-mail (faubert@stthom.edu).

Queen Dunlap Fowler, PhD, is a founding member of the Association for Multicultural Counseling and Development and served as its president from 1979 to 1980. She is a past AMCD Governing Council representative with the American Counseling Association and currently serves as the treasurer of AMCD. She is a member of ACA's By-Laws Committee, and served as chairperson of the Policies and Procedures Subcommittee, 2000-2001. Dr. Fowler is an administrator in Student Support Services, St. Louis Board of Education, St. Louis, Missouri. She has served as a visiting assistant professor at Washington University, University of Missouri at St. Louis, Webster University, Southern Illinois University, and University of Northern Colorado. She may be reached at Student Support Services, St. Louis Board of Education, 5183 Raymond Avenue, St. Louis, MO 63113.

Lisa L. Frey, PhD, is an assistant professor in the counseling psychology program of the Department of Educational Psychology at the University of Oklahoma. Prior to her move to academia, Dr. Frey had a private clinical and consulting practice as a licensed mental health practitioner, marriage and family therapist, and psychiatric nurse. Her teaching and research has been greatly influenced by this clinical experience, which focused on work with youth clients experiencing issues of trauma. Her research interests include acculturation and worldview of international students and immigrants, cross-cultural counseling, trauma experiences, assessment and treatment of juvenile sexual offenders, and relationship development in women. She may be reached at University of Oklahoma, Department of Educational Psychology, 820 Van Vleet Oval, Room 321, Norman, OK 73019-2041, or by telephone (405-325-5974), FAX (405-325-6655), or e-mail (Melissa.Frey-1@ou.edu).

Mary A. Fukuyama, PhD, received her doctorate in counseling psychology from Washington State University in 1981. She has worked primarily at the University of Florida Counseling Center in Gainesville, where she has engaged in clinical practice, training, and teaching courses in career development, multicultural counseling, and spiritual issues in counseling. She recently coauthored a book with Todd Sevig titled *Integrating Spirituality Into Multicultural Counseling*, and she is interested in exploring multidimensional ways of articulating spirituality in counseling, healing, and health. She is an active member of an interdisciplinary group at the University of Florida that has established a Center for Spirituality and Health. She may be reached at 301 Peabody Hall, P.O. Box 114100, University of Florida, Gainesville, FL 32611, or by telephone (352-392-1575) or e-mail (fukuyama@counsel.ufl.edu).

Juliann Germer, MA, is a doctoral candidate in counseling psychology at the University of Northern Colorado. She received her master's degree at the University of Nebraska–Lincoln. She is interested in the teaching and training of multicultural counseling, the concerns of biracial individuals, and in cross-cultural investigations on the eating attitudes and behaviors of girls and women. She is a Korean American.

Jane Goodman, PhD, is an associate professor of counseling and director of the Adult Career Counseling Center at Oakland University. Previously, she was a counselor educator at Eastern Michigan University and prior to that provided career counseling and organizational consulting at the Consortium Center at Oakland University. She received her bachelor's degree in sociology from the University of Chicago, and her doctoral and master's degrees in counseling from Wayne State University. She has been active in professional associations for over 25 years and was the 2001–2002 president of the American Counseling Association. Her published works include the *Career Development Casebook, Counseling Adults in Transition* (2nd ed), *Empowering Older Adults: Practical Strategies for Counselors*, several guides, monographs, book chapters, and many journal articles, primarily in the arena of career development.

Michael D. Hawkins is a graduate student in the counseling program at the University of Texas at San Antonio (UTSA). He holds a BA in business administration from UTSA and is the director of public affairs for the Air Force Center for Environmental Excellence, where he specializes in risk communications and stakeholder involvement strategies. He may be reached by telephone (210-536-3072) or e-mail (mike.hawkins@brooks.af.mil).

Jim Henderson is the head of Education Support, Assessment, and Training with Defense Activity for Non-Traditional Education Support (DANTES). He is a National Certified Counselor and has worked primarily in supervisory counseling settings in the federal government where he has directed professional academic counselors in their training endeavors. In his present position, he contracts through various companies to provide academic counselors the necessary counseling tools, such as the Myers–Briggs Type Indicator, KUDER, STRONG, and Self-Directed Search instruments. He has authored the *Strategic Air Command Counselors Guide* and the *Education Services Officers Guide*. He has served on the ACA International Collaboration Committee and also as the Military Educators and Counselors Midwest Regional Chair; and he is past president of the Association for Counselors and Educators in Government. He is presently serving as a trustee on the ACA Foundation Board. He may be reached at DANTES, 6490 Saufley Field Road, Pensacola, FL 32509, or by telephone (850-452-1884) or e-mail (jhenders@voled.doded.mil).

Canary C. Hogan, EdD, is a professional school counselor at Ewing Park Middle School, Metropolitan Nashville–Davidson County Public Schools, Nashville, Tennessee. She may be contacted by telephone (615-876-5117) or e-mail (canaryhoga@aol.com).

Arpana G. Inman, PhD, received her doctorate in counseling psychology from Temple University and is an assistant professor in the counseling psychology program at Lehigh University. Her research interests are in multicultural issues and Asian American concerns. These interests span several topics, including acculturation, biculturalism, South Asian immigrant and second generation cultural experiences, ethnic and racial identities, the psychology of women, and supervision and training. She is very involved with South Asian concerns at the community level and has presented nationally at several conferences and published in these different areas. She may be reached at Department of Education and Human Services, Counseling Psychology Program, Lehigh University, 111 Research Drive, Bethlehem, PA 18015, or by e-mail (agi2@lehigh.edu).

Kwong-Liem Karl Kwan is an associate professor in the Department of Educational Studies at Purdue University. His research focuses on the effects of perceived racial salience on cross-cultural relations, racial and ethnic identity development, and applicability of the MMPI-2 with Asians in the United States. He has served as a guest editor for the *Journal of Mental Health Counseling* issue on "Models of Racial and Ethnic Identity Development: Implications for Mental Health Counseling" (2001, 23[3]). He is an editorial board member of *The Counseling Psychologist* and *Asian Journal of Counselling*.

Judy Lewis, PhD, served as the 2000–2001 president of the American Counseling Association and is a former president of the International Association of Marriage and Family Counselors. She is currently the communications officer of Counselors for Social Justice. Lewis has published books on adolescent, family, community, substance abuse, employee assistance, health, and women's counseling. She has written and presented extensively on social justice, empowerment, and multiculturalism, which is well represented in *Advocacy in Counseling: Counselor, Clients, and Community* (2000), which she coedited with Lorretta Bradley, and in "From Multiculturalism to Social Action," a chapter coauthored with M. S. Arnold in *Social Action. A Mandate for Counselors* (1998). Lewis' community service focuses on consultation and training for community groups and agencies, with emphasis on antioppression initiatives and innovative helping strategies. She began her 30 years of experience in the field as a school counselor. She is currently a professor and program director at Governors State University in University Park, Illinois.

Jie Liu, MA, came from mainland China for graduate studies in the United States and obtained a master's degree in counseling psychology at the University of Nebraska–Lincoln. Subsequently, she became a computer programmer.

William M. Liu, PhD, is an assistant professor in counseling psychology at the University of Iowa. He received his doctorate in counseling psychology from the University of Maryland. His research interests are in multicultural competency, men and masculinity, social class, and classism. He may be reached at N328 Lindquist Center, University of Iowa, Iowa City, IA 52242, or by e-mail (william-liu@uiowa.edu).

Don C. Locke, EdD, is director of the Asheville Graduate Center and professor of counselor education at North Carolina State University. He has served as president of the Association for Counselor Education and Supervision, president of Chi Sigma Iota International, and chair of the Counseling and Human Development Foundation. He is the author of *Increasing Multicultural Understanding* and coeditor of *The Handbook of Counseling*. He received the ACA Professional Development

Award in 1996. He may be reached at Asheville Graduate Center, CPO#2140, UNCA, Asheville, NC 28804, or by e-mail (dlocke@unca.edu).

Eugenie Joan Looby, PhD, is an associate professor of counselor education and assistant dean in the College of Education at Mississippi State University. Her primary research program focuses on diversity and gender issues, sexual trauma, family, violence, and eating disorders and body image perceptions among African American girls and women. She has published and conducted numerous workshops at state, regional, and national presentations on these topics. She serves on the editorial boards of *Counseling and Values* and the *Journal of Counseling & Development*.

Erica Lynne, MA, received her master's degree in counseling psychology at the University of Nebraska–Lincoln. She is a mental health practitioner in community mental health settings in Lincoln.

Octavia Madison-Colmore, EdD, is an assistant professor of counselor education at Virginia Polytechnic Institute and State University. Dr. Madison-Colmore is a Licensed Professional Counselor and Licensed Marriage and Family Therapist. She specializes in the treatment of substance abusers and working with diverse populations. She has conducted research in the fields of substance abuse and multiculturalism and has presented both research and theory-based papers on these topics at state, regional, and national conferences. Dr. Madison-Colmore was recently invited by the People's Republic of China to teach a 3-week substance abuse course at Tainan Women's College of Arts and Technology. She may be reached at Virginia Tech, Northern Virginia Center, 7054 Haycock Road, Falls Church, VA 22043, or by telephone (703–538–8483) or e-mail (omadison@vt.edu).

Ron McLean, PhD, is an assistant professor of counselor education in the Department of Counseling, Research, Special Education, and Rehabilitation at Hofstra University. He may be reached at Hofstra University, CRSR, 212 Mason Hall, Hempstead, NY 11549.

Marcia Moody, PhD, is an assistant professor in the Counseling Psychology Division at the State University of New York at Albany. Prior to assuming this position, she worked as a secondary teacher, multicultural affairs coordinator, and college counselor. Her specialties include multicultural counseling, group counseling, and working with adolescents. She is currently doing cross-cultural research in South Africa and Ghana,

West Africa. Dr. Moody may be reached at 1400 Washington Avenue, ED 220, Albany, NY 12222, or by e-mail (mmoody@uamail.albany.edu).

James L. Moore III, PhD, is an assistant professor of counselor education at Ohio State University. Prior to coming to Ohio State University, he worked as an assistant professor in the Department of Educational Psychology at the University of South Carolina for 2 years. Dr. Moore's research interests are in Black male issues, academic persistence and achievement, cross-cultural issues in school counseling, counseling student athletes, and using innovative technological advances in counselor education. He has been frequently interviewed, cited, and featured in a number of print and video publications (e.g., *Counseling Today, Brothers of the Academy: BOTA News, Black Issues in Higher Education*) for his work. He may be reached at 356 Arps Hall, Ohio State University, 1945 North High Street, Columbus, OH 43210, or by telephone (614-292-8183) or e-mail (moore.1408@osu.edu).

Jodi J. Palensky, MA, is a doctoral candidate in counseling psychology and practices health psychology in medical clinic/hospitals in Omaha, Nebraska. She has researched the coping practices of women with breast cancer.

Paul B. Pedersen, PhD, is a visiting professor in the Department of Psychology at the University of Hawaii. He has taught at the University of Minnesota, Syracuse University, University of Alabama at Birmingham, and for 6 years at universities in Taiwan, Malaysia, and Indonesia. He has authored, coauthored, or coedited 39 books, 92 articles, and 62 chapters on aspects of multicultural counseling. He is a fellow in Divisions 9 (Society for the Psychological Studies of Social Issues), 17 (Counseling Psychology), 45 (Society for the Psychological Study of Ethnic Minority Issues), and 52 (International) of the American Psychological Association.

Tarrell Awe Agahe Portman, PhD, is an assistant professor at the University of Iowa. Her research interests are in multicultural counseling issues related to American Indian women, social justice, supervision, group work, and school counseling. She may be reached at N352 Lindquist Center, University of Iowa, Iowa City, IA 52242, or by e-mail (tarrell-portman@uiowa.edu).

S. Craig Rooney, PhD, is an assistant professor in counseling psychology at the University of Missouri-Kansas City. His research interests are in multicultural psychology with a specific emphasis on lesbian, gay, and bisexual people and issues. He teaches courses in career psychology, group therapy, and ethics and contemporary issues in counseling psychology. He is currently working on grant-funded research on the school experiences and developmental issues of lesbian, gay, and bisexual youth. He may be reached at 223 Education, University of Missouri–Kansas City, Kansas City, MO 64110-2499, or by telephone (816-235-2487) or e-mail (rooneys@umkc.edu).

Azara L. Santiago-Rivera, PhD, is an associate professor, and holds academic appointments in the Department of Latin American and Caribbean Studies and the Department of Educational and Counseling Psychology at the State University of New York at Albany. Her research interests include multicultural issues in the counseling profession, bilingual therapy, and the impact of environmental contamination on ethnic communities. She has presented on these topics at major conferences and has published in such journals as *Professional Psychology: Research and Practice, Journal of Counseling & Development*, and *Journal of Community Psychology*. She has also coauthored a recent book (with Patricia Arredondo and Maritza Gallardo-Cooper) entitled *Counseling Latinos and la Familia*. She may be contacted at State University of New York at Albany, Department of Educational and Counseling Psychology, ED 220, 1400 Washington Avenue, Albany, NY 12222, or by telephone (518-442-4988) or e-mail (arivera@uamail.albany.edu).

Deborah J. Taub, PhD, is associate professor of educational studies and coordinator of the graduate program in college student personnel at Purdue University. Her MA and PhD in college student personnel are from the University of Maryland, College Park. She has a BA in English from Oberlin College. She is chair-elect of the Professional Preparation Commission of the American College Personnel Association (2000–2004) and is a member of the editorial board of the *Journal of College Student Development.*

Nita Tewari, PhD, is a staff psychologist with the UCI Counseling Center at California State University at Irvine. She received her BA from the University of California, Irvine, and her MA in psychology and her PhD in counseling psychology from Southern Illinois University at Carbondale. Dr. Tewari is currently the co-chair for the Division on Women of the Asian American Psychological Association. Her areas of interest and research are multicultural counseling and understanding the concerns of Asian and Pacific Islander Americans, with a particular emphasis on the mental health concerns of South Asian Americans. Her master's thesis was on the acculturation and self-esteem of Indian Americans, and her doctoral dissertation was on the psychological concerns and mental health of South Asian Americans presenting at a university counseling center.

Albert A. Valadez, PhD, is an assistant professor in the Department of Education and Human Development of the University of Texas at San Antonio. He received his BA from Texas A&M University, his MEd from Southwest Texas State University, and his PhD from St. Mary's University in counseling education and supervision. Dr. Valadez's clinical experiences have included working with adults, children, and couples. His research interests are in neuroscience, counseling supervision, and emotional abuse.

Jane Uchison, BA, is a second-year doctoral student in clinical psychology at Antioch New England Graduate School. She is currently working as a practicum student at the Infant Development Center in Providence, Rhode Island, which is a clinical program and research center connected to Women and Infants Hospital. Her research interests in the area of diversity include gay, lesbian, bisexual, and transgender issues. Her present passion is the exploration of psychological and neuropsychological issues in infants and young children who are victims of violence. She may be reached at Antioch New England Graduate School, Department of Clinical Psychology, 40 Avon Street, Keene, NH 03431–3516, or by e-mail (juchison@yahoo.com).

David R. Webster, PhD, received his doctorate in counseling psychology from the University of Nebraska–Lincoln. He is a child and adolescent psychologist with the Western Arkansas Counseling and Guidance Center in Fort Smith, Arkansas. He may be contacted at Western Arkansas Counseling and Guidance Center, 3111 South 70th Street, Fort Smith, AK 72917–1818.

Yongwei Yang, MA, is a full-time statistician with the Gallup Organization's headquarters in Lincoln, Nebraska. He is working on his PhD in quantitative and qualitative measurements in education in the Department of Educational Psychology at the University of Nebraska–Lincoln. He came from mainland China to do his graduate studies in the United States. He may be reached by e-mail (yongwei_yang@gallop.com).

Part One

Counselor Multicultural Training

Chapter 1

Experiential Training in Multicultural Counseling: Implementation and Evaluation of Counselor Process

Gargi Roysircar, together with David R. Webster,

Juliann Germer, Jodi J. Palensky, Erica Lynne,

Genelle R. Campbell, Yongwei Yang, Jie Liu,

and Jason Blodgett-McDeavitt

Master's and doctoral counselor trainees (N = 16) served immigrant school children enrolled in a middle school English as a Second Language (ESL) Program for the experiential training component of a multicultural counseling course. The instructor provided broad practice guidelines, as described in the chapter, with the goals that trainees develop the competencies of cultural awareness and multicultural relationship with adolescent clients. Trainees' process notes on 10 sessions regarding their interactional process with clients were qualitatively analyzed to understand how trainees operationalized their cultural awareness and relationship competencies while offering multicultural service. Themes derived were also correlated to trainees' responses to the subscales Multicultural Skills, Multicultural Awareness, Multicultural Relationship, and Multicultural Knowledge of the Multicultural Counseling Inventory (Sodowsky, Taffe, Gutkin, & Wise, 1994), a self-report multicultural competency measure. Using a mixed-method design, the instructor attempted to evaluate experiential training in a multicultural counseling course.

S ince beginning my academic career 14 years ago, I have taught a course on concerns of racially, ethnically, and culturally different people in the United States. In the course, I apply knowledge about the psychology of race, ethnicity, and culture to the interventions and assessment methods that I impart to my trainees for work with racial and ethnic minority individuals and groups (e.g., Roysircar-Sodowsky &

3

Kuo, 2001; Sodowsky, Kuo-Jackson, & Loya, 1997; Sodowsky & Taffe, 1991). For 12 years, I have taught this course in a counseling psychology program, and since my move to a new university 2 years ago, I am teaching it in a clinical psychology program. Both are doctoral programs in predominantly White universities located in middle-class college towns.

With time and experience, I have gained certain skills and expertise in the contents and process of academic multicultural training. Notwithstanding my personal progress in this area, I find the traditional curriculum of measurement, assessment, research, and individual and group supervision much easier to work with because it is emotionally less draining. Unique to the multicultural course are the personalized reactions of some counselor trainees that suggest they have racial, cultural, and worldview disagreements with the written materials of the course, which consist of standard multicultural textbooks and journal articles. These reactions may even be projected onto me, a culturally different person, along intrapersonal and dyadic lines.

Such culture-related responses can be understood as psychological defenses operating within a trainee that either deny the sociopolitical implications of color in U.S. society or indicate overreaction to cultural differences, with both defenses representing two sides of the same coin and resulting in trainee misattributions. But if counselor trainees have defensive reactions to scholarly and clinical information, and to an instructor who is well acculturated, then how much more difficult it may be for them to work with a less acculturated, foreign-born, ethnically different person who speaks nonstandard English, is much less psychologically minded than they, and thus not disposed to help-seeking attitudes.

I have come to understand that my counselor trainees may additionally need training in a self-reflexive process of listening to and learning from the real stories of culturally different individuals. Multiculturalism recognizes the complexity of human stories, with multiple identifications and contexts, which makes us process and gain awareness into the relative nature of "what makes sense" in relation to the differing stories and perspectives of counselor and client. The crucial task set before the counselor trainee is therefore to understand the client's story and then affirm its meaning. Affirming the client's belief system is, in essence, the explicit recognition and understanding of how the client makes meaning of his or her life and the events and problems he or she faces. With their goal of attaining cultural self- and other-awareness and a positive multicultural relationship, my counselor trainees participate in sustained multicultural exposure experiences that require interpersonal exchanges.

My multicultural course consists of two components: in Component I counselor trainees gain multicultural knowledge through readings, writings, presentations, and class discussions; in Component II, the experiential component, counselor trainees develop multicultural awareness, skills, and relationship competencies through a program of systematic interactions of moderate duration with a racial or ethnic minority individual. This chapter describes Component II's operationalization and execution, and one aspect of its ongoing evaluation. The evaluation data presented herein concern the relationships between two counselor trainee self-reports: trainee process notes and trainee scores on multicultural counseling competencies.

The acquisition of multicultural knowledge and skills is the desired outcome of academic multicultural training in psychology; effecting personal change in trainees with regard to their racial and cultural attitudes is an important long-range goal. Thus the experiential component's overall goal is to raise cultural self- and other-awareness and to offer training in the formation of the multicultural relationship competency.

A Framework for Developing a Helping

Relationship With an Individual in a Local Community

Research indicates that a significant contributor to multicultural competencies is experience with racial and ethnic minority people (see Sodowsky, Kuo-Jackson, Richardson, & Corey, 1998). It is ideal to get out of the classroom and into multicultural interactions so as to experience the issues of race, ethnicity, culture, class, power, and privilege as part of everyday reality. Therefore, each counselor trainee meets and talks with one minority individual for 10 meetings of approximately 50 to 60 minutes each.

Counselor trainees are informed that this project is a multicultural exchange that is not designed to be therapeutic, but rather informative and experiential for both the trainee and the minority participant. Semi-structured guidelines are provided, so that each counselor trainee asks a minority person to exchange stories about his or her life experiences and the interface of race, ethnicity, culture, and class with those experiences. As a trainee learns to become multiculturally competent, he or she is expected to respond to the narrator's stories, so as to show the extent of understanding that has been achieved through what the trainee has heard.

5

Trainee Culturally Consistent Tasks

The counselor trainees are told that these meetings are opportunities to talk with a minority person in order for each trainee to have a multicultural interaction, exercise interpersonal and verbal skills that are culturally consistent with the minority person's perspective on issues presented, learn about an individual's multicultural experiences, and demonstrate to the minority person that the trainee can be effective and beneficial through his or her communications and efforts to serve. Examples of effective and beneficial efforts include mentoring, tutoring, life skills coaching, empowering the individual to retain his or her cultural identifications, and providing guidance for immigrants about U.S. life while stressing adaptation, practicing advocacy, and affirming biculturalism.

Trainee Benefits from Application of Cultural Knowledge

Counselor trainees can expect to gain perspective from a multicultural interaction that supplements book knowledge and challenges their comfort at an affective level. Each trainee has the opportunity to hear an individual's account of living in the United States as a minority person as well as the opportunity to address multicultural dilemmas. Examples of these dilemmas may include a minority person's perceived inequalities and oppressions, a minority person's value assumptions that differ from those of the trainee, and boundaries of comfort/discomfort when a minority individual discusses a politically charged issue or a culturally unfamiliar practice or behavior.

Method

Informed Consent, Participants, and Procedures

For the experiential training component, the general procedure is that counselor trainees inform the minority individual with whom they are meeting about the purpose of this class project, the duration of contact, and the related paperwork that is required of them. Trainees verify that the minority individual is comfortable with this interaction project. Trainees provide the individual written information about the project.

For the project reported here, 16 counselor trainees offered services in a middle school located in a low-income Midwest community for one semester. The counselor trainees offered 10 individual sessions to 16 middle schools students attending an English as a Second Language program. The mentoring and life-skills coaching service was incorporated by school administrators and teachers into study hall time. Parents were informed in writing and gave permission for this service.

Mixed Method Design: Process Notes and Self-Reported Multicultural Competencies

The counselor trainees did weekly journaling (called Multicultural Interaction Notes) for all 10 meetings with their client. Following each session, they submitted to the instructor at the next scheduled class a half- to one-page process note. Within a week of submission, the instructor provided written feedback. Ten numbered and dated notes (one for each meeting) were expected.

In addition to their journaling, the counselor trainees responded to several multicultural self-report measures. For the evaluation reported in this chapter, the relationships between the themes of the 16 counselor trainees' process notes and the trainees' scores on the Multicultural Counseling Inventory (MCI—a pretest measure; Sodowsky et al., 1994) before the experiential project started were considered. Several studies have shown the MCI to have acceptable and stable internal consistency reliabilities (e.g., Constantine & Ladany, 2000; Pope-Davis & Ottavi, 1994; Pope-Davis, Reynolds, Dings, & Nielson, 1995; Sodowsky, 1996; Worthington, Mobley, Franks, & Tan, 2000) and to predict concurrently several multicultural variables of counselors (e.g., Ottavi, Pope-Davis, & Dings, 1994; Sodowsky et al., 1998).

Qualitative Analyses of Process Notes

From the existing multicultural counseling process literature (see the literature review by Roysircar & Gard, in press) and the semi-structured guidelines provided for the multicultural interactions project, the instructor derived eight topic areas that she thought might be reported by trainees in their process notes: cultural or contextual barriers, frustrations in interethnic dyads, critical incidents, usage of critical incidents, knowledge of cultural practice and its application, awareness of value biases, client–counselor similarities, and client–counselor differences. Two individuals on the instructor's research team used this general framework and did qualitative analysis on all 10 process note entries for each trainee ($N = 16$). The qualitative method used was adapted from the methods suggested by Creswell (1994) and Hill, Thompson, and Williams (1997).

Both members of the coding team independently read and marked text passages using the general themes derived by the instructor. The two-member analysis team met after their individual coding to discuss each case and reach consensus. Matrices were constructed to facilitate the comparison of coded categories across cases. From among these categories, 10 themes presented themselves as being dominant, with dominant being defined as frequencies of endorsement over 90 times. During the coding process, the theoretical themes derived from the literature were modified. In addition, new themes emerged. The instructor and other members of the research team fine-tuned the themes in a consensual manner. For each theme, trainees' core ideas were summarized. The instructor and the remaining research team joined the analyzers to consensually identify and summarize core ideas.

Results

Qualitative

The 10 themes in order of frequency were other-awareness and reflection, self-awareness and reflection, making empathic connection through mutual self-disclosure, treatment planning and implementation, analyses of value biases, intentional exchange of cultural information, barriers, frustration with barriers, preoccupation with cultural similarities/differences, and anxiety about progress. Descriptions of these themes and summaries of their core ideas are as follows.

1. *Other-awareness and reflection*—referred to times when counselor trainees were introspective about their minority individuals' ESL learning challenges, survival trauma, conflicts between family and societal expectations, and interpersonal distance. Core ideas were
   - thinking about the minority person's experiences in being in a new land;
   - recognizing the difficulties of fleeing political persecution or ethnic cleansing from country of origin;
   - gaining understanding of the minority person's family structure and roles; and
   - monitoring the minority person's ambivalence regarding interpersonal work.
2. *Self-awareness and reflection*—indicated that trainees were introspective about the effects of their intrapersonal/interpersonal dynamics on the minority individuals, as related to trainees' privileged status, racial attitudes, U.S. citizenship, cultural values, and diverse modes of identification. Core ideas were
   - awareness of own worldview, gender attitudes;

- awareness of own cultural diversity;
- awareness of importance of immigration issues as a contrast to the counselor being a U.S.-born citizen; and
- awareness of countertransference related to racial and/or ethnic dyadic interactions, such as the counselor being overly helpful, or speaking too loudly with an ESL person.

3. *Making empathic connection through mutual self-disclosure*—referred to any time that a trainee perceived that he or she and the minority individual achieved mutual closeness through facilitative self-disclosures. Core ideas were
   - sharing ethnic food, candy, family photographs;
   - sharing personal information and finding common ground (family, hobbies, social activities);
   - minority person expressing joy at seeing trainee or being excited because something clicked; and
   - counselor using encouragement and attending to strengths.

4. *Treatment planning and implementation*—referred to being prepared with specific activities and interventions for an upcoming session on the basis of events during a previous session. Core ideas were
   - using the framework of study skills (spoken and written English; practicing vocabulary);
   - providing alternate methods of learning (Web information, library books on minority person's culture of origin);
   - incorporating creative interactive activities (structured drawings, magic tricks, games, origami, cutting pictures from ethnic magazines); and
   - using nonverbal communications to explain, give directions, express thoughts/feelings.

5. *Analyses of value biases*—included trainee examination of their American worldview with regard to issues of language, family structure and functions, positive and negative stereotypes, and intellectual aspirations. Core ideas were
   - language usage and preferences;
   - family circumstances (lack of parental supervision, nontraditional family composition; extended family);
   - positive stereotypes (about Asians); negative stereotypes (surprised that immigrants celebrate American holidays); and
   - educational achievements, sophistication, psychological-mindedness.

6. *Intentional exchange of cultural information*—included making explicit cultural norms and practices of both the client and

the counselor so as to affirm the culture of the minority individual and also to educate him or her on U.S. norms and practices. Core ideas were

- counselor and client sharing information about cultural practices in their societies;
- discussing expectations of teachers, school, and neighbors;
- discussing acculturation experiences and ethnic identifications;
- talking about why minority person left home country; about conditions "back home"; and
- discussing religious or spiritual activities.

7. *Barriers*—were any situation (language difficulties, environment, inadequate background information about the minority individual, nonclinical setting) that was perceived to impinge upon the meetings. Core ideas were

- temporal barriers (limited time with minority person);
- environmental barriers (nonclinical setting, noise, distraction, sharing of space);
- lack of initial information about the minority person's culture, demographic background, goals, expectations; and
- communication pattern differences.

8. *Frustration with barriers*—were expressed by the trainees in their notes in response to perceived barriers. Core ideas were

- distress because of miscommunications, cultural mistakes;
- wishing that the language barrier would go away;
- disappointment that closure could not be achieved because of nonclinical setting; and
- being impeded by the school's organization.

9. *Preoccupation with cultural similarities/differences*—occurred when counselor trainees made overgeneralizations about how similar they and the minority individuals were, or when the trainees compared the minority individuals to American society and found them very different. Core ideas were

- client-counselor match/mismatch in ethnicity;
- socioeconomic status differences of the client;
- seeing minority person as very different, using White society as reference group; and
- making universalistic statements to minimize differences.

10. *Anxiety about progress*—indicated that the counselor trainees were worried about clients' personal, social, or academic difficulties or were not hopeful about their efficacy or their clients' future. Core ideas were

- wanting minority person to be comfortable talking about nonacademic matters;
- feeling anxious about at-risk behaviors (disruption, bullying, potential gang membership, passivity);
- concerned about detention, missed appointments; and
- being at an impasse.

Quantitative

Cronbach's alpha ($N = 16$) for the MCI pretest administration used for this evaluation report was .85 for Multicultural Counseling Skills (MC Skills, 11 items), .81 for Multicultural Awareness (MC Awareness, 10 items), .60 for Multicultural Counseling Relationship (MC Relationship, 8 items), and .85 for Multicultural Counseling Knowledge (MC Knowledge, 11 items). The subscales showed moderate significant correlations with each other (average interscale $r = .50$).

Trainees' scores on the validity measure multicultural social desirability (Cronbach's alpha .88) had low, nonsignificant correlations with the MCI subscales and full scale. Trainees' Multicultural Social Desirability score was $M = 14.10$ ($SD = 6.21$), out of a maximum of 26 points, which was within the acceptable range, according to the developers of the instrument (Sodowsky et al., 1998). A high Multicultural Social Desirability score indicates a preference to make a good impression on others by self-reporting that one always interacts well with minorities and that one is always receptive to minority issues. This is unlikely to be true.

Frequency of endorsements of the 10 themes were aggregated for each trainee and correlated with his or her pretest MCI subscales scores, MC Skills, MC Awareness, MC Relationship, and MC Knowledge. Using the median split, trainees were categorized as high MCI scorers ($n = 8$, above a full scale score of 120) and low MCI scorers ($n = 8$, below a full scale score of 110). The two groups' frequency of themes were correlated, using Pearson product–moment correlations, with their MCI subscale scores. See Table 1.1 for the correlations.

Those who were categorized as low scorers on the MCI endorsed more frequently the themes of barriers, frustrations with barriers, preoccupation with cultural similarities/differences, and anxiety about progress than those who were categorized as higher scorers. Overall, these themes had negative correlations with MCI subscale scores. Thus these themes were labeled *negative multicultural thoughts*. Those trainees who were categorized as high scorers on the MCI endorsed more frequently the themes of other-awareness and reflection, self-awareness and reflection, empathy and self-disclosure, treatment plan-

Table 1.1

Relationships of Process Notes' Dominant Themes With High and Low Levels of
Multicultural Counseling Inventory (MCI) Subscale Scores

Dominant Theme	Category for MCI		MC Skills	MC Awareness	MC Relationship	MC Knowledge
	High	Low	r	r	r	r
Positive						
1. Other-awareness and reflection	92	73	.18	.34*	.49*	.33*
2. Self-awareness and reflection	52	39	.11	.25*	.27*	.24*
3. Making empathic connection	32	23	.54*	.30*	.43*	.22
4. Treatment planning and implementation	59	53	.24*	.30*	.23*	.05
5. Analysis of value biases	16	9	.15	.27*	.35*	.15
6. Intentional exchange of cultural information	26	20	.00	.20	.22*	.34*
Negative						
7. Barriers	19	29	-.64**	-.27*	-.42*	-.45*
8. Frustration with barriers	17	21	-.23*	-.00	-.36*	-.17
9. Preoccupation with cultural similarities/differences	21	26	-.17	-.21	-.30*	.01
10. Anxiety about progress	26	34	-.71**	.09	.23*	-.10

Note. ($N = 16$). Low MCI category indicated scores below 110.00 ($n = 8$). High MCI category indicated scores above 120.00 ($n = 8$). The values in columns are averaged frequency of theme endorsements for high and low MCI scores. Negative Pearson correlations indicate that those trainees who had lower MCI scores were more frequently concerned with barriers, frustrations, extent of progress, and issues of cultural similarities/differences. However, those with higher MCI scores were more frequently concerned with cultural other-awareness and reflection, self-awareness and reflection, empathic connection, treatment planning and interventions, analysis of value biases, and intentional exchange of cultural information. Cronbach alphas for the MCI pretest administration used for this analysis were MC Skills = .85; MC Awareness = .81; MC Relationship = .60; MC Knowledge = .85.

*$p < .05$.   **$p < .01$ (two-tailed).

ning and implementation, analyses of counselor biases, and intentional exchange of cultural information. Overall, these themes had positive correlations with MCI subscale scores. Thus these themes were called *positive multicultural thoughts*. The negative multicultural thoughts showed the most number of significant negative correlations with MC Skills and MC Relationship. The positive multicultural thoughts showed the highest number of significant positive correlations with MC Relationship and MC Awareness. Thus training experience with actual minority clients involved trainees in the multicultural relationship-building competency, in addition to working on multicultural skills- and awareness-building.

Conclusion

Multicultural training in a naturalistic setting throws light on how counselor trainees' diverse forms of self-reports, such as process notes and survey measures, can be used to guide trainees into attending to the cultural stories of their interviewees and to the interactional process of multicultural counseling. Such training results in counselor cultural self- and other-awareness, with the outcome of counselor trainees expressing more connection/closeness thoughts than disconnection/distance thoughts when working with racial and ethnic minority individuals within their respective contexts (Roysircar, Gard, & Hubbell, 2002). In experiential training, knowledge from books is translated into interpersonal engagement, as the counselor trainee and the minority individual relate to each other at a personal level. However, this training modality is challenging for beginning trainees who have had minimal exposure to minority individuals and are required by such training to interact closely with one such individual for a moderate duration of time, using a cultural, ethnic, and racial framework. Additionally, taking interpersonal risks by focusing process notes on themselves and on their interactions with the minority client, which the instructor reviews, can be threatening.

Along the lines of action research, I am developing a program of action teaching in multicultural counseling. In addition, because I believe in multicultural training making strong advances in psychology, it is important to my training vision that my course has as its centerpiece a diverse, outcome-oriented evaluation component (Roysircar, Gard, Hubbell, & Ortega, 2002). In this way I can verify that my training comprises responsible curriculum in professional psychology.

References

Constantine, M. G., & Ladany, N. (2000). Self-report multicultural counseling competence scales: Their relation to social desirability attitudes and multicultural case conceptualization ability. *Journal of Counseling Psychology*, *47*, 155–164.

Creswell, J. W. (1994). *Research design: Qualitative and quantitative approaches.* Thousand Oaks, CA: Sage.

Hill, C. E., Thompson, B. J., Williams, E. N. (1997). A guide to conducting consensual qualitative research. *The Counseling Psychologist*, *25*, 517–572.

Ottavi, T. M., Pope-Davis, D. B., & Dings, J. G. (1994). Relationship between White racial identity attitudes and self-reported multicultural counseling competencies. *Journal of Counseling Psychology*, *41*, 149–154.

Pope-Davis, D. B., & Ottavi, T. M. (1994). Examining the association between self-reported multicultural counseling competencies and demographic and educational variables among counselors. *Journal of Counseling & Development*, *72*, 651–654.

Pope-Davis, D. B., Reynolds, A. L., Dings, J. G., & Nielson, D. (1995). Examining multicultural competencies of graduate students in psychology. *Professional Psychology: Research and Practice*, *26*, 322–329.

Roysircar, G., & Gard, G. (in press). Research in multicultural counseling: Impact of counselor variables on process and outcome. In C. Lee (Ed.), *Multicultural issues in counseling: New approaches to diversity* (3rd ed.). Alexandria, VA: American Counseling Association.

Roysircar, G., Gard, G., & Hubbell, R. (2002). *Counselor trainee self-reflections in process notes on multicultural services: Within and between session analyses of alliance for clients.* Manuscript submitted for publication.

Roysircar, G., Gard, G., Hubbell, R., & Ortega M. (2002). *Relationships of client evaluations, observer reports, and counselor trainee self-reports of multicultural counseling competencies.* Manuscript submitted for publication.

Roysircar-Sodowsky, G., & Kuo, P. Y. (2001). Determining cultural validity of personality assessment: Some guidelines. In D. Pope-Davis & H. Coleman (Eds.), *The intersection of race, class, & gender: Implications for multicultural counseling* (pp. 213–239). Thousand Oaks, CA: Sage.

Sodowsky, G. R. (1996). The Multicultural Counseling Inventory: Validity and applications in multicultural training. In G. R. Sodowsky & J. C. Impara (Eds.), *Multicultural assessment in counseling and clinical psychology* (pp. 283–324). Lincoln, NE: Buros Institute of Mental Measurements.

Sodowsky, G. R., Kuo-Jackson, Y. P., & Loya, G. J. (1997). Outcome of training in the philosophy of assessment. Multicultural counseling competencies. In D. Pope-Davis & H. Coleman (Eds.), *Multicultural counseling competencies: Assessment, education and training, and supervision* (pp. 3–42). Thousand Oaks, CA: Sage.

Sodowsky, G. R., Kuo-Jackson, P. Y., Richardson, M. F., & Corey, A. T. (1998). Correlates of self-reported multicultural competencies: Counselor multicultural social desirability, race, social inadequacy, locus of control racial ideology, and multicultural training. *Journal of Counseling Psychology, 45,* 256-264.

Sodowsky, G. R., & Taffe, R. C. (1991). Counselor trainees' analyses of multicultural counseling videotapes. *Journal of Multicultural Counseling and Development, 19,* 115-130.

Sodowsky, G. R., Taffe, R. C., Gutkin, T. B., & Wise, S. L. (1994). Development of the Multicultural Counseling Inventory: A self-report measure of multicultural competencies. *Journal of Counseling Psychology, 41,* 137-148.

Worthington, R. L., Mobley, M., Franks, R. P., & Tan, J.A. (2000). Multicultural counseling competencies: Verbal content, counselor attributions, and social desirability. *Journal of Counseling Psychology, 47,* 460-468.

Chapter 2

Multicultural Competency Interventions for Building Positive Racial Identity in White Counselor Trainees

Daya Singh Sandhu and Eugenie Joan Looby

This chapter discusses the relationship between White counselor trainees' racial identity development and its impact on their multicultural counseling competencies. The chapter argues that the stronger the degree of racial identity and racial self-awareness, the greater the trainees' multicultural competence. Helms' White Identity Development Model is discussed as are the multicultural competencies. Applications of specific competencies from Domain 1: Counselor Awareness of Own Cultural Values and Biases (Arredondo et al., 1996) are provided.

Most Western plural societies are becoming multicultural societies in that there is a trend to make provisions for equal economic, political, and social participation. There is new recognition and appreciation for racial and cultural identity of different racial and ethnic groups. Despite the newly recognized advocacy and acceptance of racial identities, multicultural counseling literature continues to grow rapidly with descriptions of oppressive relationships, high degrees of alienation, and learned helplessness (Sandhu, 2001; Sandhu, Portes, & McPhee, 1996).

A number of multicultural researchers have contended that to help culturally diverse clients cope, reduce, or overcome the pain of racism, it is imperative that mental health professionals address issues related to their clients' racial and cultural identities (Cross, 1995; Gurung & Mehta, 2001; Helms, 1984; Sue & Sue, 1999). Equally important is studying White counselor trainees' racial identity development. Moreover, because the number of White counselors and trainees is significantly higher than that of counselors and trainees of color, studying White racial identity development has profound implications for multicultural training and clinical outcomes. It is postulated that if counselor trainees understand the impact of their race and ethnicity on their personality and interaction styles, they will be more cognizant of the influence of these factors on their clients' behaviors, interactions, values, and attitudes (Espin, 1987).

Research on the relationship of White racial identity development with multicultural counseling competence is still in its infancy. However, some studies (Brown, Parham, & Yonker, 1996; Ottavi, Pope-Davis, & Dings, 1994; Parker, Moore, & Neimeyer, 1998; Roysircar, Gard, & Hubbell, 2002; Vinson & Neimeyer, 2000) have suggested a correlation between levels of racial identity development and multicultural counseling competency because the manipulation of one has been shown to increase the other. For example, one study (Ottavi et al., 1994) indicated that higher levels of White racial identity development were positively correlated with higher levels of multicultural counseling competency. Another study (Roysircar et al., 2002) showed that counselor trainees' self-awareness expressed in process notes regarding their connection/ alliance with racial and ethnic minority clients (with connection/ alliance thoughts increasing in later sessions out of 10 counseling sessions) predicted combined White racial Pseudo-Independence and Autonomy subscale scores that represent nonracist White attitudes. The same counselor trainees' disconnection/distance thoughts about their clients had no relationship with these positive racial attitudes; in addition, trainees' multicultural social desirability response set (i.e., faking good) scores also did not relate with positive White racial identity attitudes. Behrens (1997) acknowledged that an understanding of White racial attitudes has the potential to transform multicultural counseling service delivery through the analysis of clinical interactions, as was done by Roysircar et al. (2002).

Conceptual writings, similarly, have suggested a link between White counselor trainees' racial identity development and receptivity to training in multicultural counseling (Sabnani, Ponterotto, & Borodovsky, 1991). Helms (1995) has pointed to the importance of training counselors to be aware of how their racial cognitions, affect, and behaviors may influence the interactional process in counseling. Thus White racial identity is considered to be an integral component in the planning of multicultural counselor training (Carter & Qureshi, 1995; Richardson & Molinaro, 1996). As Steward, Boatright, Sauer, Baden, and Jackson (1998) proposed, "We believe that if we can identify factors related to White racial identity, educators will be able to design more specific training interventions resulting in counselors' increased White racial identity and stronger counseling competencies" (p. 256).

White Racial Identity Development

The concept of White racial identity development has evolved over the last 15 years, with the work by Helms (1984, 1990, 1995, 1996) providing a major impetus to research in this field. Racial identity development is a process in which racial orientation and racial identity evolve such that the individual can accept racial aspects of self, appreciate the diversity of others, and work to eliminate racial oppression (Helms, 1984). Helms posited that because most cross-racial counseling dyads involved a White counselor and a client of color, it was necessary to study White racial consciousness as well as the identity development of people of color.

Helms'White racial identity model was developed initially to explain the stage-wise development of White counselor attitudes, worldviews, and behaviors as they explore and find fulfillment in their White race and, at the same time, recognize and ameliorate the sociopolitical oppression of people of color. She later reformulated the model in relation to concurrent ego statuses, each status gaining dominance depending upon the racial stimuli (Helms, 1996). Helms has contended that all racial groups in the United States experience a racial identity development process whose contents, however, may differ because of power differentials that exist among the racial groups in the United States. The model consists of two phases: abandonment of racism and the development of a nonracist White identity (Helms, 1990). Six specific identity statuses exist within the two phases, with each being accompanied by an Information Processing Strategy (IPS; Helms, 1996). White individuals use various information-processing strategies (IPSs), as these correspond with each identity status, to cope with their anxiety and discomfort surrounding racial issues. Helms' identity statuses and their corresponding IPSs include:

1. *Contact status.* The individual believes that racism does not exist, has limited interaction with people of color, and lacks a racial identity. The IPS is obliviousness.
2. *Disintegration status.* The individual experiences guilt, confusion, and discomfort about racial injustice and oppression. The IPS is suppression and ambivalence.
3. *Reintegration status.* The individual believes in White superiority and denigrates all other racial groups. The IPS is selective perception and negative out-group distortion.
4. *Pseudo-independent status.* The individual believes in White superiority; is aware of racial inequities, but thinks resolution

19

can occur if minority groups associate with Whites. Overintellec-
tualizing is a common behavior exhibited by individuals in this
status. The IPS is reshaping reality and selective perception.
5. *Immersion-emersion status.* The individual takes personal ownership for his or her "Whiteness" and actively seeks development
of a nonracist White identity. The IPS is hypervigilance and
reshaping.
6. *Autonomy.* The individual abandons White entitlement and practices nonracist behaviors. The IPS is flexibility and complexity.

It is logical to assume that White counselor trainees enter the field
with varying degrees of racial identity and self-awareness. Awareness
of racial identity status has significant implications for understanding
issues they must confront to develop a nonracist White identity.
Further, it is naïve to assume that the exploration of racial identity should be relegated to a specific racial group. Racial identity development has similar implications for counselor trainees of color.
All counselor trainees will have to face issues that are reflected in
Helms's model as they attempt to understand their own and their
clients' racial identities.

Developing Multicultural Competencies Through
Training in Racial Identity Development

Multicultural competency is critical to the delivery of effective mental
health services to clients of color (Arredondo et al., 1996). What is meant
by multicultural competence? Its components include counselors'
awareness of their own race, ethnicity, culture, language, and power
status, and an understanding of how these components operate in
the lives of their clients; understanding the worldview of the culturally
different client; and developing culturally appropriate interventions,
strategies, and techniques (Arredondo et al., 1996; Sue, Arredondo, &
McDavis, 1992).

The Association for Multicultural Counseling and Development,
through the work of Sue et al. (1992) and Arredondo et al. (1996), has
formulated a set of multicultural counseling competencies that delin-
eate requisite culture-specific awareness, knowledge, and skills for
becoming a culturally skilled counselor. The competencies encompass
three domains: Counselor Awareness of Own Cultural Values and Biases,
Counselor Awareness of Client's Worldview, and Culturally Appropriate
Intervention Strategies. Included in each domain are three competency

areas: beliefs and attitudes, knowledge, and skills. The competency areas are further supplemented with 117 behavioral outcome statements. Arredondo and Arciniega (2001) strongly supported the use of the competencies in curriculum planning, developing individual learning outcomes, and furthering research in multicultural counseling. For a complete listing of the competencies, the reader is encouraged to consult Arredondo et al. (1996).

In addition to having counselor trainees read the specific competencies, their instructors can develop interventions based on these competencies, which the trainees can apply to their own racial and ethnic contexts in order to work on personal biases. Training applications of select competencies from Domain 1: Counselor Awareness of Own Cultural Values and Biases are provided to show their operationalization as training interventions. Suggestions are made about the process and outcome of these interventions.

Intervention 1. Who Am I Racially and Culturally?

Domain 1. Counselor Awareness of Own Cultural Values and Biases

Competency. Attitudes and Beliefs (A1).
"Culturally skilled counselors believe that cultural self-awareness and sensitivity to one's own cultural heritage is essential" (Arredondo et al., 1996, p. 51).

Explanatory Statement (A1b).
"Can identify the specific cultural group(s) from which counselor derives fundamental cultural heritage and the significant beliefs and attitudes held by those cultures that are assimilated into their own attitudes and beliefs" (Arredondo et al., 1996, p. 51).

Application/Practice Component.
Counselor trainees are asked to create self-snapshots to facilitate exploration and understanding of how their individual identities are shaped. Snapshots are presented through various media of their choice, including music, poetry, art/drawings/paintings, video clips, television characters/ shows, books, or magazines. The exercise is structured around providing answers to questions that focus on exploration of individual cultural heritage, norms, values, and attitudes about diversity. It throws light on the influence of culture on personality and racial identity formation, and on perceptions about the racial and ethnic groups of individual trainees.

21

Processing.

Trainees compile the information and present it in a group setting. The conversations that follow allow them to explore their personal, cultural, and racial socialization; to familiarize themselves with their own cultural heritage; to examine the impact of cultural influences on their beliefs, values, and behaviors; to determine how their cultural programming will enhance or deter their ability to work with cultural differences; to examine the diversity in others; and to explore what it means to be part of a specific racial group. Trainees also enjoy the opportunity to express themselves creatively and are introduced to a variety of communication styles.

Outcomes.

Trainees become better informed about their cultural heritage and what it means to be a member of their race. The results are increased understanding of self and others, and a greater appreciation and respect for differences.

Intervention 2. My Cultural Heritage's

Strengths and Weaknesses

Domain 1. Counselor Awareness of Own Cultural Values and Biases

Competency. Attitudes and Beliefs (A1).
See Intervention 1.

Explanatory Statement (A1f).
"Appreciate and articulate positive aspects of their own heritage that provide them with strengths in understanding differences" (Arredondo et al., 1996, p. 51).

Application/Practice Component.
Counselor trainees respond to questions about the meanings of their racial and ethnic identity, things they value about their ethnic/racial identity, and things they dislike about their racial and ethnic identity. They ask themselves what their life would be like as a member of a racial and ethnic group different from their own (trainees choose the racial and ethnic group).

Processing.
Trainees dialogue with each other to glean information on important values in their own as well as other racial and ethnic groups. By identify-

22

ing positive and negative aspects of their cultural heritage, trainees realize that no cultural or racial group is superior to another, and that there are things to like and dislike about one's culture or racial group. Although choosing to be a member of a different racial or ethnic group allows trainees to step into others' lives for a day, most report being comfortable with their racial and ethnic identity while gaining an increased awareness and sensitivity to similarities and differences between self and others. Trainees discuss the significance of this knowledge to their development of culturally sensitive counseling skills.

Outcomes.
Trainees become knowledgeable about their own as well as others' ethnic or racial groups. They get information on important values of other racial or ethnic groups, and they are able to identify positive and negative aspects of their culture, cultural group, or ethnicity. Imagining life as a member of a different racial or ethnic group provides opportunities for confronting stereotypes and correcting misinformation about a cultural or racial group different from their own.

Intervention 3. The Definition of Privilege

Domain 1. Counselor Awareness of Own Cultural Values and Biases

Competency. Knowledge (B2).
"Culturally skilled counselors possess knowledge and understanding about how oppression, racism, discrimination, and stereotyping affect them personally and in their work. This allows individuals to acknowledge their own racist attitudes, beliefs, and feelings. Although this standard applies to all groups, for White counselors it may mean that they understand how they may have directly or indirectly benefited from individual, institutional, and cultural racism, as outlined in White identity development models" (Arredondo et al., 1996, p. 53).

Explanatory Statement (B2a).
"Culturally skilled counselors can specifically identify, name, and discuss privileges that they personally receive in society due to their race, socioeconomic background, gender, physical abilities, sexual orientation, and so on" (Arredondo et al., 1996, p. 53).

Application/Practice Component.
Counselor trainees read the article "White Privilege: Unpacking the Invisible Knapsack" (McIntosh, 1988) and the book *Rage of the Privileged*

23

(Cose, 1993). Both define the meaning of privilege from two differing racial perspectives. "White Privilege" presents a scorching account of how Whites systematically use "the privilege of being White" to consciously or unconsciously oppress other racial groups. *Rage of the Privileged* points out the painful disillusionment of successful African Americans who, having achieved the "American dream," are still denied full acceptance into White society because of skin color. The message of both publications is that in America, racial parity is an elusive dream.

Processing.

The articles are processed in a group discussion format. Reading and discussing "White Privilege" is very uncomfortable for White trainees because it heightens their emotional discomfort by challenging them to confront ways in which their lifestyle has consciously or unconsciously perpetuated racism and oppression of others. Reading about the African American experience provides a painful example of how a systemic, institutionalized way of life denies specific racial groups full societal participation. This is an extremely important activity because it serves to push White trainees out of their naiveté to acknowledge that being White is indeed a privileged status.

Outcomes.

Trainees have a heightened awareness that being White engenders privilege while being Black prevents full acceptance into the dominant society. Some trainees recognize, perhaps reluctantly, how White privilege perpetuates entitlement, oppression, and racism in their lives. It persuades them to confront racial issues, discuss what it really means to be White or a person of color in the United States, and how these meanings impact their racial identity attitudes and their work with racially different clients. This exercise is processed slowly, carefully, and with sensitivity. Trainees who can acknowledge awareness of individual and institutional roles in perpetuating oppression can readily work toward achieving a nonracist White identity.

Intervention 4. Racial Identity Through the Lenses of Others

Domain 1. Counselor Awareness of Own Cultural Values

Competency. Knowledge (B2).
See Intervention 3.

Behavioral Competency (B2b).

"Specifically referring to White counselors, [they] can discuss White identity development models and how they relate to one's personal experiences" (Arredondo et al., 1996, p. 53).

Application/Practice Component.

This activity involves two phases. First, counselor trainees read Helms's White racial identity development model (1984, 1990, 1995, 1996), Cross's (1995) psychology of Nigrescence, previously called Black identity development, and Sue and Sue's (1999) racial/cultural identity development model. These models are discussed and trainees identify their racial identity status. Second, they are asked to view the film *Imitation of Life* (Hunter & Sirk, 1959) and read the novel *The Color of Water: A Black Man's Tribute to His White Mother* (McBride, 1997). *Imitation of Life* chronicles the strained relationship between a Black mother and her light-skinned daughter who desperately wants to be White. It illustrates the complex issues involved in racial identity formation, the psychological destructiveness of a negative racial identity, and the dichotomous processes of racial identification and resistance. *The Color of Water: A Black Man's Tribute to His White Mother* is a story of the author's Jewish mother who married a Black man, raised 12 children, and founded a Black Baptist church. It clearly illustrates issues of biracial identity development and how the author skillfully integrated his mixed heritage into developing a positive racial identity.

Process.

Trainees discuss their reaction to the movie and the book. They also determine the characters' level of racial identity development, and articulate counseling techniques that may be helpful to clients occupying a particular phase of identity development, struggling between statuses, or struggling with racial identity issues.

Outcomes.

Trainees are provided with several different glimpses of racial identity development. They are able to conceptualize the complexity of racial identity development and factors that may impinge successful development. They are able to articulate an understanding of positive and negative racial identity development. Most important, they recognize that racial identity development is an individual process, not a group process. Finally, trainees understand the relationships among racial identity development, racial self-awareness, and acceptance of others, and the benefits of this information to enhance their multicultural counseling competencies.

Conclusion

Counselors with multicultural competencies can potentially transform the counseling profession by demonstrating how the requisite knowledge, awareness, and skills result in the delivery of effective multicultural counseling. Further, because most counselors and trainees are White, it becomes critical for them to understand the impact of their racial and cultural programming, values, beliefs, behaviors, and racial identity attitudes on their development of self and their perceptions of others who are not of their racial or ethnic heritage. All of these factors will influence their multicultural relationships with clients of color. Most importantly, the new and exciting research on the relationship between White racial identity and increased multicultural competencies will steer the profession into examining other variables that may help to explain what makes multicultural counseling work. The interventions presented here are a glimpse of the many activities, exercises, and practice applications that can be generated for increasing multicultural competencies among all counselor trainees.

References

Arredondo, P., & Arciniega, M. (2001). Strategies and techniques for counselor training based on the multicultural counseling competencies. *Journal of Counseling & Development, 29,* 263-273.

Arredondo, P., Toporek, R., Brown, S. P., Jones, J., Locke, D. C., Sanchez, J., & Stadler, H. (1996). Operationalization of the multicultural counseling competencies. *Journal of Multicultural Counseling and Development, 24,* 42-78.

Behrens, J. T. (1997). Does the White Racial Identity Attitude Scale measure racial identity? *Journal of Counseling Psychology, 44,* 3-12.

Brown, S. P., Parham, T., & Yonker, T. A. (1996). Influence of a cross-cultural training course on racial identity attitudes of White women and men: Preliminary perspectives. *Journal of Counseling & Development, 74,* 302-310.

Carter, R. T., & Qureshi, A. (1995). A typology of philosophical assumptions in multicultural counseling and training. In J. G. Ponterotto, J. M. Casas, L. A. Suzuki, & C. M. Alexander (Eds.), *Handbook of multicultural counseling* (pp. 239-262). Thousand Oaks, CA: Sage.

Cose, E. (1993). *Rage of the privileged.* New York: HarperCollins.

Cross, W. E., Jr. (1995). The psychology of Nigrescence: Revising the Cross model. In J. G. Ponterotto, J. M. Casas, L. A. Suzuki, & C. M. Alexander (Eds.), *Handbook of multicultural counseling* (pp. 93-122). Thousand Oaks, CA: Sage.

Espin, O. (1987). Issues of identity in the psychology of Latina lesbians: Explorations and challenges. In Boston Lesbian Psychologies Collective (Ed.), *Lesbian psychologies: Explorations and challenges* (pp. 35-55). Urbana, IL: University of Illinois Press.

Gurung, R., & Mehta, A. R. (2001). Relating ethnic identity, acculturation, and attitudes toward treating minority clients. *Cultural Diversity and Ethnic Minority Psychology, 7*(2), 139-151.

Helms, J. E. (1984). Toward a theoretical explanation of the effects of race on counseling: A Black and White model. *The Counseling Psychologist, 12*(4), 163-165.

Helms, J. E. (1990). *Black and White racial identity: Theory, research, and practice.* Westport, CT: Greenwood.

Helms, J. E. (1995). An update of Helms's White and people of color racial identity models. In J. G. Ponterotto, J. M. Casas, L. A. Suzuki, & C. M. Alexander (Eds.), *Handbook of multicultural counseling* (pp. 181-198). Thousand Oaks, CA: Sage.

Helms, J. E. (1996). Toward a method for measuring and assessing racial identity as distinguished from ethnic identity. In G. R. Sodowsky & J. C. Impara (Eds.), *Multicultural assessment in counseling and clinical psychology* (pp. 143-192). Lincoln, NE: Buros Institute.

Hunter, R. (Producer), & Sirk, D. (Director). (1959). Imitation of life [Motion picture]. United States: Universal International.

McBride, J. (1997). *The color of water: A Black man's tribute to his White mother.* New York: Riverhead Books.

McIntosh, P. (1988, July/August). White privilege: Unpacking the invisible knapsack. *Peace and Freedom,* 8-10.

Ottavi, T. M., Pope-Davis, D. B., & Dings, J. G. (1994). Relationship between White racial identity attitudes and self-reported multicultural counseling competencies. *Journal of Counseling Psychology, 41*(2), 149-154.

Parker, W. M., Moore, M. A., & Neimeyer, G. J. (1998). Altering White racial identity and interracial comfort through multicultural training. *Journal of Counseling & Development, 76,* 302-310.

Richardson, T. Q., & Molinaro, K. L. (1996). White counselor self-awareness: A prerequisite for developing multicultural competence. *Journal of Counseling & Development, 74,* 238-242.

Roysircar, G., Gard, G., & Hubbell, R. (2002). *Counselor trainee self-reflections in process notes on multicultural services: Within and between sessions analyses of alliance for clients.* Manuscript submitted for publication.

Sabnani, H. B., Ponterotto, J. G., & Borodovsky, L. G. (1991). White racial identity development and cross-cultural training: A stage model. *The Counseling Psychologist, 19,* 72-102.

Sandhu, D. S. (2001). An ecocultural analysis of agonies and ecstasies of my life. In J.G. Ponterotto, J. M. Casas, L. A. Suzuki, & C. M. Alexander (Eds.), *Handbook of multicultural counseling* (2nd ed.). Thousand Oaks, CA: Sage.

Sandhu, D. S., Portes, P. R., & McPhee, S. A. (1996). Assessing cultural adaptation: Psychometric properties of the Cultural Adaptation Pain Scale. *Journal of Multicultural Counseling and Development, 24,* 15-25.

Steward, R. J., Boatwright, K. J., Sauer, E., Baden, A., & Jackson, J. D. (1998). Relationships among counselor trainee's gender, cognitive development, and White racial identity: Implications for counselor training. *Journal of Multicultural Counseling and Development, 26,* 254-272.

Sue, D. W., Arredondo, P., & McDavis, R. J. (1992). Multicultural competencies/standards: A call to the profession. *Journal of Counseling & Development, 70,* 477-486.

Sue, D. W., & Sue, D. (1999). *Counseling the culturally different* (3rd ed.). New York: Wiley.

Vinson, T. S., & Neimeyer, G. J. (2000). The relationship between racial identity development and multicultural counseling competency. *Journal of Multicultural Counseling and Development, 28,* 177-192.

Chapter 3

"Walking the Talk": Simulations in Multicultural Training

Paul B. Pedersen

Simulations provide a safe place to ask dangerous questions about multicultural counseling. This chapter describes three simulations that have been used to develop multicultural counseling competencies. The first simulation is the Triad Training Model, which matches a counselor from one culture with a three-person team of coached client, procounselor, and anticounselor from a contrasting culture. The procounselor and anticounselor provide immediate and continuous feedback to the counselor about the positive and negative things a culturally different client is thinking but not saying. The second simulation is the Synthetic Culture Laboratory, in which participants are organized into four synthetic cultures of Alpha (high power distance), Beta (strong uncertainty avoidance), Gamma (high individualism), and Delta (strong masculine) based on Geert Hofstede's 80,000 international database (Hofstede, 1980, 1991). Trainees learn how to find common ground without giving up integrity. The third simulation is Critical Incidents, in which a disagreement occurs in a multicultural setting and the right response is not clear, although it is clear that a wrong response will have negative consequences. Critical Incidents is useful for bringing community resource persons into the classroom. Participants learn how to mobilize the positive learning potential in cross-cultural problems that arise. All three of these simulations highlight specific multicultural competencies toward adult development in a global context.

It is high time that we move beyond the abundant rhetorical "talk" about the importance of multiculturalism and develop competencies in the "walk" or appropriate and applied action, however dangerous that task may be. Simulations provide a safe place to ask dangerous questions about multicultural counseling. This chapter describes three simulations that have been used to develop multicultural counseling competencies. Role-play interview simulations are a well-established method of teaching counseling skills. The following three simulations go beyond role-playing a counseling interview to examining the culture-centered perspective of clients and counselors in a variety of different cultural contexts.

The three aims of this chapter are to (1) assist the counselor trainee in hearing the positive and negative internal dialogues of culturally different clients in counseling; (2) rehearse the skill of finding common ground across cultures without giving up integrity through counseling; and (3) mobilize the educational teaching/learning potential of multicultural critical incidents for counseling.

All behaviors are learned and displayed in a cultural context. Behaviors have no meaning outside of their cultural context. The framework of the three simulations allows us to experience different cultural rules in different contexts, to rehearse culture-centered counseling skills without risk to the counselor or the client in real counseling interviews. The simulations are designed to increase the accurate *awareness* of culturally different assumptions, increase the meaningful *knowledge* about culturally different perspectives, and increase the appropriate *skill* for a counseling intervention (Pedersen, 2000a). Each simulation offers the possibility of resource persons from the community being recruited to teach counselors about their cultural context in ways that might prevent misunderstandings later. All three of these simulations highlight specific multicultural competencies toward adult development in a global context.

The Triad Training Model

The first simulation is the Triad Training Model, which matches a counselor from one culture with a three-person team of coached client, pro-counselor, and anticounselor from a contrasting culture. The greater the cultural difference between a counselor and a client, the more difficult it will be to hear the client's internal dialogue. Although we cannot know exactly what the client is thinking, we can assume that some of these messages are negative or anticounselor in their orientation, and other messages are positive or procounselor in their orientation. The procounselor and anticounselor provide immediate and continuous feedback to the counselor about the positive and negative things a culturally different client is thinking but not saying (Pedersen, 2000b).

The Triad Training Model simulates a cross-cultural interview in which the client's internal dialogue is made explicit at the same time that the counseling is taking place. The anticounselor seeks to tell the negative messages a client is thinking but not saying while the procounselor is at the same time telling the client's positive messages. Their combined influence helps the counselor hear the client's hidden messages of internal dialogue in a continuous, direct, and immediate feedback loop. The confusion of voices simulates actual events from the perspective of a troubled client from a different culture. The resource persons in the team role-play the client, procounselor, and anticounselor in a 5- to 8-minute interview. When the players are articulate and authentic, and following detailed debriefing, the counselor can learn to (1) see the problem from the client's cultural perspective, (2) recognize resistance in specific terms, (3) become nondefensive when working with the culture, and (4) learn recovery skills for getting out of trouble.

The anticounselor is deliberately subversive in attempting to exaggerate mistakes by the counselor, confronting the counselor with an increased awareness of the client's perspective. The anticounselor articulates the negative, embarrassing, and impolite comments that a client might not otherwise say—much like a devil sitting on the client's shoulder.

The anticounselor might build on the positive aspects of the problem and the client's ambivalence, distract or sidetrack the counselor, keep counseling superficial, obstruct communication between the counselor and client, annoy the counselor, exaggerate differences between the counselor and client, demand immediate results, communicate privately with the client, identify scapegoats, attack the counselor's credibility, and request that someone more expert be brought in.

The procounselor is deliberately positive in attempting to exaggerate positive aspects of counseling, supporting the counselor's growing awareness of the client's cultural perspective. The procounselor articulates the positive perspective—much like an angel sitting on the client's other shoulder.

The procounselor helps reframe counseling into a helpful activity for the client, facilitates the counselor's effective responses, increases the counselor's explicit understanding of the client's culture, provides important background information, and reinforces the counselor's successful strategies.

Research demonstrating the importance of internal dialogue for the culturally different counselor and client has highlighted the clear need to incorporate more training in counselor education programs on hearing the client's internal dialogue. Most of the research evaluating the Triad Training Model has come from evaluation data by in-service training programs or from dissertation research by graduate students. The research to date gives some support for the value of the Triad Training Model, although the findings have not been conclusive:

31

More research is needed to identify the conditions under which the Triad Training Model works best. The anecdotal evidence by teachers and/or trainers using the model has been the strongest supporting evidence so far, indicating that training with the model has a positive effect, helping counselor trainees increase their awareness of self and others, strengthen their knowledge about clients from other cultures, and sharpen their skills for making appropriate interventions among clients from other cultures. (Pedersen, 2000b, p. 114)

The Synthetic Culture Laboratory

The second simulation is the Synthetic Culture Laboratory, in which participants are organized into four synthetic cultures of Alpha (high power distance), Beta (strong uncertainty avoidance), Gamma (high individualism), and Delta (strong masculine) based on Geert Hofstede's 80,000 international database (Hofstede, 1980, 1991). Trainees learn how to find common ground without giving up integrity. Pedersen and Ivey (1993) have demonstrated how the same counseling microskill can be displayed differently in each synthetic culture context. The synthetic cultures are deliberately one-dimensional and artificial. In a real culture the mix of characteristics is much more complex and confusing. This simplified framework, however, allows the participants to experience and articulate at least four contrasting perspectives on the same situation.

In the Synthetic Culture Laboratory, participants are introduced to four cultures and select one of those four as their participant role. All four cultures are confronting the same problem:

Your synthetic culture community is having a problem with outsiders from the other three synthetic culture communities who are coming into your community as refugees, visitors, tourists, students, or immigrants. These outsiders have caused serious problems in your schools, institutions, and community because they disregard your way of doing things. They do not believe the same things that you and your people believe. (Pedersen, 2001, p. 2)

The goals of the 2.5-hour Synthetic Culture Laboratory are to (1) identify shared common ground expectations across different behaviors, (2) network with other participants from different cultural backgrounds, (3) examine problems caused by outsiders across cultures, (4) enhance consultation skills in other cultures, (5) identify culturally different conflict management styles, (6) develop a framework for understanding other cultures, and (7) increase each participant's cultural self-awareness.

32

Each synthetic culture group is given a page of rules to guide them into their role. Alpha culture is a High Power Distance culture with power distance indicating the extent to which a culture accepts that power is unequally distributed in institutions and organizations. Alphas like words such as *respect, father, master, servant, older brother, younger brother, wisdom, favor, protect, obey, orders,* and *pleasing.* Alphas require that visitors show respect to their Leader. They are soft-spoken and polite, taking their responsibility as Hosts very seriously.

Beta culture is a Strong Uncertainty Avoidance culture with uncertainty avoidance indicating the lack of tolerance for uncertainty and ambiguity. Betas like words such as *structure, duty, truth, law, order, certain, clear, clean, secure, safe, predictable,* and *tight.* Betas require that visitors show respect for the Law. They are highly structured and focused on details with a tendency to treat others as either a friend or an enemy with nothing in between these polarized alternatives.

Gamma culture is a High Individualism culture with individualism indicating the extent to which a culture believes that people are supposed to take care of themselves and remain emotionally independent from groups, organizations, and other collectives. Gammas like words such as *self, friendship, do-your-own-thing, contract, litigation, self-respect, self-interest, self-actualizing, individual, dignity, I/me, pleasure, adventure,* and *guilt.* Gammas require that visitors show respect for their Freedom. They tend to be verbal and self-disclosing and measure the importance of others in terms of how useful they are.

Delta culture is a Strong Masculine culture, with masculinity indicating the extent to which traditional masculine values of assertiveness, money, and things prevail in a culture as contrasted to traditional feminine values of nurturance, quality of life, and people. Deltas like words such as *career, competition, fight, aggressive, assertive, success, winner, deserve, merit, "balls," excel, force, big, hard, fast,* and *quantity.* Deltas require that visitors allow them to Win. They tend to be competitive, dominating, sports-oriented, and quick to debate or argue every issue. They are usually macho, hero-oriented, and blame others for their mistakes.

Participants in the Synthetic Culture Laboratory interact in a series of three small groups with instructions to find common ground without sacrificing their own synthetic cultural identity. In the first round Alphas and Betas meet together while Gammas and Deltas meet together to discuss the problems outsiders are causing in their respective cultures for about 10 minutes in role. This is followed by a 10-minute debriefing in the small groups out of role and a 5-minute planning session for each separate synthetic culture before the second round. In the second round

Alphas meet with Gammas, and Betas meet with Deltas; in the third round Alphas meet with Deltas, and Betas meet with Gammas, following the same structure. When each synthetic culture has met with each other synthetic culture, there is a debriefing session for all participants together in which each synthetic culture gives feedback to the others and gives advice to outsiders wanting to visit their culture.

Hofstede and Pedersen (2000) have described some uses of synthetic cultures for learning cultural patterns and how the same message is conveyed quite differently in each cultural context. The sources of miscommunication are made more obvious and the emotional impact of culture contact is experienced. It is ironic that stereotyping can be prevented by working with four stereotyped, one-dimensional synthetic culture groups. The topic of outsiders can be changed to fit the needs of a particular training setting. On one recent occasion, the problem was changed to school violence, which sharpens the focus of the Synthetic Culture Laboratory on that particular problem. Software is also being developed using hypercard in a computer software program in which positive and/or negative responses by each synthetic culture client is determined by several thousand positive and/or negative words the trainee uses in her or his question of a particular synthetic culture on a particular problem.

Critical Incidents

The third simulation is Critical Incidents, in which a disagreement occurs in a multicultural setting and the right response is not clear, although it is clear that a wrong response will have negative consequences. Each incident is a short description of an event that took place within a brief period of time as compared with the longer case study examples. The incident involves a dilemma with no easy solution. Critical Incidents can be used in writing or in role-played hypothetical situations for classroom discussion. Critical Incidents does not imply a single best solution. Critical Incidents is useful for bringing community resource persons into the classroom. Participants learn how to mobilize the positive learning potential in cross-cultural problems that arise.

The Critical Incidents technique is widely used in training doctors, lawyers, managers, and other professionals (Pedersen & Hernandez, 1997) and is closely related to the case study method for evaluating the behavior of a person in a decision-making setting. The primary advantage of Critical Incidents is the focus on observable behaviors. The disadvantages are that it requires considerable time and effort to collect the incidents and to translate them in a meaningful way. The incidents also tend to emphasize the extraordinary rather than the typical situation, which exaggerates aspects of that context. It is sometimes hard to generalize from the incidents to the real world. It is also difficult to get consensus about the right response to any particular multicultural incident (Brislin, Cushner, Cherrie, & Young, 1986; Pedersen, 1995; Sue & Sue, 1999).

Critical Incidents is particularly popular for teaching or training about multicultural relationships. In part, this happens because more specific and focused situational tests are more likely to impose a cultural bias. In part, it is because Critical Incidents is more open-ended and includes the complexity of real-life situations in which persons from more than one culture come into contact. The Critical Incidents methodology has been used to develop and measure several multicultural competencies, as follows.:

1. *Information source development.* Students develop the ability to use many different information sources within a social or cultural context, encouraging their information-gathering skills for observing, questioning, and careful listening.
2. *Cultural understanding.* Students' awareness of feelings, attitudes, and ways those feelings or attitudes influence people are clarified. It becomes more apparent how attitudes and feelings are connected with values and behaviors.
3. *Interpersonal communication.* Listening well and paying attention to nonverbal messages are highlighted to students as important aspects of an incident.
4. *Commitment to persons and relationships.* The opportunity to get involved with people from different cultures is enhanced through gathering incidents. This involves inspiring trust and confidence and establishing a basis for mutual liking or respect.
5. *Decision making.* Problems are turned into learning opportunities. Students learn how others may draw different conclusions from the same information and different solutions for similar problems.

There is no substitute for actual experience. The Critical Incident technique is an attempt to bring actual experiences or events into the classroom as a resource. The incident is critical—meaning important, essential, or valuable—in the way that a part of a machine might be critical to the smooth operation of that machine.

Conclusion, Implications, and Recommendations

Think of simulations as simplified examples of the more complicated culturally learned structures that guide our lives. Simulations have become a recognized way of training to minimize risk of making mistakes in the real world. The three examples of simulations in this chapter provide a safe context for risk taking in learning about multiculturalism. There are several implications for culture-centered counselors wanting to "walk the talk" or otherwise go beyond their supportive rhetoric about multiculturalism toward decisive action, skills, and competence as counselors. These implications are as follows.

1. People can be trained to increase their multicultural awareness, knowledge, and skill. Multicultural skills are teachable and learnable, given the proper setting.
2. The more similarity between training and real life, the more impact that training is likely to have on changing behaviors. Multiculturalism is not an abstraction.
3. Learning how to learn from real-life experience is more important than the mere transfer of information in a classroom. Simulations engage the participant personally.
4. Complexity is your friend. Attempts to find simple answers to complex questions are likely to fail and are dangerous.
5. Behavior has no meaning until and unless it is seen in the cultural context in which that behavior was learned and is being displayed.

There are also several recommendations that the reader of this chapter might consider. (1) Cultural encapsulation by our own self-reference criteria is a continuing risk and danger for us all. (2) Look at the reasonable opposite of what you have always believed true, and you will be surprised by how insightful that alternative might be from the perspective of another culture. (3) You are in greatest danger when you believe you have already discovered your biases. Never underestimate the power of social groups to capture memberships.

References

Brislin, R. S., Cushner, K., Cherrie, C., & Young, M. (1986). *Intercultural interactions: A practical guide.* Beverly Hills, CA: Sage.

Hofstede, G. (1980). *Culture's consequences: International differences in work-related values.* Beverly Hills, CA: Sage.

Hofstede, G. (1991). Cultures and organizations: *Software of the mind.* London: McGraw Hill.

Hofstede, G. J., & Pedersen, P. B. (2000). Synthetic national cultures: Intercultural learning through simulation games. *Journal of Simulation and Gaming, 30,* 415–440.

Pedersen, P. (1995). *The five stages of culture shock: Critical incidents around the world.* Westport, CT: Greenwood Press.

Pedersen, P. (2000a). *Handbook for developing multicultural awareness* (3rd ed.). Alexandria, VA: American Counseling Association.

Pedersen, P. (2000b). *Hidden messages in culture-centered counseling: A triad training model.* Thousand Oaks, CA: Sage.

Pedersen, P. (2001). *Working cross-culturally: Preparing for differences: A Synthetic Culture training program.* Unpublished manuscript, East West Center, Honolulu, HI.

Pedersen, P., & Hernandez, D. (1997). *Decisional dialogues in a cultural context: Structured exercises.* Thousand Oaks, CA: Sage.

Pedersen, P., & Ivey, A. E. (1993). *Culture-centered counseling and interviewing skills.* Westport, CT: Greenwood Press.

Sue, D. W., & Sue, D. (1999). *Counseling the culturally different: Theory and practice* (3rd ed.). New York: Wiley.

Chapter 4

Engaging Students in the Quest for Competence in Multiculturalism: An Expanded View of Mentoring

Azara L. Santiago-Rivera and Marcia Moody

The chapter begins with a brief discussion of the role of the mentor and a mentoring relationship in multicultural competency development. Various ways in which the authors have engaged students in their development through mentoring opportunities are described. Examples are drawn from the authors' personal experiences as educators, and from the observations of others who have successfully engaged students in this process. These strategies and activities are described in the context of learning environments that foster and promote self-exploration, enhanced awareness, and the acquisition of new knowledge and skills.

I t is well recognized that one of the biggest challenges facing counselor educators is helping students increase multicultural competence in their professional training. Proponents of the multicultural competency movement agree that much of the focus in training has been on developing competencies through formal coursework and research, and, to some extent, practica and supervision (e.g., Ponterotto, 1997; Sue et al., 1998). Although there has been significant progress in creating opportunities that promote multicultural competency development through these educational experiences, little attention has been given to the role of mentoring.

Galbraith and Cohen (1995) provided a fairly comprehensive perspective, defining mentoring as

a process within a contextual setting; involves a relationship of a more knowledgeable individual with a less experienced individual; provides professional networking, counseling, guiding, instructing, modeling, and sponsoring; is a

developmental mechanism (personal, professional, and psychological); is a socialization and reciprocal relationship; and provides an identity transformation for
both mentor and mentee. (pp. 90–91)

Generally, a mentor can be a role model, an educator, and/or a supervisor
who models desirable attitudes and behaviors. However, mentoring in
the context of the development of multicultural competency requires
additional considerations.

First, no one can teach another to become culturally competent.
Although a mentee can be exposed to information and specific strategies through a mentor, ultimately real learning takes place by doing (i.e.,
interacting with people from culturally diverse backgrounds). Second,
everyone approaches multiculturalism differently based on his or her
background and experiences. Therefore, an important aspect of mentoring is recognizing the diversity among mentees and allowing them to
subjectively interpret and personalize their educational experiences.
Third, given the complexities of multiculturalism, cultural competency
cannot be gleaned from one person. Rarely can a mentee develop the
complex array of attitudes and skills that constitute cultural competency
after being mentored by a single individual. Therefore, one of our primary goals in mentoring is to lay a foundation so that the mentee can
learn from multiple sources of cultural experiences. Last, before a
mentoring relationship can evolve, a prerequisite for the development
of a successful mentoring relationship is that the mentee be willing to
place himself or herself in the role of learner without the expectation of
becoming a master of another culture. That is, we can never become an
expert on someone else's culture, and even within our own culture of
origin, it is important to recognize that our knowledge base and experiences are limited.

In spite of these complexities, a mentor in an academic setting may
be considered a trusted advisor who provides learning opportunities
that extend beyond the traditional classroom environment. In particular,
Kiselica (1999) pointed out that mentoring students in multicultural
development requires a commitment to guide students through the
process by not only creating a safe learning climate but also exposing
students to experiences that do not normally occur in their academic
training.[1] In this regard, a mentor must be willing to self-disclose experiences and struggles with becoming more sensitive and aware of his or
her biases and attitudes toward other groups (e.g., religious, ethnic,

---

[1] The authors are referring to the process of multicultural development of *all students* in
training.

racial, gay, lesbian), strive to establish new contacts with people of different backgrounds, and model behaviors that demonstrate respect and genuine caring (Rooney, Flores, & Mercier, 1998). As such, the mentor's role may be considered central in the student's multicultural professional development.

The purpose of this chapter is to describe various ways in which the authors have engaged students in the quest for multicultural competence through mentoring opportunities. The examples are drawn from the authors' personal experiences as educators, and from the observations of others who have successfully engaged students in this process. The strategies and activities described center on learning opportunities that (1) take place in safe learning environments that foster and promote self-exploration and enhanced awareness, and (2) are designed to heighten knowledge and increase skill level. The chapter first overviews recent and current perspectives on multicultural competency development and then discusses two general multicultural development strategies: creating a learning environment that promotes collectivism, and providing opportunities that simultaneously enhance professional and multicultural development. The chapter next examines important considerations in teaching multicultural competencies in courses and concludes with specific recommendations for strategies to facilitate cultural learning when developing multicultural courses.

Recent and Current Perspectives on
Multicultural Competency Development

In the early 1980s, Derald Wing Sue and colleagues (1982) presented a compelling argument on the need to develop multicultural competencies, and introduced a conceptual framework in the context of culture-specific attitudes, knowledge, and skills in counseling. This landmark publication set the stage for more recent perspectives. Specifically, Sue, Arredondo, and McDavis (1992) developed competencies that were organized into three specific domains: Counselor Awareness of Own Values and Attitudes, Counselor Awareness of Client's Worldview, and Culturally Competent Strategies and Interventions. Then Sodowsky, Taffe, Gutkin, and Wise (1994) constructed a set of competencies that center on four domains: Multicultural Counseling Skills, Multicultural Awareness, Multicultural Counseling Relationship, and Multicultural Counseling Knowledge. Subsequently Sue et al. (1998) described a broader framework for multicultural competence in the context of three domains: Counselor Awareness of Own Assumptions, Values, and Biases; Understanding the Worldview of the Culturally Different Client; and Developing Appropriate Intervention Strategies and Techniques.

Although there are variations in these conceptualizations of specific competencies, the common denominator among them is the importance of increasing awareness, knowledge, and skills in multicultural counseling. Therefore, we follow the working definition proposed by Sue et al. (1992):

> A culturally skilled counselor is one who is actively in the process of becoming aware of his or her own assumptions about human behavior, values, biases, preconceived notions, personal limitations, and so forth; actively attempts to understand the worldview of his or her culturally different client without negative judgments; [and] is in the process of actively developing and practicing appropriate, relevant, and sensitive intervention strategies and skills in working with his or her culturally different clients. (p. 481)

One of the most important roles for a mentor is to model successful ways of developing a professional identity that incorporates and integrates multicultural competency. As Sodowsky, Kuo-Jackson, and Loya (1997) cogently stated, multicultural competency requires two essential ingredients: self-exploration about one's own culture and racial identity, and the development of what they call a political ideology (p. 15), which refers to taking on advocacy roles within communities. With respect to the advocacy role, for example, we bring social justice perspectives to the attention of our mentees, such as the inequality in access to health care and the emerging concern that low income and minority communities are disproportionately exposed to environmental contamination (e.g., Molina & Aguirre-Molina, 1994; Pilisuki, 1998; Santiago-Rivera, 2000).

The mentoring role requires that the educator join with students in local, state, and national advocacy activities in support of specific causes. In a recent publication, McGoldrick, et al. (1999) outlined specific ways that the Family Institute of New Jersey has infused social justice perspectives in family therapy training, demonstrating an expanded view of multicultural competency development. They also openly address the effects of White privilege from social and historical contexts on people of different cultural, ethnic, and racial groups, and examine social inequities in contemporary U.S. society. McGoldrick and colleagues also critically examine theories of human and family development with respect to their applicability across diverse populations while highlighting the impact of oppression and race on family functioning.

Another attempt to bring social justice perspectives to the forefront as a necessary component of the multicultural counselor advocacy role is the recent creation of Counselors for Social Justice (CSJ), a new division within the American Counseling Association. A fundamental guiding principle of CSJ is to promote individual and collective responsibility in addressing issues of oppression and inequalities in working with clients, as well as in the counseling profession. One of CSJ's goals is to create a support network for counselors to engage in social justice issues.

Multicultural Competencies Development Strategies

Strategies effective in promoting multicultural competencies in student mentees include creating a learning environment that promotes collectivism, such as through a multicultural research team, and providing opportunities that simultaneously enhance professional and multicultural competency development, such as through field work and organizing diversity conferences.

Providing a Learning Environment That Promotes Collectivism

One of the most important activities in mentoring students is creating a learning environment that promotes collectivism, a value held by many ethnic/cultural groups that is in contrast to the Eurocentric value orientation of individualism. We have promoted this perspective on our campus by structuring a research team on multicultural issues. The research team meets monthly, is held on the university campus, publicized at the beginning of each semester, and open to both undergraduate and graduate students. These meetings serve as an avenue for students to present their own ideas on research while promoting collaboration as an essential goal in the development of multicultural competence. In many instances, their involvement has led to individual student research projects, including doctoral dissertation work, and conference presentations. In addition, students have opportunities to work with faculty members who have ongoing research projects. Some of these projects have included studies on Black and White race relations, spirituality, and acculturation processes.

The multicultural research team approach not only fosters a collectivist orientation but also allows students to observe the interaction of educators from different racial/ethnic backgrounds. Specifically, the faculty members who participate in the research team are of different ethnic/racial heritage, and intentionally model effective cross-cultural communication, risk-taking behaviors, and teamwork.

Providing Opportunities to Enhance Professional and Multicultural Competency Development

Effectively engaging students in activities that are part of their overall professional development is undeniably one of the most important goals in training. Our position is that mentors must provide opportunities that enhance professional development and multicultural development simultaneously. In other words, certain activities lead to general professional development (e.g., learning how to prepare and present a paper at national conference) while also increasing competencies in multicultural areas.

Two ongoing projects, one on bilingual therapy with Latino clients and the other on environmental contamination in a Native American community located in the Northeast, are directed by one of the authors of this chapter. Both projects require fieldwork, which means that visiting these communities to meet with people and attend social gatherings is necessary. In essence, the fieldwork provides students an opportunity to experience, firsthand, another culture. The end result has been considerable cultural learning through interaction with individuals from these distinct communities in settings that promote positive experiences.

An annual Diversity Conference is another activity that has been successful in bringing together students and faculty across the campus. The conference is organized by graduate students in the Department of Educational and Counseling Psychology, Division of Counseling Psychology, at the State University of New York at Albany. It is unique in that graduate students take the lead in all aspects of conference planning, from seeking funds to organizing, implementing, and evaluating sessions. Faculty members serve as advisors. Now in its second decade, the conference has featured renowned keynote speakers who have presented on such topics as racial and ethnic identity development, multicultural family therapy, spirituality, and social class. In many respects, the conference not only teaches students about conference planning (a professional development activity) but also exposes them to issues and topics associated with multiculturalism in the helping professions. Equally important, students work collaboratively and take on different leadership roles in the planning of the conference such as fundraising and publicity (A. Tully, personal communication, July 6, 2001).

Considerations in Teaching Multicultural Competencies in Courses

As stated earlier, an expanded view of mentoring as it relates to multicultural competency development requires a commitment to guide students through a complex process by creating opportunities for cultural learning. It is quite common for these opportunities to occur in formal coursework. Therefore, when teaching courses with a multicultural emphasis, particularly multicultural counseling classes, a variety of issues need to be considered, including the developmental levels of students, the philosophical framework guiding course construction, and how students typically progress when developing multicultural competency.

The Developmental Levels of Students

We conceptualize development in two primary domains: psychosocial development and cognitive development. *Psychosocial development* refers to the management of developmental milestones such as choosing a career, adapting a spiritual belief system, or selecting a life partner. Factors that influence psychosocial development include age, family of origin, social and work history, self-esteem, and identity issues (Chickering & Havighurst, 1981). Other important aspects to consider, such as those in the psychosocial student development model proposed by Chickering (1969), include achieving competence, managing emotions, becoming autonomous, establishing identity, developing intimate relationships, and clarifying purpose.

The other domain is *cognitive development*. William Perry (1981) proposed a model of cognitive and ethical development that consists of three primary phases. The first phase is characterized by dualistic all-or-nothing thinking in which the student views the teacher as expert. In this phase, students are most comfortable being passive recipients of knowledge. They simply want to know the right answers or, in the case of cultural competence, want the instructors to tell them what to do. Subsequent phases of Perry's model reflect more complex ways of thinking and learning that are less rigid and include multiple perspectives. Moreover, students in the latter stages take more active roles in the learning process. In our classes, one of our primary goals is to shift students away from dualistic thinking.

The Philosophical Framework Guiding Course Construction

The second consideration in course development is the philosophical framework that guides course construction. As mentioned previously, collectivism is stressed in our work with students. When designing courses, collectivism takes the form of feminist and multicultural approaches that are more egalitarian and collaborative. For instance, rather than viewing ourselves, the instructors, as multicultural experts, we see ourselves as facilitators of learning. Often this is reflected in the participatory nature of our classes; students are expected to help create class agendas based on the readings and are responsible for presenting course materials. The primary strategy for facilitating this type of active learning is to avoid straight lecturing. We stress that the student is responsible for reading outside of class in order to acquire a theoretical and empirical foundation. This allows for experiential activities and lively discussions during class.

How Students Progress When Developing Multicultural Competency

The third consideration revolves around how students typically progress when developing multicultural competency. We believe it is important to prepare students for the multicultural education process by reviewing common reactions experienced by most students when they take multicultural courses, such as guilt, anger, and insecurity. Given the nontraditional nature of multicultural learning, we believe it is essential to prepare students for the emotionally charged experience of developing multicultural competence. Because these emotions are discussed at the onset, students tend to feel less discomfort as the course progresses and are therefore more receptive to cultural learning.

We also consider students' level of multicultural competence as it relates to racial or ethnic identity (Helms & Cook, 1999; Helms & Richardson, 1997). Hoopes (1979) theorized that intercultural learning progresses from ethnocentrism (i.e., believing your culture is the best and being unaware of other cultures) to an awareness, understanding, and eventual acceptance of other cultures, and then to appreciating and selectively adopting diverse cultural perspectives. It is not until the final stage that multiculturalism is achieved, and even when that phase is reached, multiculturalism is considered an ongoing process in which a person is open to new experiences.

As in Hoopes' (1979) model, racial identity theorists (Cross, 1991; Cross, Parham, & Helms, 1991) have described a process in which individuals start out being relatively unaware of race, racism, and other cultures. Next, critical events spiral the person into a racial identity crisis. These events can be positive (e.g., the Black Power Movement of the

1970s) or negative (e.g., perceived acts of discrimination and/or incidents, which contribute toward feelings of marginalization). The events facilitate an immersion into the person's culture of origin in order to understand and experience more fully what it means to be a member of his or her race or ethnic group. If the person continues to progress through the model and the racial identity crisis is resolved, the person adopts a more affirmative racial/ethnic identity. We have found it important to consider the multicultural backgrounds of our students in terms of their intercultural learning style (or multicultural competence) as well as their racial/ethnic identity. Although we cannot precisely adjust our pedagogical strategies to comply with all students' developmental needs, we have found it useful to consider where the majority of students fall at the beginning of our class and where we would like them to be upon completion of the course.

Strategies to Facilitate Cultural Learning in Multicultural Competencies Courses

When developing courses with a multicultural emphasis, it is useful to consider strategies that help facilitate cultural learning. Our specific recommendations are as follows.

- Get people talking about multiculturally sensitive and sometimes controversial topics right away. Provide models for giving and receiving feedback to facilitate the difficult dialogues destined to take place.
- Model the specific skills, attitudes, and behaviors that reflect cultural competence. Based on our feminist/multicultural philosophies, this may sometimes involve self-disclosure and the willingness to share power.
- Establish guidelines for discussion so that students go beyond the superficial by exploring genuine feelings while also taking others' feelings into consideration.
- Provide outlets for student catharsis of feelings of disequilibrium that may result from readings, classroom activities, discussions, and experiences such as journals, private conversations when appropriate, or exploratory classroom exercises.
- Incorporate experiential classroom activities such as simulations, role plays, and debates.
- Use nontraditional modes of education such as plays, music, dance, and other genres that do not rely exclusively on verbal communication.

47

- Give and receive ongoing feedback. It is especially important to provide positive feedback to students who may have had their worldviews shaken. Also, as an instructor, it is helpful to get feedback in order to know what is working and what needs to be modified in order to maximize the learning experience.
- Realize that conflict is normal and that the instructor may not be able to reach all students. Have a plan in place for resolving volatile interactions that may erupt within and out of the classroom.

Conclusion

We have outlined an expanded view of the role of a mentor to include promoting social justice and advocacy work, and engaging students in professional development activities that focus on collaboration and teamwork. In the context of teaching courses with a multicultural orientation, the mentor must consider the complex interplay of the students' psychosocial and cognitive development to determine their readiness for cultural learning. We have argued that mentoring students in their quest for competence in multiculturalism is a complex process; however, in spite of these complexities participating in a mentoring relationship can be a rewarding professional development experience for both the mentor and the mentee.

In addition, it is important to keep in mind that although educational settings provide opportunities for learning, in reality the quest for multicultural development is a lifelong process that will undoubtedly extend beyond the training that students receive in academic institutions. We encourage our students to continue their journey toward multiculturalism long after the completion of their degree.

References

Chickering, A. W. (1969). *Education and identity*. San Francisco: Jossey-Bass.

Chickering, A. W., & Havighurst, R. J. (1981). The life cycle. In A.W. Chickering & Associates (Eds.), *Modern American college* (pp. 16–50). San Francisco: Jossey-Bass.

Cross, W. E., Jr. (1991). *Shades of Black: Diversity in African American identity.* Philadelphia: Temple University Press.

Cross, W. E., Parham, T.A., & Helms, J. E. (1991). The stages of Black identity development: Nigrescence models. In R. L. Jones (Ed.), *Black psychology* (pp. 319–338). Hampton, VA: Cobb & Henry.

Galbraith, M. W., & Cohen, N. H. (1995). Issues and challenges confronting mentoring. In M. W. Galbraith & N. H. Cohen (Vol. Eds.), *New directions for adult and continuing education: Vol. 66. Mentoring: New strategies and challenges* (pp. 89–93). San Francisco, CA: Jossey-Bass.

Helms, J., & Cook, D. (1999). *Race and culture in psychotherapy.* Pacific Grove, CA: Brooks/Cole.

Helms, J. E., & Richardson, T. Q. (1997). How "multiculturalism" obscures race and culture as differential aspects of counseling competency. In D. Pope-Davis & H. L. K. Coleman (Eds.), *Multicultural counseling competencies: Assessment, education and training, and supervision* (pp. 60–79). Thousand Oaks, CA: Sage.

Hoopes, D. S. (1979). Intercultural communication concepts and the psychology of intercultural experience. In M. D. Pusch (Ed.), *Multicultural education: A cross-cultural training approach* (pp. 9–38). La Grange Park, IL: Intercultural Network.

Kiselica, M. (Ed.). (1999). *Confronting prejudice and racism during multicultural training.* Alexandria, VA: American Counseling Association.

McGoldrick, M., Almeida, R., Garica Preto, N., Bibb, A., Sutton, C., Hudak, J., Moore Hines, P. (1999). Efforts to incorporate social justice perspectives into a family training program. *Journal of Marital and Family Therapy, 25,* 191–209.

Molina, C. W., & Aguirre-Molina, M. J. (Eds.). (1994). *Latin health in the U.S.: A growing challenge.* Washington, DC: American Public Health Association.

Perry, W. P. (1981). Cognitive and ethical growth: The making of meaning. In A. W. Chickering & Associates (Eds.), *Modern American college* (pp. 76–116). San Francisco: Jossey-Bass.

Pilisuki, M. (1998). The hidden structure of violence: Peace and conflict. *Journal of Peace Psychology, 4,* 197–216.

Ponterotto, J. G. (1997). Multicultural counseling training: A competency model and national survey. In D. Pope-Davis & H. L. K. Coleman (Eds.), *Multicultural counseling competencies: Assessment, education and training, and supervision* (pp. 111–130). Thousand Oaks, CA: Sage.

Rooney, S. C., Flores, L. Y., & Mercier, C. A. (1998). Making multicultural education effective for everyone. *The Counseling Psychologist, 26,* 22–32.

Santiago-Rivera, A. (2000). Ecological violence: Impact of environmental degradation and contamination on psychological health and well-being. In D. Sandhu (Ed.), *Faces of violence: Psychological correlates, concepts, and intervention strategies* (pp. 129–142). Huntington, NY: Nova Science.

Sodowsky, G. R., Kuo-Jackson, P. Y., & Loya, G. J. (1997). In D. Pope-Davis & H. L. K. Coleman (Eds.), *Multicultural counseling competencies: Assessment, education and training, and supervision* (pp. 3–42). Thousand Oaks, CA: Sage.

Sodowsky, G. R., Taffe, R. C., Gutkin, T. B., & Wise, S. L. (1994). Development of the Multicultural Counseling Inventory: A self-report measure of multicultural competencies. *Journal of Counseling Psychology, 41,* 137–148.

Sue, D. W., Arredondo, P., & McDavis, R. J. (1992). Multicultural counseling competencies and standards: A call to the profession. *Journal of Multicultural Counseling and Development, 20,* 477–486.

Sue, D. W., Bernier, J. E., Durran, A., Feinberg, L., Pedersen, P., Smith, E. J., & Vazquez-Nutall, E. (1982). Position paper: Cross-cultural counseling competencies. *The Counseling Psychologist, 10,* 45–52.

Sue, D. W., Carter, R. T., Casas, M., Fouad, N. A., Ivey, A. E., Jensen, M., LaFromboise, T., Manese, J. E., Ponterotto, J. G., & Vazquez-Nutall, E. (1998). *Multicultural counseling competencies: Individual and organizational development.* Thousand Oaks, CA: Sage.

Chapter 5

Cultural Considerations in Counselor Training and Supervision

Marie Faubert and Don C. Locke

This chapter focuses on the teaching of multicultural counseling in counselor education. The authors, both counselor educators and members of the Association for Counselor Education and Supervision, write from their combined experiences teaching about cultural diversity. We explore the nature of the multicultural debate in the classroom, communicate efforts for inclusion of diverse voices in discourse, advocate for liberation, and do so with integrity.

This chapter considers procedures for providing an educational environment that develops competence and confidence (Locke, 1998) among students from various cultural and language groups. Suggestions for maximizing opportunities are made, with a focus on how to make all students feel welcome and be successful. We agree with an assessment of education presented by Canfield and Lafferty (1974):

> Education is squarely speared on the horns of an old dilemma, an ancient conflict that lies below the surface of all inquiry into the teaching/learning process. On one side we are convinced that people are different. Some emphasis upon individual differences is found in almost every pedagogical work. The concept is established virtually beyond refute. Our continuing subtle but pervasive search for the best represents the other way to teach. If it is true that everyone is different, then it cannot be true that there is one way that is best for everyone. (p. i)

This chapter also addresses effective teaching and supervising strategies, many of which require rethinking of teaching and supervision, and focuses on reciprocal pedagogy and reciprocal supervising. The measurement of minimal competency in issues of culture and diversity will secure the counseling profession.

51

Reciprocal Pedagogy

Before reciprocal pedagogy (Freire, 1970, 1993a, 1993b) can take place, students must be recruited and retained. The quality of recruited students is dependent upon the quality of the recruiting practices. The success of retention is dependent upon the quality of the counselor education program, among other things. The quality of the program is dependent on the soundness of the theoretical underpinnings espoused by the program. This chapter's consideration of reciprocal pedagogy includes recruitment, retention, theoretical foundations, classroom learning, and assignments.

Recruitment

One of the best methods for recruitment of diversity is word of mouth. If counselor educators are seen in diverse communities, are active in neighborhoods, and invite current and former students to help with recruitment, then counselor educators will have success in diversifying their student bodies. Influencing potential students and their families by personally inviting them to come and see will result in serious investigations of a counselor education program. Making sure that people of color and members of other groups are active members of advisory committees and speakers in classes as well as among the faculty facilitates diversification of students.

Personal contact with all prospective students is essential. In a city where there are several counselor education programs, competition for students is intense. When potential students call seeking information, it is important that inquiries be directed to a person, and not to a machine. When students are wondering about how they might fit into a program, personal contact can aide in communicating a sincere invitation to potential students.

Personal contact is essential for effective recruitment. Where counselor education programs are targeting large numbers of students in a particular setting, visits to the setting by counselor educators should prove to be useful in recruiting all students, but especially students of color.

Retention

Students of color, students whose first language is other than English, students who might wonder if they will be accepted because of their sexual orientation, students who practice a religion different from the majority in the community or university, and students with a variety of other circumstances want to know if they will be valued for who they are. Successful directors of programs and professors who are proactive facilitate embracing the culture, language, and various realities of the students in the program.

A relative on the advisory committee on admissions of a counselor education program had convinced one African American student to enroll in that program. This student later shared with the director of the program and with other students that she had been in two master's programs before coming to this one. She asserted that she had left both of them because she felt unwelcome and alienated and felt that the programs were not preparing her to become a professional school counselor in the real world.

The first night of the first class this student sat with her arms folded and her eyes down. The students were sitting in a circle as is customary in this particular program. The student was sitting directly opposite the professor. The professor took the challenge of getting her to open up, at least to get her to speak, before the first class was over. It took 45 minutes to invite her gently to speak and get a response.

After the student felt comfortable in the program, she became very active. She served as president of Chi Sigma Iota International and became a leader in the service components of the counselor education program. She told the professor that if she had not been welcomed and encouraged in that first class and in subsequent classes of the program's courses, she would have left it and never tried again for a master's degree. This student is now a successful professional school counselor valued by students, parents, colleagues, and principal.

The professor was proactive in encouraging another student whose first language is Arabic, and who is from Egypt, to use Arabic in class. Spanish was a common language in that particular counselor education program. It was important that the Arabic-speaking student did not feel left out. Her *language of the heart* needed to be affirmed and valued as well as the first language of the Spanish-speaking students. In addition, it was important to include in the curriculum aspects of her history and culture pertinent to counseling.

There is an expression in Spanish—*Conosco a mis hennanos*—that means that a person knows another so well that his or her needs and desires can be anticipated. Successful professors know their students this way. They can anticipate their needs and desires in such a way that they can use the uniqueness of each student to develop each as a culturally competent and confident counselor. The grist for reciprocal pedagogy is present in every class of the program as it is in any counseling group (Yalom, 1995).

Successful retention is conscious and committed. Professors who design interventions that include all students for every aspect of the program will be successful in establishing a culture of appreciation for diversity. All students will benefit. Students will become culturally competent and confident.

Theoretical Foundations

What is reciprocal pedagogy? In a counselor education program it means that all are teachers and all are learners. The professor and students bring to the classroom history, culture, tradition, language, and collective life experiences. All are rich sources of content for developing an understanding of theory and skills in counseling.

This perspective might look esoteric until the background for this approach is considered. In this age of inclusiveness, counselor educators utilize the gifts that all students bring to the table. When recruitment for a diverse student body has been successful, drawing on the strengths of the students is rather easy because each comes with a distinctive set of benefactions. Rather than being esoteric, reciprocal pedagogy becomes almost unlimited in possibilities.

In order to use this rich source of potential for the development of content and practice, a theory of pedagogy that gives legitimacy to reciprocal pedagogy is essential. Furthermore, pedagogy can be called a profession and can be effective only if it has a strong theoretical base. A theoretical foundation, supporting the perspective of reciprocal pedagogy, was proposed by Paulo Freire, the universally recognized Brazilian educator (1970, 1973, 1985, 1993a, 1993b, 1994, 1998; Chonchol, 1973; Escobar, Fernandez, Guevara-Niebla, & Freire, 1994; Gadotti, 1994; Shor & Freire, 1987).

In his books *Pedagogy of the Oppressed* (1970), *Pedagogy of the Oppressed: New Revised 20th-Anniversary Edition* (1993b), and *Pedagogy of Hope* (1994), Freire set the groundwork for his theories, and in *Education for Critical Consciousness* (1973), he outlined the practical ways of implementing the theory. Locke and Faubert (1999) and Faubert and Locke (in press) have profiled the application of Freire's theory to counselor education.

When Freire was asked by the Brazilian government to raise the literacy level in one part of rural Brazil, he sent his graduate students into the rural areas to listen. From what they heard, Freire and his students developed a vocabulary of what they called *generative words* (for example, *favela* — slum) that were part of the everyday vocabulary of the residents whom Freire and his students were mandated to teach to read

(Freire, 1973). The meanings of generative words were shared in a reciprocal dialogue. The words were divided into syllables (fa-ve-la), and the phonemic families were introduced. Reading had begun.

We have very briefly glanced at Freire's methods. What do his methods have to do with preparing professional counselors to be culturally competent and confident? The remainder of this chapter addresses this question.

Classroom Learning

When Freire sent his graduate students into the countryside to be with the people, he commissioned them to listen and hear. The dominant United States culture does not develop skills of listening and hearing. Sound bites, and responding and reacting to talk, are common, but people are not encouraged to listen and hear people different from themselves. Counselor educators have the countercultural challenge to consciously enhance the ability of students to listen and hear. There is no better place to begin to listen to and hear one another than in the classroom.

However, until students feel heard, they will not be motivated to sharpen their abilities to listen and hear. At the beginning of each semester and many classes, activities can be prepared to enhance the feeling of being heard and the skills of listening and hearing. In classes on sociocultural/family issues in counseling, professors might begin with the following activity:

> I remind you that in this class we are going to discuss issues that are emotionally close to us. There is no issue more emotional than that of family. In addition, we are going to talk about race, substance abuse, and culture. I want you to feel secure that you will not be asked to share anything that you are not relaxed about sharing or do not wish to share. Sometimes there might be some feeling of discomfort; you might be willing to venture sharing in areas that you feel safe. Sometimes growth requires challenge. Be assured of support to accompany your challenging yourself in this class.
>
> I invite you to participate in this activity: Write the first five words that come into your mind when you think of each of these phrases: family, race, substance abuse, social behavior, and culture.

After giving the students time to think and write, invite them to share on whatever level they feel comfortable and safe. One way of saying this might be, "Using your responses to these phrases, tell us your name and anything else you would like us to know about you."

This first activity is more challenging than the one that follows because courses in sociocultural/family issues in counseling are advanced courses in programs. Students are already listening and hearing and know the philosophy and culture of respective programs. Most will feel more comfortable venturing later than earlier in their programs.

The next activity is more appropriate for courses nearer to the beginning of a program when students are not so experienced with listening and hearing, the philosophy and culture of the program, and the professors and other students. This activity has been used in group counseling classes:

> Place your name in the middle of a piece of paper. On the top left-hand corner write your favorite color. On the top right-hand corner write one place you have visited. On the lower right-hand corner write one goal you have for this course. On the lower left-hand corner write one of your values.

This activity gives students the chance to share on many levels. On one hand, maybe the only thing that will be learned is the favorite color. On the other hand, a significant number of students may want to share their values with others present in the class. At least professors and students are listening to one another and are on the road to hearing one another.

A third activity that has been fruitful in helping students feel heard and in honing their skills of listening and hearing involves asking them to think of the geometric figure that best represents them, such as a straight line, circle, spiral, square, or hexagon. Then invite them to share the reasons for choosing the figure that they chose. The geometric figure is not threatening and provides an opportunity for students to share in a way in which they feel comfortable and at the same time invites some risk taking at a suitable level. If the professor models the behavior, students will understand how much self-disclosure is appropriate.

These three activities, and many others, give students the opportunity to be heard with respect and to sharpen their skills in listening and hearing. The subjects introduced are theirs just as the generative words belonged to the peasants of Brazil. When students are heard and required to hear, then courses are beginning to develop culturally competent and confident professional counselors who can listen with respect and hear people like them and different from them.

It is important that the classroom be arranged in a circle. Sitting around a table is helpful if the class is small enough. Some have the privilege of teaching from 7 to 15 students in a class, but others have classes with as many as 28 students in them.

How students seat themselves in a classroom can be related to culture or diversity. Sensitivity to issues of culture and diversity encourages students' exploration and sharing of their reasons for choice of seats. An Egyptian student once remarked that she sits beside the professor because it would not be polite to sit opposite her and make eye contact. Other students like sitting opposite a professor. They say that they feel connected when they can make eye contact.

Meta-discussions on classroom discussions enhance listening and hearing activities. Students reflect on how the males and females in the class hear one another. They consider different communication styles and who are the initiators, carriers, and summarizers of conversation. They concentrate on who speaks after a general invitation and who needs a specific invitation from the professor or another student. There are many other aspects of communication that can be examined, and generalizations may be made to professional counseling.

The level of comfort in sharing personal stories helps students concentrate on issues of culture, gender, or others that are germane. Permission to be discrete or open is essential. Students may not always feel perfectly relaxed, but they must always feel safe. Professors must provide a place in which students feel sufficiently comfortable to practice new ways of thinking, feeling, and behaving, and, at the same time, feel safe.

One way of achieving content learning while providing an environment of discourse is to have the students reflect on the readings, the professor comment on the reflections, and after every student has spoken, add any salient content that has been omitted. As one student said, in order to be able to do this effectively, professors must have command of the content.

The difference between independent and interdependent construal of self (Matsumoto, 1994) is an important idea in developing culturally competent and confident counselors. Often an occasion arises in class that provides the opportunity to teach an important concept like this one serendipitously. Professors use these teachable moments to enhance cultural competence and confidence.

A student role-playing a counselor listened but did not hear a student role-playing a client when she told him that she was worried that she was not meeting the needs of her students, her family, and her faith. She elaborated on her statement by giving the counselor many examples. The "counselor" asked the "client" about her own needs and suggested that she needed to meet them before she worried about being approved by all the other people she mentioned.

The "client" came from a culture with an interdependent construal of self. She had been in the United States for just a few years and had not acculturated to an independent construal of self. When the "counselor" suggested that the "client" think of herself, she had a puzzled and anxious look on her face. The "counselor" did not notice the expression.

This experience gave the student counselor and his colleagues an opportunity to develop an understanding of the difference between independent construal of self and interdependent construal of self and the importance of reading nonverbal cues. The professor modeled for the class, and the student was thanked for the courage to learn and teach.

In a professional issues and ethics course, students were instructed to go to an agency that serves the economically poor and just sit for 20 minutes. They were directed to see, hear, smell, and feel as much as they could and then write a paper about the experience. One student did more than was asked. She dressed down, with no makeup, and in a house dress, sandals, and no stockings. She went to the agency and sat down. No one paid any attention to her. In a week or two, she went back to the same agency. This time she was dressed up, with makeup and in business suit, heels, and stockings. She was asked three times if anything could be done for her.

From in vivo assignments students learn from one another what is going on in agencies and schools. From research assignments students learn from one another the content and process of research, and learn to "speak" research as well as "write" research. From activity-creating assignments, students share techniques that they can use in classroom guidance situations.

When students come to class with a first language other than English, professors have the opportunity to enhance knowledge of how language influences thinking, feeling, and behaving.

A student once asked, "What do I do if I cannot speak the language of the client?" The professor gave a demonstration by inviting an Arabic-speaking student to speak in her native language. The Arabic-speaking student enjoyed the opportunity to speak the language of her home in class, and the students saw demonstrated methods of inviting clients to speak in their first language. Students with experiences like this leave counselor education programs feeling more confident about how they will handle clients whose first language is not English or who may have limited English proficiency.

In a career counseling class, the professor invited an undergraduate college student to role-play being a client for career counseling so that the professor could demonstrate the various stages of career development. The students got a chance to see the professor actually introduce professional disclosure information to the client, discuss confidentiality and its limitations, and present other pertinent information related to informed consent. Students saw goals being set and short-term counseling done.

After each of the sessions, the professor and students wrote their reflections about the experience in their journals and then engaged in a meta-discussion about what happened in the session. The importance of record keeping was discussed, and legal and ethical implications of record keeping were considered.

In summary, the classroom is a place where cultural considerations are the grist for thoughts, feelings, and behaviors. Students think from cultural perspectives, name their feelings from cultural perspectives, and respond and react to content, one another, and the professor from cultural perspectives. Culture permeates everything going on in the classroom. Culturally competent and confident professors use culture, especially the culture in the classroom, as the source for reciprocal teaching and learning.

Assignments

Traditional assignments can be used in new ways. New assignments can move teaching and learning to a more reciprocal experience. Competing with communication methods in a society that entertains students with sound bites and voyeurism provides challenges to professors that can be met with reciprocal pedagogy.

The traditional research paper is still important. It can be used to teach about research writing and to speak on research. It can also be used to enhance understanding of the limitations of research in all areas, but especially in generalizing to cultures not represented in the samples or in methods not appropriate to the samples. Conclusions drawn by researchers can also be evaluated in the context of cultural variables (Locke, 1998).

Research papers provide the opportunity to recommend to students that they become familiar with action research (Mills, 2000; Selner, 1997) as they complete literature searches. Action research provides the investigator with tools to make the examinee the subject as opposed to the object of the discourse. Mills (2000) pointed out that action research enhances change. Willingness to change is essential in nurturing cultural competence and confidence.

When assigning research papers, professors have the opportunity to introduce students to journals, books, and other sources that originate in populations not always well represented in commonly known sources. Counselor education students should become familiar with African American, Latin American, Asian American, and Native American professionals in the field. Research papers can help them achieve this important goal for enhancing cultural competence and confidence.

In addition, in vivo visits and writing and sharing about them are also helpful in developing cultural competence and confidence. Classroom role-plays of counseling give students the opportunity to feel and do counseling before prepracticum, practicum, or internship.

Preparing and facilitating class discussions on the part of students are also meaningful. As with the conversation between the woman who made pottery and Paulo Freire (Freire, 1973), they provide opportunities for codification, decodification, and recodification. Students rethink their points of view regarding people unlike themselves. They move to new ways of feeling and behaving in situations that are unfamiliar. In addition, what students create for the counselor education classroom can be sources for insightful workshops to be replicated at state and national professional growth conferences at which students have the opportunity to share with professors as presenters. Here they enhance their cultural competence and confidence by applying their skills at reciprocal pedagogy and meeting people from other parts of the United States and world.

Other effective assignments include book reports of primary sources. A counseling program is a graduate program, and in this setting, students will benefit from being introduced to primary sources in addition to journal articles. This is an occasion to introduce students to sources not found in many of their textbooks (Guthrie, 1998).

One policy that is essential is that the professor carefully thinks out all assignments. Each assignment must have a specific purpose, and it is astute to share that intention with students. When they know the rationale for an assignment, no matter how challenging, they work very hard at it, and they benefit maximally from it.

Reciprocal Supervision

The roles of professors and supervisors are not mutually exclusive, but they are somewhat different. Professors and supervisors are facilitators of discussions and meta-discussions on content and practice. Supervisors provide a more intense degree of support than professors. Supervisees need more encouragement in supervision than in the classroom.

New counselors meeting clients for the first time look to supervisors for support and concrete help in making counseling successful.

Supervisees succeed in an atmosphere of support and challenge. Supervisees flourish when there is open communication between supervisors and supervisees and among students in practice. Supervision, like teaching, is most constructive if the supervision is reciprocal. When professor-supervisors meet with students one-on-one, the students are given the opportunity to suggest the skills they want to concentrate on.

Reciprocal supervision is not unstructured. Students may be given a list of counselor and client behaviors. They can use this list to choose the skills on which they want to work. When supervisees and supervisors are finished discussing the skills on which they agreed to work, supervisors might suggest skills on which to concentrate that they think will benefit supervisees. Supervisors and supervisees work on these skills together by pointing them out on videotapes, practicing them, and planning how they will put them into practice in the next session with the client.

Supervisees who are in a counselor education program that integrates cultural competence and confidence will be aware of issues of culture between themselves and their counselees. An African American supervisee was counseling an Iranian American client. The client had come into counseling hostile toward her parents who would not let her date and who chose her college major for her. She felt angry because they had chosen her future spouse.

She was dating outside her ethnic group and had chosen a major different from the one that they thought she was majoring in. She felt guilty, shameful, anxious, resentful, and confused. The practicum student listened while the client told her story. There did not seem to be a solution.

While discussing the situation in practicum class, the supervisee realized that the struggle this client was having was related to acculturation. She had been influenced by the United States much more than her parents had been. When the client's issues were reframed as ones relating to acculturation, the client let go of some of her guilt, shame, anxiety, resentment, and confusion, and began filtering what about her was traditionally Iranian and what about her was becoming American. The rest of the counseling time was spent helping the client sort out her feelings and make some decisions with which she could feel comfortable.

In the sessions, the client struggled with acculturation, with the questions she had to face in her life: What were the cultural traits that

61

would remain Iranian? What were the cultural traits that she wanted in order to become American? How was she going to talk with her parents about her choices? Would they listen to her or think she was being disrespectful and ungrateful? How important was family to her? How much could she deviate from family expectations and still remain part of the family?

The sessions took place in the counseling laboratory on campus, so all the students in the practicum class could watch the sessions through a one-way mirror. Because all practicum students shared the experience of the student counselor grappling with cultural issues, there was ample opportunity for the supervisor to use the experience to sharpen the skills of the students.

In a way all counseling is cross-cultural. No two people are exactly alike, even in the same family or cultural group. In multicultural counseling classes, the students learned that within-group differences are always greater than between-group differences. Therefore, astute supervisors always have grist for cultivating cultural competence and confidence. Attention is always paid to the cultural issues in counseling sessions.

Conclusion

This chapter has examined recruitment and retention of potentially successful students, a theoretical foundation for effective pedagogy, strategies for success in the classroom, and helpful assignments. New ways of thinking, feeling, and doing vis-à-vis supervision have been explored. Now it is time to turn to the issues of minimal competency and how a state should measure it in order to protect the public and the practitioner.

References

Canfield, A. A., & Lafferty, L. C. (1974). *Learning Styles Inventory*. Birmingham, MI: Humanics Media.

Chonchol, J. (1973). *Extension or communication* (M. B. Ramos, Trans.). New York: Continuum. (Original work published 1969)

Escobar, M., Fernandez, A. L., Guevara-Niebla, G., & Freire, P. (1994). *Paulo Freire on higher education: A dialogue at the National University of Mexico*. Albany, NY: State University of New York Press.

Faubert, M., & Locke, D. C. (in press). Language diversity in counselor education. In R. T. Carter (Ed.), *Handbook on racial-cultural psychology*. New York: Wiley.

Freire, P. (1970). *Pedagogy of the oppressed* (M. B. Ramos, Trans.). New York: Continuum. (Original work published 1968)

Freire, P. (1973). *Education for critical consciousness* (Study of Development and Social Change, Cambridge, MA, Trans.). New York: Continuum. (Original work published 1969)

Freire, P. (1985). *The politics of education: Culture, power, and liberation* (D. Macedo, Trans.). South Hadley, MA: Bergin & Garvey.

Freire, P. (1993a). *Pedagogy of the city* (D. Macedo, Trans.). New York: Continuum.

Freire, P. (1993b). *Pedagogy of the oppressed: New revised 20th anniversary edition* (M. B. Ramos, Trans.). New York: Continuum.

Freire, P. (1994). *Pedagogy of hope: Reliving pedagogy of the oppressed* (R. R. Barr, Trans.). New York: Continuum. (Original work published 1992)

Freire, P. (1998). *Teachers as cultural workers: Letters to those who dare teach* (D. Macedo, D. Koike, & A. Oliveira, Trans.). Boulder, CO: Westview.

Gadotti, M. (1994). *Reading Paulo Freire: His life and work* (J. Milton, Trans.). Albany, NY: State University of New York Press.

Guthrie, R. V. (1998). *Even the rat was White: A historical view of psychology* (2nd ed.). Boston: Allyn & Bacon.

Locke, D. C. (1998). *Increasing multicultural understanding: A comprehensive model* (2nd ed.). Thousand Oaks, CA: Sage.

Locke, D. C., & Faubert, M. (1999). Innovative pedagogy for critical consciousness in counselor education. In M. S. Kiselica (Ed.), *Confronting prejudice and racism during multicultural training* (pp. 43-58). Alexandria, VA: American Counseling Association.

Matsumoto, D. (1994). *People: Psychology from a cultural perspective*. Pacific Grove, CA: Brooks/Cole.

Mills, G. E. (2000). *Action research: A guide for the teacher researcher*. Upper Saddle River, NJ: Merrill.

Selner, D. (1997). *Participatory action research and social change*. Ithaca, NY: Cornell University Press.

Shor, I., & Freire, P. (1987). *A pedagogy for liberation: Dialogues on transforming education*. South Hadley, MA: Bergen & Garvey.

Yalom, 1. D. (1995). *The theory and practice of group psychotherapy* (4th ed.). New York: Basic Books.

Part Two

---

*Multicultural
Interventions*

Chapter 6

Women of Color and Substance Abuse: A Counseling Model for an African American Woman Client

Octavia Madison-Colmore and James L. Moore III

Nearly 3 million women in the United States are substance abusers. Women of all races and socioeconomic statuses use and abuse alcohol and other drugs. Unfortunately, researchers and counseling practitioners know little about the extent of substance abuse among women, especially women of color, because few studies have focused on this population. For counseling to be effective, practitioners must understand the cultural values, norms, and beliefs regarding alcohol and other drug use among different racial, ethnic, and gender groups. One method that might be helpful to practitioners in working with women of color is the History, Empowerment, Rapport, and Spirituality (H.E.R.S.) model, which is discussed in this chapter. This particular model, although not empirically tested, draws from the literature on counseling women of color.

Women of all races and socioeconomic statuses suffer from the serious illness of drug addiction. According to the Center for Substance Abuse Prevention (2000), women make up one of the fastest growing substance abusing populations in the United States, with nearly 3 million American women abusing alcohol and/or other drugs (25% of all abusers). Unfortunately, little is known about the prevalence of alcohol and other drug use in women because few studies have adequately focused on them and have seldom included representative numbers of women from different racial and ethnic minorities (Blumenthal, 1998; Canino, 1994; Dowdall, Crawford, & Wechsler, 1998; Herd, 1993; Hughes, Day, Marcantonio, & Torpy, 1997; Lo & Globetti, 1993; Padgett, Patrick, Burns, & Schlesinger, 1994; Womble, 1990). The vast majority of research on women and, specifically, on substance abuse has been conducted on European American, middle-class women, with the assumption that findings on this population could be generalized to all women regardless of their race, class, gender, or other variables (Eliason, 1999).

In spite of the paucity of research regarding substance abuse and women of color, some studies have been carried out. Most of these studies have not focused on African American, Hispanic/Latino, American Indian, or Asian American women, but have mostly consisted of descriptions of drinking patterns and behaviors of a minority population in comparison with the dominant culture. Also, the findings of these studies are inconclusive. For example, Herd (1993) examined alcohol-related problems in both Black and White women drinkers and found that there were similar drinking behaviors and alcohol-related problems in the two groups; but Hughes et al. (1997) studied gender differences in alcohol and other drug use and found rates of "heavy" alcohol consumption to be higher among White women than African American and Hispanic women. Chatham (1990) posited that drinking patterns among Black women with increased socioeconomic status and education tend to parallel those of the White female population.

Other researchers have found alcohol among the Asian population, regardless of gender, to be less frequently used compared with American Indians, Whites, Hispanics, and African Americans (Collins, 1993; D'Avanzo, Frye, & Froman, 1994; Kim, McLeod, & Shantzis, 1995; Zane & Hub-Kim, 1998). However, Asians, owing to the constraints of such cultural values as social shame, may be underreporting or underutilizing substance abuse treatment. Results from the National Institute on Drug Abuse (1998) found European American women between the ages of 15 and 24 to have the highest (45%) lifetime rate of alcohol and drug use, followed by Hispanic (31.4%), African American (29%), and women of other races (24.2%).

As a result of the limited meaning of cross-ethnic group research and inconclusive findings, working with women of color can be challenging to counseling practitioners. As Taylor (1999) noted, traditional psychological concepts offer little to address effectively the intersection of race, gender, and mental health. This chapter presents one method, the History, Employment, Rapport, and Spirituality model, which is designed for working with women of color. The chapter begins with the story of Shala, an African American college student who uses alcohol and other drugs to cope with college life. Therapeutic models designed for working with minority clients are briefly presented, followed by a discussion of the H.E.R.S. model in which the model is defined, delineated, and demonstrated using a case study of Shala. The chapter culminates with implications for future research.

Shala's Story

Hello, my name is Shala, and I am an alcoholic. I am a 21-year-old college student, majoring in pre-med. I began drinking at the age of 16, around the same time I first attempted suicide. It was also during this time that two of my brothers started molesting me. I grew up in a small rural town with my six brothers and sisters, including myself. I am the youngest. Our home was nice, but small: three bedrooms, two baths, and a huge backyard. My parents shared one of the three bedrooms, and the other two rooms were divided by gender, girls in one and boys in the other. Because there were so many of us, I learned early what it was like to share.

As we all got older, space became less of a problem. My siblings either moved out on their own, enlisted in the military, or got married. At age 16, I finally had my very own room. Two of my brothers, who were still living at home, would come in my room at night, after my Mom and Dad had gone to bed. At first, I thought it was fun. We drank beer, I taught them the steps to the latest dance, and they molested me. I knew in the back of my mind what they were doing to me was wrong, but I never told them to stop. One day while listening to the local news, I heard about the arrest of a father who had molested his daughter. I began wondering what would happen to my parents and my brothers if they found out that I, too, was being molested. As I pondered on these thoughts, I kept saying to myself, well, if I were dead they would never know. For nearly 2 weeks, I thought about ways to end my life. I finally got the urge to take some pills. I took about 20 or 30 pills, whatever my mother had in the medicine cabinet. I did not know what they were or what they were prescribed for. I just wanted my life to be over. My little brother found me passed out on my bed with prescription bottles on the floor. He thought I was dead. He telephoned my mother at work who instructed him to call the ambulance. I was rushed to the hospital where they pumped my stomach. I stayed overnight and was discharged the next day. The doctor suggested to my parents that I seek counseling. My parents took me to the local community mental health center, which was located about 2 or 3 miles from our home. My parents did not have insurance, so private therapy was out of the question. I met with a counselor for about six or seven sessions. She was really getting frustrated with me because I would not discuss the suicide attempt. My parents tried to get me to talk as well. They even tried to get our neighbor, a lady whom I called Aunt Shirley, to talk with me along with our minister. I was really resistant to talking with anyone. I was mad because I failed at something I really wanted to do.

At age 18 when I entered college, I began feeling lonely and depressed. I called home daily telling my parents how much I hated college and how I wanted to come home. My parents thought I was homesick, something that I would get over in a few days. Those few days came and went and I still felt the same. I had no one to talk to. I was shy and withdrawn. I just didn't fit in. I tried once again to end my life. This time I cut my wrist. My roommate walked into the room just as I ran the razor blade across my wrist. I remember her saying, "Woman, are you crazy?" She immediately wrapped my wrist with a towel and rushed me over to the infirmary. I told the nurse that it was an accident, that my hand had slipped. I guess she believed me since she didn't refer me to counseling or call my parents. When I returned to my room I kept wondering why God would not let me die. Meanwhile, my roommate and I began spending more time together, going to parties and meeting new friends.

I met this guy at one of the parties that I really liked. We started hanging out and having a good time. He was one of those big time guys who always kept brandy and liquor in the room. I started drinking with him and later he introduced me to marijuana and cocaine. I was feeling really good about myself at this point. Approximately 6 months into the relationship, I learned that I was pregnant. When I shared this with my friend, his immediate response was to get an abortion. I was totally against abortions, but I really wanted to hold on to this guy because I loved him. I decided to have the abortion to maintain the relationship. Shortly after the abortion, he decided to end the relationship. I was so angry. I began drinking more and more alcohol and using drugs. I attended classes maybe once a week, sometimes once every 2 or 3 weeks. I also missed a lot of time from my part-time job. My grades suffered and I was eventually fired from my job. I started hanging out with some of the guys on campus, drinking and doing drugs. Occasionally, I would sleep with them for drugs.

During the fall semester of my junior year, I "hit bottom." I visited my doctor to get something to help me relax because I was feeling very anxious. Final exams were coming up and I wanted to do well. I had used some cocaine to help me stay awake and study. But I needed something to help me relax. My doctor, unaware of my drug use, wrote me a prescription for Valium. Not knowing the dangers of mixing Valium with alcohol and cocaine, I passed out and was rushed to the hospital. Although I was not trying to kill myself, my doctor was convinced that I was and demanded that I seek counseling. He arranged for me to see the psychologist at the hospital. The next thing I remembered was being admitted to the psych ward at the hospital. I was thinking to myself that this must be a dream. I am not crazy. Why do they have me here with all of these crazy people? After a week in the hospital I decided to leave against the advice of my doctor. Although he could not make me stay, he did suggest that I seek further counseling. This was interesting because my roommate had shared with me a while back that I needed to go and get some counseling. After much resistance and weeks of wondering whether or not I should go to counseling, I decided to seek professional help. Since money was a factor, I sought help from the counseling center on campus.

> When I entered the counseling center, I was taken back by the lack of African American counselors. Since my freshman year, all I heard was "Diversity this" and "Diversity that," so I wondered where the diversity was at the center. I started to leave until I heard a soft little voice saying, "May I help you?" I responded quite loudly by stating, "Yes, I need to see an African American counselor." Surprisingly, there were no African American counselors and no counselors of color working at the center. I said to myself, "How can they help me? They do not have a clue to what I am all about. I am an African American woman in need of an African American counselor." Despite the lack of African American counselors at the counseling center, I sought the help that I needed, and I stand before you today to say, I am clean and I am sober and I have been this way for the last 2 years.

Shala's story is one of thousands of stories shared by women across the country who have survived the deadly disease of alcoholism and drug addiction. Women who drink and use drugs put themselves at risk for dangerous behaviors, including suicidal thoughts and attempts, unwanted and unsafe sex, and poor academic performance. They also suffer from low self-esteem, feelings of loneliness, helplessness, and powerlessness. Unfortunately, when it comes to seeking professional help, women, including women of color, are often faced with several barriers, such as transportation, childcare, and financial assistance. Women of color may face additional cultural and language barriers that could hinder the counseling process. Women who find themselves in double jeopardy, that is, they are members of two oppressed groups because of race and gender, are especially prone to being misunderstood and misrepresented in the field of psychology (Taylor, 1999).

Therapy Models Designed for Minority Clients

Several models have been developed to assist counseling practitioners in working with minorities. However, these models do not adequately address the unique needs of women of color. For instance, the Deficit Model conceptualizes minorities as being intellectually flawed, socially disadvantaged, and culturally deprived (Ridley, 1995). The Medical Model, which has dominated the helping profession, views psychological problems as a disease (Ridley, 1995). The Conformity Model contends that problems can be normally distributed, and thus excludes cultural background (Ridley, 1995). The Biopsychosocial Model, which is used quite frequently in the counseling profession, focuses on the whole person (e.g., physical, psychological, social, and emotional well-being). The Systemic Model, a more active, innovative approach to counseling, is

71

designed to "help Black people provide for themselves, rather than receive traditional treatment which causes them to be dependent" (Gunnings & Lipscomb, 1986, p. 22). Finally, the Affirmation Model focuses on the characteristics of the counselor, such as responding in a nonthreatening manner, being genuine and empathic, paraphrasing, using open-ended questions, building rapport, and becoming an advocate for the client (Larrabee, 1986). The one method that takes into account the unique needs of women of color and is believed to be helpful to counseling practitioners is the H.E.R.S. model, which is described in detail in the next section.

H.E.R.S. Model

The History, Empowerment, Rapport, and Spirituality model was developed following a thorough review of the literature in which several recurrent themes were noted on counseling African American women. These themes included understanding the cultural *history* (Gainor & Forrest, 1991; Jordan, 1997; McNair, 1992, 1996; Sanchez-Hucles, 2000; Vontress & Epp, 1997); motivating women to change through a process of *empowerment* (Brown, 1995; Brown, Lipford-Sanders, & Shaw, 1995; Jordan, 1997; Mehra, 1997; Raheim & Bolden, 1995; Rubenstein & Lawler, 1990; Sanders, 1996; Williams & Frame, 1999); challenging women to increase interpersonal skills through a process of building *rapport* (Cook, 1993, Gainor, 1992; McDavis, Parker, & Parker, 1995; Sanchez-Hucles, 2000); and incorporating *spirituality* into the clinical process (Ahia, 1997; Baer, 1993; Cook, 1993; Dunn & Dawes, 1999; McRae, Thompson, & Cooper, 1999; Richardson & June, 1997; Sanders, 1996). Also, following the development of the History, Identity, and Spirituality (H.I.S.) model, a therapeutic strategy designed for counseling African American males (Madison-Colmore & Moore, 2002), the authors were compelled to design and develop a method for counseling the African American woman client.

The first step in the H.E.R.S model is gaining an understanding of the client's cultural history/herstory, including the values, beliefs, life experiences, worldviews, and customs. The words *history/herstory* are used collectively to symbolize the importance of understanding culture from a feminist perspective. Several resources are available to assist counselors in finding information about the cultural history of women of color. Counselors can research the literature, attend special seminars and conferences, go to cultural events, and/or seek special training in working with women of color. One tool that may be helpful is the cultural genogram. Similar to the traditional genogram, which gathers information on the basic structure of the family, the demographics, the functioning level, and the relationship among members of the family of origin, the cultural genogram takes this process a step further by including the extended and unrelated family members (e.g., friends in the community, neighbors, church members) and asking questions pertaining to the clients' cultural history. The extended genogram serves two major purposes: (1) the role of individuals beyond the family of origin is emphasized, and (2) it identifies individuals who can provide both instrumental and emotional support (Paniagua, 1996).

The second step in this model is empowerment. According to Aspy and Sandhu (1999), empowerment is defined as a process in which people develop the skills and capacity for gaining control over their lives. Empowerment techniques that may be helpful to counseling practitioners include bibliotherapy, Bible stories, motivational training, and community involvement (Williams & Frame, 1999).

The third step is building rapport. Rapport is defined as a relationship, especially one of mutual trust or emotional affinity. Without rapport, it is difficult to connect or establish a trusting relationship. Group experience is one of the most effective tools to use to establish rapport. Groups provide a relatively safe environment for women to express themselves. Groups designed for women of color, specifically African American, provide "a sense of belonging, an immediate sense of sisterhood, a shared history, and an opportunity for personal growth" (Gainor, 1992, p. 235). Being connected to others and helping others to meet their needs is an important value shared by many women of color.

The fourth and final step in this model is spirituality. For many racial and ethnic minority groups, spirituality is a very important component in their lives. Spirituality is often associated with religion. However, not all women of color adhere to spirituality or recognize its importance. Therefore, practitioners must use caution when exploring or incorporating spirituality.

Applying the H.E.R.S. Model to the Case of Shala

Therapist: Shala, hi, my name is Anne. (Anne extends her hand to shake Shala's hand.)

So, what brings you in today?

Client: A lot of things. I have been drinking and using drugs, which has resulted in poor academic performance and the loss of my job. My boyfriend broke up with me, I have no friends, and I am feeling lonely and depressed. Besides all of that, my doctor is convinced that I am trying to kill myself after attempting suicide twice. And you people do not have an African American counselor here to help me. You are always talking about "Diversity this" and "Diversity that." Where is the diversity in this center?

Therapist: It sounds like you have several issues going on. Before we go any further, two thoughts come to mind. First, I was wondering if you had thoughts of harming yourself today?

Client: No! I have no immediate or future thoughts of harming myself and I do not have a plan. I have been in counseling before and was asked that same question.

Therapist: My second thought is . . . I noticed that you mentioned the lack of African American counselors, and I know that is important to you. I was wondering if you would be comfortable working with me, knowing that I am a White female counselor.

Client: It bothers me that there are no African American counselors on staff here. Since freshman year, all I have heard is "Diversity this" and "Diversity that"; yet there is no diversity here in the center. I am aware that I could probably go out in the community and find someone of color to work with me, but what the heck, my tuition covers the counseling here, so I might as well take advantage of it. But, just so you will know, I am not biased toward your culture and I hope that you are not biased toward mine. As long as we are clear on the biases, then I think we can work together.

Therapist: OK. Let's get started. Tell me about your alcohol and drug use.

Client: I began using at age 16. It started off as being something fun to do, and over the years, it has gotten progressively worse. I missed a lot of classes and my GPA [grade point average] is the pits. I also got fired from my job because I simply would not go to work. My boyfriend and I had problems, which I don't want to talk about. Since the breakup I have been drinking and using drugs a lot. But I like to drink and do drugs. It really makes me feel good. I know I am putting myself in danger, but I am not sure if I really want to stop using. Why give up something that makes you feel so good? Besides, drinking and using drugs have been the only way I could survive on this campus.

Therapist: Shala, has there ever been a time when you did not drink or use drugs?

Client: Yes, the first couple of months of my freshman year.

Therapist: What were those months like for you?

Client: Miserable. I had no friends, no one to talk to. I was homesick and wanted desperately to go home.

Therapist: What made you stay?

Client: I really don't know. I guess the suicide attempt. Following the last attempt, my roommate began spending more time with me; taking me to parties, introducing me to her friends. I met this guy whom I fell in love with. We drank and used some drugs. We are no longer together, but I do not want to talk about that.

Therapist: Shala, have you had a drink of alcohol today or used any drugs?

Client: No, not today.

Therapist: Just to share a bit of information with you, discontinuing the use of alcohol and other drugs can be difficult. There are a number of theories about the reasons people drink and use drugs. One theory, which is discussed quite frequently in the literature, is genetics. There are some researchers who say that people drink and use drugs because of a genetic link. I was wondering if there are people in your family that drink and/or use drugs?

History

Using the cultural genogram, Anne proceeds to gather information on Shala, her family, and her cultural history/herstory. Anne learned that Shala is the youngest of six siblings. During her upbringing, Shala's father drank heavily and her brothers also engaged in the use of alcohol. None of the sisters drank or used drugs, to her knowledge. She also learned that Shala was molested by two of her brothers at age 16. Shala had no close friends, either at school or in the neighborhood. However, Shala did baby sit for Aunt Shirley, a friend in the neighborhood, not related by blood. She also attended church with Aunt Shirley and, occasionally, with her family. Shala does not appear to be very close to either her sisters or her parents. However, she does appear to be close to the two brothers who molested her. Anne suspects that Shala may have played the role of the lost child in an alcoholic family. After gathering the history on Shala, her family, and her culture, Anne begins to explore ways to empower her.

Empowerment

Therapist: Shala, if I had a magic wand and could change your life, what would your life look like?

Client: I would be like Oprah Winfrey. Oprah strikes me as being someone who is always positive, full of life, and confident. She is also very generous.

Therapist: So what I hear you say is that you would like to feel more positive about yourself and more confident.

Client: Yes!

Therapist: So what do you think would make you feel more positive and more confident?

Client: Getting off of drugs permanently and not dealing with these crazy men. I think if I can get rid of those two things in my life, I can stay focused and concentrate more on my studies. The problem is, drugs make me feel good.

Therapist: I am wondering if you will be willing to attend a meeting where people, such as yourself, have problems with alcohol and other drugs. In these meetings, Alcoholic Anonymous or AA, people share their stories about their drinking and drug use and what they are doing not to drink and use drugs.

Client: The AA meeting sounds interesting. But what if I am not ready to stop drinking? You see, I really like to drink and use drugs.

Therapist: That's the purpose of the meeting, to help those who may not be ready to quit drinking and using drugs and to support those who have stopped.

Rapport

Anne introduced AA as a method not only to help Shala in understanding her addiction to alcohol and other drugs, but also to build Shala's confidence and increase her interpersonal skills. Anne believes that as Shala becomes involved in AA, she will develop friendships, which will assist her in building rapport and establishing healthier relationships. Anne also remembers how Shala enjoyed going to church with Aunt Shirley and introduces spirituality into the counseling process.

Spirituality

Therapist: Shala, another thing that comes to mind, which might be helpful to you in feeling more positive and more confident, is attending church. From what I have learned and observed, the church is a place where people can openly express their feelings without fear of reprisal. It is also a place to meet others who may have had similar experiences and thus serve as role models for you. You mentioned earlier that you attended church with Aunt Shirley and, occasionally, with your family. I am wondering if you would be interested in attending church now?

Client: I loved attending church with Aunt Shirley and with my family. Unfortunately, I have not been to church in quite some time. However, I am very spiritual. I love reading my Bible, listening to my gospel music, and meditating every now and then. For now, I would prefer to try AA and see how it goes; maybe later I shall think about attending church.

Therapist: OK. Before we end the session, I want to give you a list of AA meetings. The ones that I have highlighted are for women only. I think you will really enjoy these meetings. I am also attaching a list of resources in case you need to talk to someone before our meeting next week.

Client: OK. Thanks.

Conclusion/Future Directions

As mentioned, the research on women of color and substance abuse is limited and inconclusive. Therefore, further research is needed and must take the following into account: (1) cultural groups and subgroups and their knowledge of family roles, kinship bonds, commitment to religion, education and employment orientation, endurance of suffering, and their perception of alcohol and other drug use; (2) regional influences; and (3) levels of acculturation, which are often positively correlated with substance abuse. Although the research is scarce, substance abuse among women, especially women of color, is increasing. Traditional alcohol treatment models do not take into account the unique needs of women of color. The H.E.R.S. model, however, is one alternative method that may be helpful to counseling practitioners in working with women of color. Although the model has not been empirically tested, it draws from the literature on counseling women of color. Researchers and counseling practitioners may want to explore the usefulness of the H.E.R.S. model to determine its effectiveness. Finally, counseling practitioners must become aware of their own biases and stereotypes, which can negatively impact the counseling process.

References

Ahia, C. B. (1997). A cultural framework for counselors. In C. C. Lee (Ed.), *Multicultural issues in counseling: New approaches to diversity* (2nd ed., pp. 73-80). Alexandria, VA: American Counseling Association.

Aspy, C. B., & Sandhu, D. S. (1999). *Empowering women for equity: A counseling approach*. Alexandria, VA: American Counseling Association.

Baer, H. (1993). The limited empowerment of women in Black spiritual churches: An alternative vehicle to religious leadership. *Sociology of Religion, 54*, 65-82.

Blumenthal, S. J. (1998). Women and substance abuse: A new national focus. In C. L. Wetherington & A. B. Roman (Eds.), *Drug addiction research and the health of women* (pp. 13-32). NIH Publication No. 98-4290. Rockville, MD: U.S. Department of Health and Human Services.

Brown, C. (1995). Empowerment in social work practice with older women. *Social Work, 40*, 358-364.

Brown, S., Lipford-Sanders, J., & Shaw, M. (1995). Kujichagulia—uncovering the secrets of the heart: Group work with African American women on predominantly White campuses. *Journal for Specialists in Group Work, 20*, 151-158.

Canino, G. (1994). Alcohol use and misuse among Hispanic women: Selected factors, processes, and studies. *International Journal of the Addictions, 29*(9), 1083-1100.

Center for Substance Abuse Prevention. (2000). *Substance abuse resource guide: Women*. Publication No. (SMA) 94-2097. (Revised 2000). Rockville, MD: U.S. Department of Health and Human Services.

Chatham, L. R. (1990). Understanding the issues: An overview. In R. C. Engs (Ed.), *Women, alcohol, and other drugs* (pp. 3-14). Dubuque, IA: Kendall/Hunt.

Collins, R. L. (1993). Sociocultural aspects of alcohol use and abuse, ethnicity, and gender. *Drugs and Society, 8*(1), 89-116.

Cook, D. A. (1993). Research in African American churches: A mental health counseling imperative. *Journal of Mental Health Counseling, 15*, 320-333.

D'Avanzo, C. E., Frye, B., & Froman, R. (1994). Culture, stress, and substance abuse in Cambodian refugee women. *Journal of Studies on Alcohol, 55*(4), 420-426.

Dowdall, G. W., Crawford, M., & Wechsler, H. (1998). Binge drinking among American college women: A comparison of single-sex and coeducational institutions. *Psychology of Women Quarterly, 22*, 705-715.

Dunn, A. B., & Dawes, S. J. (1999). Spirituality-focused genograms: Keys to uncovering spiritual resources in African American families. *Journal of Multicultural Counseling and Development, 27*, 240-254.

Eliason, M. J. (1999). Nursing's role in racism and African American women's health. *Health Care for Women International, 20*, 209-219.

Gainor, K. A. (1992). Internalized oppression as a barrier to effective group work with Black women. *Journal for Specialists in Group Work, 17*(4), 235-242.

Gainor, K. A., & Forrest, L. (1991). African American women's self-concept: Implications for career decisions and career counseling. *Career Development Quarterly, 39*, 261-272.

Gunnings, T. S., & Lipscomb, W. D. (1986). Psychotherapy for Black men: A systemic approach. *Journal of Multicultural Counseling and Development, 14*, 17-23.

Herd, D. (1993). An analysis of alcohol-related problems in Black and White women drinkers. *Addiction Research, 1*(3), 181-198.

Hughes, T. L., Day, L. E., Marcantonio, R. J., & Torpy, E. (1997). Gender differences in alcohol and other drug use among young adults. *Substance Use and Misuse, 32*(3), 317-342.

Jordan, J. M. (1997). Counseling African American women from a cultural sensitivity perspective. In C. C. Lee (Ed.), *Multicultural issues in counseling: New approaches to diversity* (2nd ed., pp. 109-121). Alexandria, VA: American Counseling Association.

Kim, S., McLeod, J. H., & Shantzis, C. (1995). Cultural competence for evaluators working with Asian American communities: Some practical considerations. In M. A. Orlandi (Ed.), R. Weston & L. G. Epstein (Assoc. Eds.), *Cultural competence for evaluators: A guide for alcohol and other drug abuse prevention practitioners working with ethnic/racial communities* (pp. 203-260). DHHS Publication No. (SMA) 95-3066. Rockville, MD: U.S. Department of Health and Human Services.

Larrabee, M. L. (1986). Helping reluctant Black males: An affirmation approach. *Journal of Multicultural Counseling and Development, 14*(1), 25–38.

Lo, C. C., & Globetti, G. (1993). Black college students' drinking patterns: The roles of family religious affiliation and parental guidance during the first drinking experience. *Sociology Spectrum, 13*(3), 343–363.

Madison-Colmore, O., & Moore, J. (2002). Using the H. I. S. model in counseling African American men. *Journal of Men's Studies, 10*, 197–208.

McDavis, R. J., Parker, W. M., & Parker, W. J. (1995). Counseling African Americans. In N. Vaac, S. DeVaney, & J. Wittmer (Eds.), *Experiencing and counseling multicultural and diverse populations* (3rd ed., pp. 217–250). Bristol, PA: Accelerated Development.

McNair, L. (1992). African American women in therapy: An Afrocentric and feminist synthesis. *Women and Therapy, 12*, 5–17.

McNair, L. (1996). African American women and behavior therapy: Integrating theory, culture, and clinical practice. *Cognitive and Behavioral Practice, 3*, 337–349.

McRae, M. B., Thompson, D. A., & Cooper, S. (1999). Black churches as therapeutic groups. *Journal of Multicultural Counseling and Development, 27*, 207–220.

Mehra, R. (1997). Women, empowerment, and economic development. *Annals of the American Academy of Political and Social Science, 554*, 136–149.

National Institute on Drug Abuse. (1998). *Drug use among racial/ethnic minorities.* Publication No. 98-3888. Rockville, MD: U.S. Department of Health and Human Services.

Padgett, D. K., Patrick, C., Burns, B. J., & Schlesinger, H. J. (1994). Women and outpatient mental health services: Use by Black, Hispanic, and White women in a national insured population. *Journal of Mental Health Administration, 21*(4), 347–360.

Paniagua, F. A. (1996). Cross-cultural guidelines in family therapy practice. *The Family Journal: Counseling and Therapy for Couples and Families, 4*(2), 127–138.

Raheim, S., & Bolden, J. (1995). Economic empowerment of low-income women through self-employment programs. *AFFILLIA, 10*, 138–154.

Richardson, B. L., & June, L. N. (1997). Utilizing and maximizing the resources of the African American church: Strategies and tools for counseling professionals. In C. C. Lee (Ed.), *Multicultural issues in counseling: New approaches to diversity* (2nd ed., pp. 73–80). Alexandria, VA: American Counseling Association.

Ridley, C. R. (1995). *Overcoming unintentional racism in counseling and therapy: A practitioner's guide to intentional intervention.* London: Sage.

Rubenstein, M., & Lawler, S. K. (1990). Toward the psychological empowerment of women. *AFFILIA, 5*, 27–38.

Sanchez-Hucles, J. (2000). *The first session with African Americans: A step-by-step guide.* San Francisco: Jossey-Bass.

Sanders, C. J. (1996). Hope and empathy: Toward an ethic of Black empowerment. *Journal of Religious Thought, 52*, 1-17.

Taylor, M. J. (1999). Changing what has gone before: The enhancement of an inadequate psychology through the use of an Afrocentric—feminist perspective with African American women in therapy. *Psychotherapy, 36*(Summer), 170-179.

Vontress, C. E., & Epp, L. R. (1997). Historical hostility in the African American client: Implications for counseling. *Journal of Multicultural Counseling and Development, 25*, 170-184.

Williams, C. B., & Frame, M. W. (1999). Constructing new realities: Integrating womanist traditions in pastoral counseling with African American women. *Pastoral Psychology, 47*(4), 303-314.

Womble, M. (1990). Black women. In R. C. Engs (Ed.), Women, alcohol, and other drugs (pp. 127-135). Dubuque, IA: Kendall/Hunt.

Zane, N. W. S., & Hub-Kim, J. (1998). Addictive behaviors. In L. C. Lee & N. W. S. Zane (Eds.), *The handbook of Asian American psychology* (pp. 527-554). Thousand Oaks, CA: Sage.

Chapter 7

Multicultural Issues in Assessment: Assessment Procedures With a Latina

Robert M. Davison Avilés

Assessment underlies nearly every interaction between counselor and client. Multicultural variables that moderate the assessment process include person-based contextual factors, environmental factors, and process factors. This chapter includes these factors within a comprehensive and systematic multicultural assessment procedural model with six steps. A college-counseling center case, a Puerto Rican Latina, is presented within this assessment procedural model. Additional recommendations are provided for assessment practice.

Assessment underlies nearly every interaction between counselor and client. We watch, listen to, and evaluate our clients in formal and informal ways. Counselors judge interpersonal skills, determine cognitive or affective functioning, or investigate interests, ideas, and behavior patterns. Our clients often watch us just as closely. Throughout this process, counselors and clients make decisions regarding the utilization of the data they have obtained. Thus assessment is typically conceived as a counseling process wherein a diagnosis is made that will guide treatment (Roysircar-Sodowsky & Kuo, 2001).

Moreover, Ridley, Hill, and Li (1998) have suggested that assessment and therapy may be similar pursuits in that assessment unfolds over an extended period of time in the context of forming a trusting relationship.

Multicultural Variables Moderating the Assessment Process

It is well known that multicultural variables moderate the assessment process and include person-based contextual factors (e.g., client and counselor language, acculturation, ethnicity, gender, and socioeconomic status), environmental factors (e.g., racism, test bias, discrimination in educational and occupational access), and therapy process factors (philosophy, theory, and application of assessment; for more details see Baruth & Manning, 1999; Roysircar-Sodowsky & Kuo, 2001). These three factors interact with one another, presenting counselors with a seemingly impossible task of bringing together an enormous amount of data in a sensible way. Ridley, Li, and Hill (1998) acknowledged the challenges of using broad-based, multilevel assessment strategies and offered a comprehensive, systematic method of multicultural assessment. Their system is presented here as a way to unify the various aspects of multicultural assessment.

Person-Based Factors in Multicultural Assessment

Person-based factors deal with counselor and client attributes. Roysircar-Sodowsky & Kuo (2001) called these *assessor barriers* and *assessee cultural barriers*. For counselors, Sedlecek (1994) called this an issue of *I'm okay, you're not* (p. 551).

Counselors.

According to Ridley, Li, and Hill (1998), person-based qualities relevant to counselors are cultural self-awareness, culturally related defenses, credibility, subjectivity in decision making, cognitive complexity and behavioral flexibility, validating the client's belief system, and linguistic competency.

1. *Cultural self-awareness* refers to the counselor's understanding of culture and her or his own biases and how the confluence of these factors affects the counselor's beliefs and behaviors. Roysircar-Sodowsky & Kuo (2001) echoed these concepts, citing the need for counselors to control their value assumptions inconsistent with the client's worldview and learn more about the client's relevant cultural characteristics.
2. Ridley, Li, and Hill (1998) defined *culturally related defenses* as psychological mechanisms operating within the counselor that deny the existence of color or overreact to cultural differences. According to Roysircar-Sodowsky & Kuo (2001), these defenses result in misattributions, a Type II error, such as underdiagnoses that fail to distinguish between healthy cultural syndromes (e.g., hypervigilance due to repeated encounters with racism) and true mental disorders, such as paranoia.

82

3. The converse of cultural defensiveness is counselor *credibility*. Thought to enhance the therapeutic relationship, credibility is defined as a function of expertness (perceived competence or capability), trustworthiness, nondefensive behaviors, and willingness to self-disclose (Sue & Sue, 1990).
4. Counselors often make several decisions during assessment, many of which are based upon objective data such as test results and clinical or academic records. However, even when using objective data, counselors make subjective decisions regarding which data to access or which inventory or test to administer. Moreover, *subjectivity in decision making* allows for creative human understanding in addressing the complex issues of multicultural assessment (Ivey, D'Andrea, Ivey, & Simek-Morgan, 2002).
5. *Cognitive complexity* is a counselor attribute that allows for multidimensional thinking and integrative problem solving, that is, the ability to perceive client behaviors in the context of multiple criteria and to incorporate many dimensions into proposed assessments and interventions. Increased cognitive complexity facilitates diagnostic accuracy, leading to counselor *behavioral flexibility* in providing treatment and seeking out information. Pedersen (1994) observed that complexity is a fundamental fact of multicultural life.
6. Ivey et al. (2002) noted that counseling is fundamentally a process of listening to and learning from stories. Postmodern multiculturalism recognizes the complexity of human stories and the relative nature of truth as it relates to the differing stories and perspectives of counselor and client. Thus, one of the crucial tasks set before the counselor is to understand the client's story and then validate its meaning. *Validating the client's belief system* is, in essence, the explicit recognition and understanding of how the client makes meaning of her or his life and the events and problems she or he faces.
7. *Linguistic competency*, whether in English or in bilingualism, is important to every counselor–client interaction. Language serves as the means by which knowledge is constructed, flavoring the process and outcome of multicultural assessment. Santiago-Rivera (1995) indicated that language is tied to cultural beliefs and history, thereby becoming an ally in accurate assessment. Counselors need to assess language preference and dominance, language proficiency, and learning key idioms and phrases specific to the client's preferred language (Altarriba & Santiago-Rivera, 1994; Santiago-Rivera, 1995).

Clients.

Client factors also influence assessment.Aponte and Johnson (2000) outlined eight general cultural variables affecting how clients understand and act upon their reality: level of enculturation (socialization within one's cultural group), racial and ethnic identity development, acculturation (interaction with a second, dominant culture), social characteristics (economic status, family networks, role flexibility) oppression and sociopolitical factors (immigrant status, accessibility to education, employment), racism and discrimination, language, and individual characteristics (spirituality, childrearing, locus of control).

Ramirez (1999) used a more generalized approach, suggesting that cultural values were linked to field sensitive and field independent styles of thinking, learning, and interacting. Field sensitive styles are allocentric (other- or group-centered) and collectivist, emphasizing cooperation and spirituality and following traditional, non-Western cultural preferences for communication and social interactions. Ramirez described field independent styles as "modern" (p. 21), emphasizing individualism and competition, and valuing science. Most people have a preference for one style; however, persons who are able to shift styles according to environmental demands are thought to be academically and interpersonally more successful.

Environmental Factors

Accurate and useful assessment requires the counselor to consider the effects of legal and educational systems, including immigration and affirmative action laws and policies, educational policies (especially regarding special education and language minorities), and government initiatives on poverty, substance abuse, employment, and housing. Social attitudes in the client's environment are often related to systemic policies and include individual and group discrimination, stereotypes in the media, and local community attitudes toward people of color and/or diverse ethnic groups.

Process Factors

Process factors involve philosophy, theory, and application of assessment procedures. The central questions for counselor and client are What is the purpose of assessment? What do counselor and client believe are the appropriate sources of knowledge? And how is that knowledge accessed and used? From a practice standpoint, this means that counselors use emic (culture-centered) criteria, etic standardized instruments (e.g., normed instruments having relevant racial and ethnic groups in normative samples), and nonstandardized methods (client narratives, journaling). Counselors and clients negotiate and agree upon problem definition, purpose, and meaning of assessment (Pedersen, 1994; Ramirez, 1999; Ridley, Li, & Hill, 1998).

Effective Multicultural Assessment

Ridley, Li, and Hill (1998) proposed a four-phase Multicultural Assessment Procedure (MAP) that attempted to systematize and operationalize an assessment procedure that identifies, interprets, and incorporates cultural data, and that culminates in making a sound decision. Ramirez (1999) posited a personality theory in which cognitive and cultural abilities to shift styles of thinking and interacting ("flexes") are assessed. These abilities involve purposeful moving between traditional (collectivist-cooperative-spiritual) and modern (individual-competitive-science) values in thinking, communicating, and relating to others. Taken together, Ridley, Li, and Hill's procedure and Ramirez's theory of personality flex offer a comprehensive balance of behavioral, data-driven, and intrapersonal process-oriented approaches to multicultural assessment.

Two additional steps have been added to Ridley, Li, and Hill's four phases: establishing rapport and postassessment feedback from the client. It is important to explicitly indicate that both relationship and client feedback are necessary for accurate and valid assessment.

Step One: Establish Rapport and Begin Data Gathering

Wehrly (1995) adapted an explanatory medical model for understanding the client and remaining culture-centered. She suggested the following open questions to begin the assessment process:

- What name do you give to your problem? What caused your problem?
- When did your problem begin? How serious is your problem?
- How does this problem affect your life? How does this problem affect the lives of those around you? What worries you about this problem? (For clients who are immigrants or who are not living with the natural support system in which they were socialized): How would you solve this problem if you were living back in _____?
- What kind of help or treatment do you think you should receive? (p. 156)

Step Two: Identify Cultural Data

During this phase of assessment counselors conduct a clinical interview using multiple methods of data collection. Counselor and client enter this phase by taking a short life history (Ramirez, 1999). A life history is the client's story of her or his life told in chapters of early childhood, elementary and middle school years, high school years, and post high school years. During each developmental stage, the counselor asks the client about how he or she expressed him- or herself, how he or she related to family and others, what was rewarding or motivating, and how he or she learned or solved problems. In addition, counselor and client together determine cultural style. Using Ramirez's field-based model, counselors can ascertain the client's preferred cultural style of interacting. Counselors can determine cultural style by listening for the following cues: traditional-oriented clients usually behave deferentially toward the counselor, carefully observe the social environment, and often focus on important others when giving reasons for seeking therapy. Modern-leaning clients tend to see equal status between themselves and the counselor, appear assertive, and focus on self when giving reasons for seeking therapy.

Ridley, Li, and Hill (1998) identified cultural style as the client's cultural and idiosyncratic data. The former are culturally normative behaviors, and the latter, recognizing within-group variability, consist of the client's individual expression of cultural identity. Knowledge of the client's cultural background, gleaned from the client (but within ethical bounds; it is not the client's responsibility to teach the counselor everything about his or her culture) and study and preparation, can assist the counselor in gathering these data.

Step Three: Interpret Cultural Data

At this point the counselor must attend to all collected data as relevant. Later in the process of cointerpreting data with the client, counselors may begin to differentiate significant from insignificant information. These decisions must be made with discernment gained from patterns derived from client input and information from appropriate environmental sources (family, school, employment).

Having gathered normative and idiosyncratic data and determined traditional and modern styles, the counselor now needs to apply base rate information to cultural data. Base rate data are statistical norms and/or research findings about particular data. For instance, if a Native American client presents with symptoms of depression, it will be useful to know that Native Americans have the highest rate of completed suicide of any ethnic group (Porter, 2000).

The counselor encourages the client to become an active partner in assessment. Essentially, this is a negotiation between counselor and client about the cultural meaning of client behavior vis-à-vis traditional versus modern thinking, communication, and relating to others. Through assessment by informal means (client narratives, journaling), counselor and client seek to discover a pattern of preferred style.

On the basis of data gathered and interpreted thus far, counselors at this step can begin to formulate a working hypothesis on the determinants and consequences of client behavior. Do client behaviors result in growth or self-defeat? Is there a mismatch between the cultural (interacting, motivational) style of the client and the important persons in his or her life? It is critical at this point to reframe apparent idiosyncratic or cultural deficits into strengths. Assessment too often falls into an epidemiological mire, at the expense of empowering the client (Davison Avilés & Montero, in press).

It is likely that some combination of client dispositional factors and environmental and sociocultural stressors will inform a working hypothesis regarding the client's problems.

Step Four: Incorporate Data

In this phase of Ridley, Li, and Hill's (1998) model, counselors and clients refine their working hypothesis (multicultural assessment is, to the greatest extent possible, coproduced) by incorporating other clinically relevant data. Counselors now rule out organic or medical explanations for the client's condition. Appropriate standardized testing is used. Referral to competent professionals is required if the counselor is not skilled in administering or interpreting necessary instruments. It is at this point that appropriate use of the *Diagnostic and Statistical Manual of Mental Disorders* (4th ed.; *DSM-IV*; American Psychiatric Association, 1994) is considered. Ridley, Li, and Hill advised comparing all the relevant cultural data up to this point with possible *DSM-IV* diagnoses. Hypotheses based upon comparative analyses of cultural, medical, and *DSM-IV* criteria will reveal points for interventions and help counselors arrive at a sound clinical decision.

Step Five: Decide

Once the working hypotheses of counselor and client are tested, a decision is made regarding appropriate treatment. Counselors should avoid becoming bogged down in data gathering, in wondering if they have enough information to intervene effectively. Unwilling to risk imperfection, sometimes counselors put off deciding what to do, at the peril of their clients' well-being.

Step Six: Postassessment Feedback

Multicultural assessment is an iterative activity, recycling information gained during the process of gathering data. In addition, an important therapeutic aspect of assessment is to empower the client by using her or his feedback regarding the accuracy and effectiveness of the process, thus validating the client. Assessment and therapy are twin processes that often overlap. Regular, evaluative feedback from clients and other relevant persons is necessary to arrive at sound clinical decisions and interventions.

Using Effective Multicultural Assessment:
A Case Example

Graciela, aged 18, was born in Puerto Rico to native Puerto Rican parents. Currently, she is a first-year college student at a large state university in the Midwest. Graciela, who is demographically a White Latina, has lived in Puerto Rico all her life and attended Catholic K–12 schools. Graciela is bilingual, knowing Spanish and English, although her first language is Spanish. Graciela's parents and 12-year-old brother live in Puerto Rico. Initially referred to the college counseling center by a professor, Graciela's presenting concerns included failing grades and crying while in class. Graciela reports few friends, but recently she has become close with a female student at the university. Graciela describes being close to her parents, especially her mother, and admits to frequent feelings of homesickness. She indicates that her relationship with her father is less close, yet she describes him as loving, though temperamental, and openly affectionate with his wife and children. Lately Graciela has been cutting classes and staying in her room watching TV.

Step One: Establish Rapport and Begin Data Gathering

Prior to her appointment, Graciela had filled out an intake form, noting her place of birth, family circumstances, and bilingualism. She arrived at her appointment on time and appeared appropriately groomed and dressed for the season. Her hair was pulled back in a ponytail. Graciela had a moderate case of facial acne with visible scars. She addressed the counselor as Mr. and made appropriate eye contact.

The counselor, a White Latino, greeted her in Spanish and English and invited her into the office. Upon hearing the counselor speak Spanish, Graciela smiled briefly and replied in Spanish. Most of the session was conducted in English, but during times of apparent emotional stress, (e.g., when discussing academic problems), Graciela code-switched, switching from English to Spanish in midsentence. The counselor responded with a few words in Spanish, then reverted to English. In addition, when speaking to the counselor in Spanish, Graciela used the formal *usted*, indicating respect for age and/or position. The counselor addressed Graciela using Ms., but changed when Graciela asked him to use her first name.

Graciela's cultural style appeared to be a mix of traditional and modern characteristics. On one hand, she was deferential to the counselor and used both Spanish and English. It appeared that the counselor's knowledge of Spanish facilitated Graciela's willingness to discuss her concerns. When she learned there was a Latino counselor, Graciela requested an appointment with him. On the other hand, Graciela was punctual, made consistent eye contact, and wore typical college student clothing.

Step Two: Identify Cultural Data

In addition to establishing rapport, early sessions with Graciela were spent discussing her experiences at college, her family background, and her years growing up in Puerto Rico. Graciela's childhood was unremarkable, with developmental and relational milestones being met appropriately. Discipline was strict and sometimes physical, with occasional spankings. As a teen and young adult, her musical and entertainment preferences were contemporary rock, rap, and movies. Using open questions similar to Wehrly's (1995) suggested queries, the counselor asked Graciela what brought her to counseling. Graciela replied that she was worried about her grades (she was in danger of failing three classes) and found talking in class difficult: "I get nervous, you know, *me pongo muy nerviosa cuando tengo que hablar* (I get very nervous when I have to speak [in class])."

Although Graciela was academically successful in high school, she reported college courses were very difficult. When asked to expand on her nervousness in class, Graciela indicated that although in Puerto Rico both English and Spanish were spoken in school, most often she, her friends, and teachers spoke Spanish. Graciela noted through tears that at college she could go weeks without hearing someone speak Spanish, and when she was pressed to speak in class she sometimes used the wrong words. When the counselor asked Graciela what she thought might be causing her academic challenges, she expressed great anxiety over shaming her parents by failing and guilt over the money they spent to send her to college. Graciela's response did not answer the counselor's question; however, it revealed the predominant feelings she was experiencing. Graciela indicated that her parents were very proud and supportive of her. Although Graciela said that while growing up she and her mother could talk about *casi todo*, almost everything, she was fearful about her parent's feelings and what they might do when they found out she was failing. The counselor focused again on Graciela's academic concerns. Graciela responded by reporting frequent feelings of overwhelming sadness and homesickness, some days so great that she skipped classes to stay in her dorm room and watch TV all day. She admitted difficulty in focusing on course lectures and told the counselor that she often had no energy or desire to complete class assignments.

Graciela's roommate Annie was White, the same age as Graciela, and from a small town in the Midwest. Graciela reported to the counselor that she tried to avoid disagreements with Annie, but arguments did occur. Occasionally they escalated, which usually resulted in Annie shouting and Graciela crying and leaving the room. Graciela suspected that her roommate disliked her because she is Puerto Rican, although the only evidence of this was an occasional "you people" comment from Annie. Graciela reported her academic strengths to be in art (she excels in drawing) and physical education (she played volleyball in high school). She also reported good relationships with her professors.

Over the next few sessions, Graciela reported a few casual acquaintances, no romantic interests, and only one close friend, Barbara, a student she met playing volleyball. Graciela reported that in the past few weeks her tense roommate situation caused her to spend increasing time with Barbara, and as a result, they were becoming close friends. At one point Barbara, who was older and lived alone in an apartment, asked Graciela to spend the night in her apartment. Graciela refused, but admitted to the counselor about having confusing feelings toward Barbara and wondering whether Barbara's interests were platonic or romantic.

Salient cultural data include Graciela's consistent mix of traditional and modern styles, with perhaps a preference for her more traditional Latina background. Noting that she could talk to her mother about her problems, Graciela showed a traditional problem-solving style. Her interdependent family upbringing and occasional preference for Spanish was also more traditional (Ramirez, 1999). However, she enjoyed the same music as most of her peers and, until college, related easily with others, regardless of race or ethnicity. It was important to recognize that Graciela's avoidance of conflict might be interpreted as a cultural strength, as an effort to maintain harmony.

Graciela also evidenced some individual behaviors that were not necessarily typical of only Latina/os. Homesickness is common among first-year college students living away from home, and strained roommate relations are frequent. However, her tense relations with her roommate might have been caused, in part, by cultural differences in managing conflict. In addition, Graciela's social withdrawal, class cutting, and self-seclusion were not culturally normative but rather symptomatic of a possible adjustment or mood disorder.

Step Three: Interpret Data

During this phase of assessment, the counselor seeks to identify cultural flex and individual vs. cultural vs. social determinants of behavior. Tentative hypotheses about the cause of client problems are drawn. Graciela's ability to manage her academic and interpersonal stressors appeared inconsistent. The absence of her native language appeared to be causing additional stress, as did the possibility of shaming her parents by failing academically. Recall that Ramirez (1999) theorized that cultural flexibility is important to interpersonal success. Despite good relations with professors, Graciela seemed to be rigid in her style of communications and problem solving. In a traditional sense, professors were authority figures to Graciela, and thus she respected and sought positive relationships with them. However, she seemed unable to be assertive in either asking for help with her classes or during disagreements with Annie. Moreover, there were hints of racism in her roommate's comments, to which she responded with avoidance. There was a mismatch between Graciela's cultural style and the important people in her life. Finally, Graciela appeared to be on the verge of questioning her sexual orientation. Although the recognition of a different sexual orientation might be normative for some college-age students, Graciela's traditional upbringing precluded this process as an option for her.

A working hypothesis might be that certain of Graciela's dispositional factors (withdrawal, questioning) combined with cultural mismatches (preference for the Spanish language, inadequate conflict management) and environmental factors (racism and living in an unfamiliar place) caused problems in academic persistence and interpersonal relations. In addition, it is possible to hypothesize that what was a cultural strength, her family, had become inaccessible either through geographic distance or through Graciela's fear of disappointing her parents.

Step Four: Incorporate Data

It was clear that Graciela's most recent behaviors and feelings—withdrawal, an overwhelming sense of sadness, and homesickness—were cause for concern. The wise counselor should seek to rule out organic causes in developing a treatment plan. Indeed, Graciela's counselor wished to rule out possible medical causes while at the same time suspecting a possible mood disorder. Graciela was referred to the college health center for a physical and was found to be slightly underweight. Her counselor gave the following diagnosis:

Axis I:	309.28 Adjustment Disorder, acute, with Mixed Anxiety and Depressed Mood
V code:	Acculturation Difficulties
Axis II:	v71.09 none

Axis III: None

Axis IV: Educational problems, problems related to racism, social environment, relocation losses and grief

Axis V: GAF = 60 (current)

Graciela was cooperative in coming to therapy and rarely missed an appointment. The counselor assessed for suicidal ideation. Graciela denied suicidal thoughts or behaviors, but reiterated her sense of loneliness and homesickness.

Step Five: Decide

Graciela's statements about homesickness prompted the counselor to ask if she had spoken with her parents lately. She had not, fearful of crying on the phone with her mother. *"Los quiero llamar, pero no se si puedo* (I want to call them, but I don't know if I can)." Graciela was also concerned with the cost of a call to Puerto Rico.

After discussing the benefits and problems with a phone call to parents in Puerto Rico (i.e., Graciela needed her parents' support but they might be angry), it was decided that Graciela could call from the counselor's office. If necessary the counselor might even talk to her parents with Graciela's consent. To some counselors this may seem a boundary violation, but to Graciela and her counselor, the counselor's possible intermediary role was consistent with a relationship based in part upon shared cultural values or worldviews. In addition, it was agreed that if Graciela did not feel as if she was improving within 2 weeks or that she felt worse, she would return to the health center for a psychiatric consultation and possible antidepressant medication. Graciela was hesitant to discuss her feelings about Barbara and wanted to focus on school and her parents. The counselor followed Graciela's lead, but asked permission to bring up Graciela's relationship at a later time, pointing out that although it seemed uncomfortable at present, it might turn out to be an important source of self-knowledge and strength in the future. Graciela agreed.

Graciela and her counselor called the parents who responded with great concern for Graciela and appreciation for the counselor's assistance. When Graciela told her mother about her loneliness and roommate problems, both parents decided to fly out the next day. A family appointment was set for the day following the parents' arrival. Graciela's mother brought the counselor a gift basket containing Puerto Rican coffee and baked goods, which the counselor accepted. Following this and one other family session, Graciela decided to remain in school, reduce her course load, and seek help in her studies. She requested a roommate change and sought information about the Latino/a student group on campus. Graciela's parents returned to Puerto Rico after giving Graciela permission to call every weekend. (Graciela's father insisted upon the lower weekend rate time, unless there was an emergency during the week).

Step Six: Feedback From the Client

After her parents returned home, Graciela admitted that she felt uneasy about the counselor's suggestion to call her parents. She changed her mind based upon the therapeutic relationship and the fact that *"aunque usted habla español con acento, me parece que [usted] tiene razón* (although you speak Spanish with an accent, it seems to me that you are right"). In addition, learning to give feedback to her counselor taught Graciela how to be more flexible in asserting her needs with current and future roommates. The counseling experience revealed a growing personal strength and a willingness to learn how to adapt her style to meet the demands of her environment. Graciela also revealed growing cultural pride, evidenced in her gentle teasing about the counselor's accent and her interest in the Latina/o student group.

Recommendations for Practice

The following are recommendations for counselors based upon the multicultural assessment literature cited herein and the author's clinical experience:

1. Learn about your culture and your own styles of interacting, communicating, and thinking. This should be a purposeful attempt to develop self-insight and develop the ability to manage greater amounts of cognitive complexity, which is necessary for counselors.
2. Learn about as many cultures as you can. Although this is a daunting task, there is no other alternative to sound clinical practice in the modern world. The face of the future is colored with a multicultural palette; you may as well learn to paint.
3. Assess every client from a multicultural perspective.
4. Learn to discern between cultural and idiosyncratic data by seeking experiences firsthand with people who look, act, and sound like you and people who do not. Expect to learn that we are not all the same, and that this knowledge may cause you some discomfort. After a while you will learn so much that you'll forget what it was like when you knew only one culture.
5. Seek alternative explanations for your data. Consider the opposite of what you believe.
6. Include your clients in the assessment process. They are the experts about who they are, what they mean, and what they can do.

93

7. Seek out testing instruments designed for or normed on different racial and ethnic groups. The numbers of such instruments are growing rapidly, and many are well researched.
8. Use qualitative data to give context to the numbers you get from standardized instruments.
9. Use the *DSM–IV* cautiously under any circumstances. Diagnoses are only effective if they are accurate, and take into account client contextual variables.
10. Think deliberately. Be slow to judgment, but once you have decided, act.
11. Test hypothesis and give yourself a chance to prove yourself wrong.
12. Recycle your hypothesis testing. After several sessions your client will not be the same; why should you be the same?

Conclusion

Effective multicultural assessment is a multifactor, comprehensive process. In this chapter, professional standards act as a foundation for a multicultural assessment model that includes person-based, environmental, and process components. Within each component multicultural variables moderate the assessment process. A six-step multicultural assessment procedure allows a balance of behavioral, data-driven, intrapersonal process-oriented approaches to multicultural assessment. A case example using this procedure is provided, as are recommendations for practice.

References

Altarriba, J., & Santiago-Rivera, A. L. (1994). Current perspectives on using linguistic and cultural factors in counseling the Hispanic client. *Professional Psychology: Research and Practice, 25*, 388–379.

American Psychiatric Association. (1994). *Diagnostic and statistical manual of mental disorders* (4th ed.). Washington, DC: Author.

Aponte, J. F., & Johnson, L. R. (2000). The impact of culture on intervention and treatment of ethnic populations. In J. F. Aponte & J. Whol (Eds.), *Psychological intervention and cultural diversity* (pp. 18–39). Boston: Allyn & Bacon.

Baruth, L. G., & Manning, M. L. (1999). *Multicultural counseling and psychotherapy* (2nd ed.). Upper Saddle River, NJ: Prentice Hall.

Davison Avilés, R. M., & Montero, H. (in press). Career counseling with Latinos in the United States. *Career Planning and Adult Development Journal.*

Ivey, A. E., D'Andrea, M., Ivey, M. B., & Simek-Morgan, L. (2002). *Theories of counseling and psychotherapy: A multicultural perspective* (5th ed.). Boston: Allyn & Bacon.

Pedersen, P. (1994). *A handbook for developing multicultural awareness* (2nd ed.). Alexandria, VA: American Counseling Association.

Porter, R. Y. (2000). Understanding and treating ethnic minority youth. In J. F. Aponte & J. Whol (Eds.), *Psychological intervention and cultural diversity* (pp. 167–182). Boston: Allyn & Bacon.

Ramirez, M. (1999). *Multicultural psychotherapy*. Boston: Allyn & Bacon.

Ridley, C. R., Hill, C. L., & Li, L. C. (1998). Revisiting and refining the multicultural assessment procedure. *The Counseling Psychologist, 26*, 939–947.

Ridley, C. R., Li, L. C., & Hill, C. L. (1998). Multicultural assessment: Reexamination, reconceptualization, and practical application. *The Counseling Psychologist, 26*, 827–910.

Roysircar-Sodowsky, G., & Kuo, P. Y. (2001). Determining cultural validity of personality assessment. In D. B. Pope-Davis & H. L. K. Coleman (Eds.), *The intersection of class and gender in multicultural counseling* (pp. 213–239). Thousand Oaks, CA: Sage.

Santiago-Rivera, A. L. (1995). Developing a culturally sensitive treatment modality for bilingual Spanish-speaking clients: Incorporating language and culture in counseling. *Journal of Counseling & Development, 74*, 12–17.

Sedlecek, W. E. (1994). Advancing diversity through assessment. *Journal of Counseling & Development, 72*, 549–553.

Sue, D. W., & Sue, D. (1990). *Counseling the culturally different*. New York: Wiley.

Wehrly, B. (1995). *Pathways to counseling competence*. Pacific Grove, CA: Brooks/Cole.

Chapter 8

The Power of Context: Counseling South Asians Within a Family Context

Arpana G. Inman and Nita Tewari

Family therapy has typically focused on interventions being systemic rather than being directed at the individual. The emphasis is on an appropriate balance between individual, family, and group goals and the give-and-take within and between systems. This notion of a systemic perspective inherent in family therapy lends itself to examining issues within a context. Within the counseling profession there has been an increased awareness of contextual variables such as culture, race, ethnicity, sexual orientation, socioeconomic status, religion, and gender, and their influences on the individual. The importance of these contextual variables led to the development of multicultural counseling competency standards, providing guidelines for effective and ethical clinical practice. In keeping with the framework of multicultural counseling competency, this chapter focuses on developing awareness and understanding of South Asian families and delineating family-based interventions that have been beneficial in working with this group.

In appreciating the experience of South Asian communities, it is essential to be mindful of four issues: The first is that the largest group of immigrants has typically been from India and Pakistan (U.S. Census, 2001), and therefore, there is limited literature on people from other South Asian countries (e.g., Bangladesh, Sri Lanka, Nepal, Bhutan). The second issue to be mindful of is that there is great diversity within this population with regard to religious affiliations, languages abilities, immigration history, socioeconomic status, education, and acculturation levels.

A third issue is that although many South Asian Americans might fit the model minority image, many recent immigrants may not share the successes of immigrants that arrived upon the 1965 Immigration Act. It is not uncommon for the recent immigrants to be less educated, be employed in lower paying and unskilled jobs, and have financial obligations to extended family members who remain in their countries of origin. However, irrespective of their immigration and socioeconomic status, many have experienced prejudices similar to other cultural groups (Gupta, 1999; Kuo & Roysircar-Sodowsky, 1999).

The fourth issue to be mindful of is that despite the diversity within the South Asian population, there are common cultural factors among individuals from this group. It is these commonalities that are the focus of this chapter.

Factors Impacting South Asians

When examining the experiences of South Asians, factors need to be considered within the context of culture, immigration, and acculturation (Roysircar-Sodowsky & Kuo, 2001). Acculturation poses significant pressures on South Asian immigrants (Roysircar-Sodowsky & Maestas, 2000). For instance, the literature reveals that many South Asian immigrant families tend to maintain traditional values while selectively adapting to the sociocultural norms of the dominant culture (Prathikanti, 1997; Ramisetty-Mikler, 1993). This process of selective acculturation is likely to create different choices and pressures for parents and their children, which means there is potential for family conflict (Sodowsky, Kwan, & Pannu, 1995). Thus it is imperative to gain an awareness of the family's culture, values, preimmigration socialization, level of connection with ethnic and dominant societies, and the extent of social and familial support in the United States and in countries of origin in South Asia. Additional cultural characteristics relevant to U.S. South Asian families that need to be examined within the family context include family relations, intimacy/sexuality issues, and educational/career issues.

Family Relations and Gender Roles

A significant factor influencing family relations among South Asians is the influence of a patriarchal society. Both males and females in the South Asian community have well-defined and structured role expectations. Women have been considered to be the carriers of tradition and primary family caregivers. Among conservative subgroups and in the middle class, education for South Asian women may be seen as a marketable commodity for marriage, with their status primarily coming from marriage and having children (Almeida, 1996). The careers of these women may be sacrificed in favor of their husband or family's priorities. Men, however, are traditionally identified as the primary breadwinner and caretaker of the family, and elders are accorded much respect and seen as the carriers of wisdom (Tewari, Inman, & Sandhu, in press).

Traditional gender expectations may be placed upon second generation South Asians in the United States (henceforth called U. S. South Asians), given the trend in their countries of origin to raise male and female children differently. Females may be expected to take on more domestic responsibilities in the household in comparison to males, and males tend to have more freedom and less stringent rules. U.S. South Asian women have labeled these differences in gender role as *double standards*.

Within this patriarchal context, South Asian families typically deemphasize individuation from the family unit. It is not uncommon for a family to emphasize an individual's social, emotional, and psychological development as secondary to the preservation of family needs, relations, and/or a South Asian cultural identity (Sodowsky, 1991; Sodowsky et al., 1995). This emphasis on the family is generally evident in child-rearing practices, which differ from those of the U.S. dominant culture. For example, U.S. South Asian children are often pampered and taken care of well beyond their childhood. In the country of origin, such as India, it is not uncommon to see adult sons living in their parents' home despite being married and earning a good living. Also, children feel a responsibility towards parents (i.e., taking care of parents by moving in with them or having parents move in with them). Thus family roles within the South Asian community tend to be hierarchically based on gender, age, birth order, and socioeconomic status in the family (Jayakar, 1994; Ramisetty-Mikler, 1993; Sodowsky & Carey, 1987).

Because of the hierarchical context, boundaries among family members may appear enmeshed, with parents, who have the most status and economic responsibility, expecting to know everything their child is involved in or expecting their children to share information with them. Many U.S. South Asian adolescents and young adults growing up in the United States that value independence may struggle with their lack of privacy (Inman, Constantine, & Ladany, 1999).

A related parenting challenge for U.S. South Asian families is the loss of their extended familial and societal support systems that assist in socializing and reinforcing South Asian cultural values in their children. These families may perceive themselves as having the sole responsibility to impart these values and beliefs, which results in restrictive/conservative behaviors on the part of parents (Sodowsky & Carey, 1988).

Intimacy and Sexuality

Dating and intimate relations can be complex and full of conflict for many U.S. South Asians. Dating brings up issues of sex, issues that are perceived as being American concepts, and thus there is a lack of discussion or acknowledgement of sexuality within the South Asian culture. In the countries of origin, although discussions about sexuality are avoided, it is portrayed symbolically through Bollywood films. (Bollywood, the Indian film industry, is headquartered in Mumbai, the city previously known as Bombay. The name *Bollywood* is derived from America's *Hollywood*.) Sex/sexuality is a characteristic of the villain (male or female) who has a western name and wears revealing western clothes, whereas the hero/heroine adheres strongly to South Asian cultural values.

Public displays of affection, premarital sexual relations, and physical intimacy are generally unacceptable within the cultural context, unlike the U.S. dominant culture (Sodowsky et al., 1995), which acknowledges and supports the growing sense of masculinity and femininity at different stages of life through social avenues such as mixed parties, proms, and homecoming dances. South Asian immigrant parents raising their children within this cultural context experience these social events as dangers that encourage preoccupation with sexual behavior and create a potential risk for poor academic achievement, less successful career pursuits, and limited future marriage prospects (Mehta, 1998).

An added issue of intimacy is related to arranged marriages (i.e., an expectation for marriages to occur within the same geographical region in South Asia, religion, language group, and levels of education, class, and caste), a tradition that poses significant challenges for both generations in the U.S. South Asian communities, for both immigrant parents and their U.S. second-generation children.

Skin color is another issue for South Asian families with regard to marriage and race-based discrimination (Mehta, 1998). As is true in most cultures that have varying shades of skin color, assumptions about socioeconomic status, education, beauty, and success have been attached to skin color in the immigrants' South Asian countries of origin as well (Tewari, 2000). These assumptions have led to discrimination against people of darker color in South Asia as elsewhere. Skin color is more salient for women than for men, as can be seen in matrimonial advertisements for arranged marriages that suggest the extent to which marriages are premised on a woman having a fair skin, the hallmark of beauty. The issue of skin color may continue to trouble South Asians socialized within the United States, a society that is also race/color focused.Thus implications of skin color can be seen with regard to self-perceptions of attractiveness, familial feelings about interracial marriages, and the family's ability to deal with race-based discrimination (Mehta, 1998).

Educational and Career Issues

Education within the South Asian culture is greatly respected. South Asian parents seem to hold higher educational aspirations and discuss grades and college plans with their children more often than other Asian parents, for example, Korean, Filipino, and Chinese (Hsia & Peng, 1998). Thus it is quite likely for parental expectations for educational achievements to factor into pressures felt by second-generation U.S. South Asians attempting to make independent academic decisions. U.S. South Asian families see successes in academics as well as in careers as familial accomplishments rather than as a process of individuation. Second-generation U.S. South Asians may defer to their parents in making academic and career choices out of respect for their parents' age, authority, wisdom, and economic support, and out of familial obligation (Sodowsky, 1991).Therefore, they may sacrifice their own vocational desires and interests.

Historically, and even currently, experiences of discrimination and racism have influenced many parents to push their children toward prestigious, highly respected, autonomous professions such as medicine or engineering in hopes to see their children live a financially secure lifestyle (Mehta, 1998;Tewari et al., in press). Many South Asians believe that a higher education degree, wealth (financial security), and a respectable profession will help minimize the prejudicial experiences that numerous South Asian immigrants have faced (Tewari, 2000).

Interventions With South Asian American Families

Four specific interventions—cultural genograms, stories or narratives, self-disclosure by the therapist, and bibliography or psychoeducation—are delineated here, followed by a case example illustrating their use.

The Four Interventions

Cultural genogram.
Because the family is an important source of support for South Asians, whether a client comes in for individual therapy or family therapy, issues need to be examined within a familial context. One technique useful to

clients and counselors in understanding immigration history, family structure, and alliances that exist in the extended family and with friends is the use of a cultural genogram. In using the genogram, patterns of communication, gender role socialization, levels of acculturation and ethnic identification, religious affiliations, and indications of socioeconomic and educational levels often emerge (Hardy & Laszloffy, 1995).

Stories or narratives.
Relational, emotional expression is commonly kept to a minimum among South Asians because there is an emphasis on showing modesty in behavior and emotions in therapy (Das & Kemp, 1997). As life difficulties are discussed and experienced, parents might typically present their challenges through narratives, stories, and metaphors, as opposed to personally disclosing their emotions (Almeida, 1996). Therefore, encouraging families to share their experiences and struggles related to immigration through the use of stories or narratives can be a beneficial tool for families negotiating intergenerational conflicts and challenges. This can allow immigrant parents not only to acknowledge their own losses through the immigration process (Mehta, 1998) but also to explore their expectations and relationships with their children within this context.

Self-disclosure by the therapist.
Because South Asians are relational in their interpersonal orientation (Das & Kemp, 1997; Roysircar-Sodowsky & Kuo, 2001), the use of self-disclosure by the therapist may increase trust levels in the South Asian client–counselor relationship. A silent counselor who expects the client to reveal his or her darkest secrets and fears may be perceived as voyeuristic and distant from the client. Therefore, sharing of personal challenges that might have been similar to the ones experienced by the client can prove beneficial.

Bibliography or psychoeducation.
The use of bibliography or psychoeducation can be another important supplement in therapy for both first- and second-generation South Asian clients. Reading materials help to provide some objectivity and distance to concerns while normalizing what may be seen as shameful or stigmatizing issues.

The Case Example: Seema's Story

Seema, a 23-year-old, second-generation Asian Indian female reported experiencing depression for over 6 months with some passive suicidal ideation due to conflicts with her parents. Seema's experience of her parents was that they were very strict and controlling about their children's socialization with peers (e.g., who Seema could go out with, how long she could be out of the house), and that they had strong expectations for academic excellence. In addition, Seema was expected to live at home until she married someone whom the parents would help to select. Seema, however, indicated a desire to find herself an apartment as soon as she was able to save up some money. Also, Seema reported that she was dating a Chinese American man but had not revealed this to her parents. Her parents suspected that Seema was dating him and made comments about the importance of staying focused on her education and the significance of marrying someone within the South Asian community.

Seema saw her parents keeping regular contact with their families in India as well as being very connected and involved with the Indian community in the U.S. city where they lived. She described her mother to be "very Indian," describing an incident in which her mother had returned to India for a visit and was touched by her family's comments that she had not become Americanized because she had not cut and styled her hair short (the mother's hair was still long in the traditional sense). Seema's mother saw cultural involvements, such as attending Indian celebrations and wearing Indian clothes, which Seema loathed, as important ways of maintaining connection with cultural heritage.

This case illustrates some typical intergenerational conflicts for second-generation children and their parents. In working with Seema, the genogram was used as a way to understand the organizing principles (e.g., gender messages/roles, messages about education, sexuality) that guided her family. Her struggles were explored, discussed, and normalized in the context of acculturative difficulties and the implicit demands of a multicultural identity (Inman et al., 1999). By sharing her own personal struggles with negotiating the two cultures and its impact on her relationship with her parents, the therapist (first author) was able to join Seema in her experience. An additional intervention that helped to normalize Seema's experience was providing her with readings on the cultural value conflicts that can occur within the bicultural context.

Seema was encouraged to talk to her parents about their pre- and postmigrational experience (e.g., reasons for migration; potential sacrifices made in leaving family and friends; changes in social status; struggles with holding onto ethnic identities) and talking to her mother about her mother's gender role socialization within her family of origin and issues related to sexuality. These narratives not only allowed Seema to explore parental expectations within the context of their immigration history and acculturation but also provided her parents with an opportunity to voice their fears and struggles in raising children within a culture different from the one in which they were raised. The parents' fears—that Seema was losing her cultural identity (thus they were imposing strong pressures on her to engage in culturally specific ways), and that Seema would bring shame to her family and jeopardize future marriage prospects through dating (and potentially engaging in pre-marital sex)—were revealed.

Overall, helping Seema to understand her experiences/behaviors within an ethnic cultural context served to validate both Seema's and her parent's experiences as well as bring them closer to each other. The family's ability to externalize felt pressures, by locating their existence in societal contexts, and to attribute their challenges to acculturative factors rather than to view problems as inherent only within the family or to attribute failures to themselves and to Seema, allowed Seema and her parents to negotiate cultural challenges and adapt to each other in the process.

Implications for Counseling South Asian Americans

In working with South Asians, it is important to note that members of this group vary in their cultural identity, worldviews, and levels of acculturation based on generational status, education, class, ethnic identification, experiences with racism, and sexism (Ibrahim, Ohnishi, & Sandhu, 1997; Roysircar, in press). All these factors have an impact on their openness to seeking counseling. For second-generation individuals seeking counseling, counselors need to be mindful that South Asians are socialized within a collective orientation. In therapy, these individuals socialized within both the dominant and ethnic cultural contexts may be reluctant to focus on developing an individual sense of self due to family loyalty and obligations (Das & Kemp, 1997). Further, there continues to be a stigma associated with mental health problems in the South Asian community, resulting in a denial of issues within South Asian families. Despite this denial, first- and second-generation South Asians are faced with challenges that are specific to their generational status and that need to be acknowledged.

First-generation South Asians may experience isolation and a lack of support due to leaving their support systems behind and guilt related to obligations and responsibility to care for elderly parents back home; they have concerns over children dating and marrying outside of their caste and culture and over conflicts rising from in-law interactions (Almeida, 1996). Additionally, they have conflicts related to gender role reversals arising from males having difficulty establishing themselves in a chosen career, being laid off or being unemployed, or being discriminated against based on race (Roysircar-Sodowsky & Kuo, 2001). Conversely, second-generation South Asian Americans may experience distress related to intergenerational conflicts (Almeida, 1996; Tewari, 2000), cultural value conflicts in relation to dating/sexuality, sex-role expectations (Inman, Ladany, Constantine, & Morano, 2001; Roysircar, in press), educational and career goals, identity issues, self-esteem, and self-criticism (Tewari, 2000). In addition, compartmentalization of roles/behaviors may create stress in both generations (Inman et al., 1999).

Conclusion

In providing mental health services, it is important to note that cultural differences can heighten the ambivalence of choosing one culture over another. Individuals and families may push to resolve this ambivalence by seeking advice from the counselor. The task of the therapist is to not resolve the ambivalence but rather to explore, process, and hold the paradox while helping families appreciate contributions of both cultures to the self and family.

This chapter's intent is to highlight the importance of developing multicultural counseling competence when working with South Asian families within a familial context. Specific challenges of South Asians around acculturation and immigration are addressed. Further, effective interventions are identified for families that consist of foreign-born immigrant parents and U.S.-born second-generation children or children who came to the United States with their parents at a young age, with parents and children endorsing traditional gender roles variously.

References

Almeida, R. (1996). Hindu, Christian, and Muslim families. In M. McGoldrick, J. Giordano, & J. K. Pearce (Eds.), *Ethnicity and family therapy* (pp. 395–423). New York: Guilford Press.

Das, A. K., & Kemp, S. F. (1997). Between two worlds: Counseling South Asian Americans. *Journal of Multicultural Counseling and Development, 25,* 23–33.

Gupta, S. R. (1999). *Emerging voices: South Asian American women redefine self, family, and community.* Walnut Creek, CA: AltaMira.

Hardy, K. V., & Laszloffy, T. A. (1995). The cultural genogram: Key to training culturally competent family therapists. *Journal of Marital and Family Therapy, 21,* 227-237.

Hsia, J., & Peng, S. S. (1998). Academic achievement and performance. In L.C. Lee & N.W.S. Zane (Eds.), *Handbook of Asian American Psychology* (pp. 401–432). Thousand Oaks, CA: Sage.

Ibrahim, F., Ohnishi, H., & Sandhu, D. S. (1997). Asian American identity development: A culture specific model for South Asian Americans. *Journal of Multicultural Counseling and Development, 25,* 34-50.

Inman, A. G., Constantine, M. G., & Ladany, N. (1999). Cultural value conflict: An examination of Asian Indian women's bicultural experience. In D. S. Sandhu (Ed.), *Asian and Pacific Islander Americans: Issues and concerns for counseling and psychotherapy* (pp. 31-41). Commack, NY: Nova Science.

Inman, A. G., Ladany, N., Constantine, M. G., & Morano, C. K. (2001). Development and preliminary validation of the cultural values conflict scale for South Asian women. *Journal of Counseling Psychology, 48,* 17-27.

Jayakar, K. (1994). Women of the Indian subcontinent. In L. Comas-Diaz & B. Greene (Eds.), *Women of color: Integrating ethnic and gender identities in psychotherapy* (pp. 161-181). New York: Guilford Press.

Kuo, P. Y., & Roysircar-Sodowsky, G. (1999). Political ethnic identity versus cultural ethnic identity: An understanding of research on Asian Americans. In D. S. Sandhu (Ed.), *Asian and Pacific Islander Americans: Issues and concerns for counseling and psychotherapy* (pp. 71-90). New York: Nova Sciences.

Mehta, P. (1998). The emergence, conflicts, and integration of the bicultural self: Psychoanalysis of an adolescent daughter of South Asian immigrant parents. In S. Akhtar & S. Kramer (Eds.), *The colors of childhood: Separation-individuation across cultural, racial, and ethnic differences* (pp. 129-168). Northvale, NJ: Aronson.

Prathikanti, S. (1997). East Indian American families. In E. Lee (Ed.), *Working with Asian Americans: A guide for clinicians* (pp. 79-100). New York: Guilford Press.

Ramisetty-Mikler, S. (1993). Asian Indian immigrants in America and sociocultural issues in counseling. *Journal of Multicultural Counseling and Development, 21,* 36-49.

Roysircar, G. (in press). Immigrants from South Asia and international students: Therapy for acculturation and ethnic identity concerns. In T. Smith & P. S. Richards (Eds.), *Practicing multiculturalism.* Boston: Allyn & Bacon.

Roysircar-Sodowsky, G., & Kuo, P. Y. (2001). Determining cultural validity of personality assessment. In D. B. Pope-Davis & H. L. K. Coleman (Eds.), *The intersection of class and gender in multicultural counseling* (pp. 213-239). Thousand Oaks, CA: Sage.

Roysircar-Sodowsky, G., & Maestas, M. (2000). Acculturation, ethnic identity, and acculturative stress: Evidence and measurement. In R. H. Dana (Ed.), *Handbook of cross-cultural and multicultural personality assessment* (pp. 131-172). Mahwah, NJ: Erlbaum.

Sodowsky, G. R. (1991). Effects of culturally consistent counseling tasks on American and international student observers' perception of counselor credibility: A preliminary investigation. *Journal of Counseling & Development, 69,* 253-256.

Sodowsky, G. R., & Carey, J. C. (1987). Asian Indian immigrants in America: Factors related to adjustment. *Journal of Multicultural Counseling and Development, 15,* 129-141.

Sodowsky, G.R., & Carey, J.C. (1988). Relationship between acculturation-related demographics and cultural attitudes of an Asian Indian immigrant group. *Journal of Multicultural Counseling and Development, 16*, 117–136.

Sodowsky, G. R., Kwan, K. L., & Pannu, R. (1995). Ethnic identity of Asians in the United States. In J. G. Ponterotto, J. M. Casas, L. A. Suzuki, & C. M. Alexander (Eds.), *Handbook of multicultural counseling* (pp. 123–154). Thousand Oaks, CA: Sage.

Tewari, N. (2000). *Asian Indian American clients presenting at a university counseling center: An exploration of their concerns and a comparison to other groups.* Unpublished doctoral dissertation, Southern Illinois University at Carbondale.

Tewari, N., Inman, A. G., & Sandhu, D. S. (in press). South Asian American mental health. In J. Mio & G. Iwamasa (Eds.), *Culturally diverse mental health: The challenges of research and resistance.* New York: Brunner/Routledge.

U.S. Census Bureau. (2001, May 1). *Table DP-1 Profile of general demographic characteristics: 2000 census of population and housing.* Washington, DC: U.S. Department of Commerce.

Chapter 9

Deconstructing Black Gay Shame: A Multicultural Perspective on the Quest for a Healthy Ethnic and Sexual Identity

Ron McLean

Counselors who are skilled in multicultural helping can provide much needed assistance to persons who are members of a racial or ethnic minority group and who identify as gay, lesbian, transgendered, or bisexual men and women (GLTB). This chapter focuses on some of the concerns associated with the often-conflicting identities of ethnicity and GLTB sexual orientation. Although integrating these two central identities are likely to be similar for many people of color, the focus of this discussion centers on African American individuals who also identify as GLTB. Attention is given to a literature review that includes such aspects as issues of race and ethnicity, GLTB identity development, the sociopolitical context of being African American and a sexual minority, psychological aspects of stigma and prejudice, and the beneficial components of a multicultural and diversity counseling perspective. In addition, specific multicultural strategies and outcomes are presented.

When a dominant group in society exercises its power to impose norms that view minority groups as aberrant, differences between these groups become institutionalized. Difference is often viewed as "less than," pathological, or deviant because a minority individual fails to meet the standards of the dominant group. Carmen de Monteflores (1993) suggested that "The institutionalization of differences between individuals and between groups creates stereotypes which reduce the full humanity of the individual to a few selected deviant traits" (p. 218). Stereotyping of individuals or groups because of minority status or difference frequently progresses to discriminatory practices that interfere with the individual or group's psychological health. An individual who is a member of an ethnic minority group and identifies as a gay, lesbian, transgendered, or bisexual man or woman may be discriminated against because he or she lives with two stigmatized identities. Such dual identities are often also in conflict, causing distress both from pressures within the individual and from societal pressures without. Loiacano (1993) has suggested that Black gay males experience prejudice in the Black community as well as the gay community, and that the Black gay male is challenged to integrate two highly charged identities.

Shame is internalizing messages that state that a person is deficient or flawed, until eventually the person feels negatively about him- or herself. Chronic shame causes alienation and isolation, and promotes the development of a false self or a more acceptable self. This splitting of the self is an emotionally painful experience and may lead to self-destructive behaviors, such as substance abuse, sexual compulsivity, or other addictions (Isensee, 1997). Chronic shame cultivates low self-esteem and interferes with healthy development as culturally transmitted perceptions, feelings, and behaviors constantly assault the person's core self.

In U.S. society, Black gay men, and to varying degrees other ethnic and sexual minorities, are not viewed favorably because of rigid cultural attitudes related to race and ethnicity and, especially, to sexual orientation. Indeed, the dominance of values such as the preference for a European heritage or the practice of heterosexuality has been integral in the oppression and marginalization of Black gay men. The U.S. society's power over and prejudice against racial, ethnic, and sexual minorities cause "perceived traits of inferiority in Black gay men and significantly contribute to their psychological distress, perpetuation of shame, and unequal treatment" (Everett, Chipungu, & Leashore, 1991, p. 16).

Racism and homophobia foster at least three debilitating conditions for Black gay males. First, they propagate misinformation about Black gay males that promotes self-hate (e.g., internalized shame, idealized heterosexism) and encourages others to hold prejudicial beliefs about Black gay males (e.g., Black gay men are seen as more unusual than other minority men and other sexual minority persons; Herek, 1993; Isensee, 1997). Second, racism and homophobia contribute to the powerlessness and second-class citizenry of Black gay men because they deny access to goods and services or rights and privileges that are taken for granted by heterosexual persons (e.g., being denied a family membership at a local fitness center because a gay family constellation is not recognized by the facility). Third, racism and homophobia offer no support for Black gay men to develop and be valued for who they are (e.g., there are few role models that portray Black gay men positively in the media). The significant lack of cultural support and existing cultural sanctions increase the potential for feelings of shame, alienation, isolation, and depression (Loiacano, 1993).

This chapter discusses how a counselor, working from a multicultural perspective, can facilitate a climate in which Black gay men can deconstruct their shame-based personalities and begin to create new ways of being, valuing who they are and integrating their salient identities. The chapter first describes principles for a framework in which this can take place, in which Black gay men can deconstruct shame and develop a healthy identity. The chapter then discusses five issues important for counselors to consider in this endeavor. I am guided in this writing by my practice with Black gay men.

The Framework

The themes or principles basic to providing a framework for cultivating cultural sensitivity, understanding the individual client, and forming a personal commitment to a collective responsibility for healing psychological wounds are becoming a culturally aware counselor, having a theoretical grounding, building a multicultural relationship, deconstructing shame, and operating flexibly.

Becoming a Culturally Aware Counselor

Counselors must increase awareness of their own biases related to racial, ethnic, and sexual diversities, and change damaging attitudes and behaviors in their work with Black gay men. Culturally skilled counselors actively work to understand their own worldview about Black gay men and how these views are reflected in their work. Increasing self-awareness provides an opportunity for counselors to acknowledge personal biases, and to acquire accurate knowledge about Black gay men.

Sue and his associates (1998) argued that "culturally skilled counselors actively attempt to understand the worldview of their culturally different clients without negative judgments. It is crucial that counselors understand and share with respect and appreciation the worldviews of their culturally different clients" (p. 39). Ethically, counselors who are unable or unwilling to accept the Black gay experience as valid should refrain from working with them, and may want to reevaluate their motives for being in the human services profession.

Having a Theoretical Grounding

It is imperative to have a theory-based rationale for counseling practice to facilitate conceptualization of clients' issues, formation of counseling goals, and use of interventions. In my model of counseling, I draw heavily from four theoretical frameworks: multiculturalism, Africentrism, family systems theory, and humanism. I believe that these theories sufficiently address client issues in at least two important areas: interpersonal (or environmental) and intrapsychic (or personal). Briefly, these theories/models and their relation to helping Black gay men create a healthy identity are as follows.

1. *Multiculturalism.* The multicultural perspective respects differences and embraces the validity of multiple contexts and worldviews. This theory advocates facilitating social justice for marginalized groups and valuing diversity not only in race, ethnicity, and culture but also in sexual orientation. At its best, it speaks to personal and environmental practices that provide equal opportunities to all groups in society (Sue et al., 1998). Multicultural theory helps a Black gay male recognize that his differences are not something to pathologize or be ashamed of. Rather, his experiences are valid, and he deserves access to opportunities for healthy growth and development along with members of other groups.

2. *Africentrism.* The "Africentric perspective is a reflection of the real experiences and mind-set of African Americans" (Everett et al., 1991, p. 16). The interconnection of all things; oneness of mind, body, and spirit; collective identity; and a sense of spirituality are its common characteristics. This model provides insights into how a Black gay male may develop self-esteem by increasing self- and group knowledge, finding support through collective action, and finding meaning and purpose in activities that transcend him.

3. *Family systems theory.* The family systems perspective explores how family members mutually affect each other through their interactions and interconnectedness. Causality is believed to be circular rather than linear, and symptomatic problems are best understood from an interactional point of view (Gladding, 2001). Systems theory helps the counselor to address internalized homophobia and shame by showing how negative messages about race and sexual orientation are often transmitted through the family unit. These negative messages can be seen as

112

societal constructions with the intent to oppress, but these imposed constructions should not hold any merit regarding a Black gay male's sense of self-worth.

4. *Humanism.* Humanism addresses the worth and potential of the individual and examines the dynamics and traits that propel the individual toward self-actualization, which is a striving toward achieving full potential (Gladding, 2001). Humanism provides insight about self-acceptance and self-worth. Further, a Black gay male is helped to learn to accept that his selfhood is valuable in and of itself and to take responsibility for nurturing himself.

These four theories/models are useful for counseling Black gay male clients. Together they suggest that each person is simultaneously living in his or her subjective world (personal) in a larger external community (interpersonal context). To understand how Black gay shame develops, the client becomes aware of the interactions between himself and his cultural contexts, the White dominant society as well as his African American cultural group, and examines how cultural messages have been transmitted to him through various societal contexts concerning race, ethnicity, and sexual orientation. Then the client decides whether these messages are valid. This positive reframing of cognitions begins the process of deconstructing Black gay shame. Negative messages about the self are reframed as messages that are more productive or positive. Then, as they reach their full potential, Black gay men accept personal responsibility for their own health and participate in collective action for social justice.

Building a Multicultural Relationship

Counselors establish trusting relationships with Black gay clients and create an affirming climate. These two therapeutic characteristics are necessary for Black male clients if they are to eliminate shame and build an identity of self-worth, positive potentials, and good health—and replace an identity of internalized self-hatred and self-destructive responses. Because counseling research has consistently pointed to the cultural mistrust of African Americans, counselors need to face the challenge of developing trusting multicultural relationships with Black gay clients. Counselors who are viewed as a member of a gay association or as an ally gain credibility and foster trust with Black gay males.

In order to develop the necessary trusting relationship, counselors might start by acquiring what theorists have described as essential characteristics of therapists: (a) high levels of self-awareness and acceptance, (b) open-mindedness, (c), trustworthiness, (d) flexibility, (e) objectivity, (f) personal integrity, (g) genuineness (h) empathy, (i) capacity for intimacy, (j) ability to function autonomously, and (k) respect for others (Nugent, 2000; Pipes & Davenport, 1999; Srebalus & Brown, 2001). Conversely, rigidity, overcontrol, ineptness, and virtuosity or "showing off" are characteristics that hinder the helping process (Srebalus & Brown, 2001). These characteristics suggest that counselors should be committed to their own self-work, and because of ongoing self-work, they will actively convey sensitivity or acceptance of the experiences of Black gay men.

Counselors are confident in their ability to assist Black gay men, and yet remain open to different ways of thinking about a gay client's problems, thus preserving their individuality. A counselor's skills and interpersonal style are presented in such a way that a Black gay male experiences him or her as real, trustworthy, and as a person of good will. It is at this point that the work of counseling or psychotherapy can begin.

Deconstructing Shame

Systemic marginalization and oppression can be seen in legal sanctions against sexual minorities (e.g., inadequate hate crime legislation), homophobia (e.g., unmerited fear of nonheterosexuals), racism (e.g., inequities in health care for racial and ethnic minorities), and institutional practices that create barriers to reaching one's full potential (e.g., religious and family practices and work benefits that are prejudiced against GLTB individuals). One result of chronic marginalization is the development of a cycle of shame in Black gay men (Isensee, 1997).

Isensee (1997) has described the cycle of shame as a five-part process: internalization of shame, isolation and suppression of one's feelings, development of a false self, self-destructive behavior to avoid emotions, and lowered self-esteem. His discussion serves as a useful model for counselors to help them understand the tasks required to successfully deconstruct Black gay shame: First, a Black gay male must use the therapeutic process to acknowledge and express the pain caused by shame (e.g., address internalized homophobia, abuse, negative cultural messages), and how this has led to his alienation, isolation, and the belief that his true self must remain invisible. Second, a Black gay male needs to begin to see how distorted thinking regarding himself and feelings of alienation and isolation may lead to self-destructive behaviors (e.g., compulsive sexual activity, substance abuse), which further deepen the feeling of shame. Third, it is important for a Black gay male to seek support from others, either within his own community (e.g., Black gay social clubs) or in the larger community (e.g., affirming churches, 12-step programs, coalition groups) where he can experience validation without suppressing either of his salient identities. Fourth, a Black gay male must develop the capacity to restructure distorted thinking about himself, construct a way of thinking, feeling, and being that integrates his salient identities (e.g., begin to see himself as a valuable Black person and gay male rather than as one who is pathological or inferior). Fifth, a Black gay male should commit to something meaningful that transcends himself and is beneficial to other people (e.g., community service, a spiritual path) to gain a sense of purpose and overcome feelings of shame and unworthiness. Lastly, when Black gay males and their allies challenge cultural myths about race, ethnicity, and sexual orientation; develop the supports necessary for individual and group esteem; and commit to a purpose that is beneficial to a larger cause, then they may eliminate shame because they have developed mental and cultural structures inconsistent with the maintenance of shame.

Operating Flexibly

In addition to traditional office visits, alternative methods of helping are essential. Pedersen (1991) argued that counseling the culturally diverse frequently occurs in an informal setting (e.g., home, street corner, hallway) and often uses an informal method of assisting (e.g., discussion, daily encounter, presentation). Culturally sensitive counselors are willing to utilize a variety of methods to provide services to a Black gay male. In addition to office visits, I have met regularly with Black gay male clients in coffee shops, parks, and public agencies (e.g., social service organizations). Moreover, to augment talk therapy, I have utilized a variety of communication or contact methods that include letter writing, telephone counseling, emails, and voicemail contact.

Counseling Implications

How can the multicultural counselor facilitate the deconstruction of shame in a Black gay male? This section presents five issues that are important for the counselor to address in order to work efficaciously with Black gay male clients. The first four issues relate primarily to the relationship between the counselor and the client, and the fifth issue relates more to a global concern.

First, competent multicultural counselors provide safe space that is affirming and nonjudgmental for a Black gay male, maximizing the client's capacity to heal. The meeting location and mode of communication should be as flexible as possible.

Second, competent multicultural counselors use treatment modalities that are sensitive to the needs of a Black gay male. In particular, I prefer the cognitive restructuring (Nugent, 2000) model. Cognitive restructuring provides a way to create a narrative or self-talk that affirms a Black gay identity. That is, the client (a) becomes aware that at the root of shame is a distorted thinking process, (b) learns how internalized cultural messages become established as negative self-talk, (c) is taught how to listen to negative self-talk and observe his dysfunctional behavior, (d) is taught how to develop a more positive dialogue or self-talk, and finally (e) learns new coping skills to manage oppressive and stressful situations directed at him by the larger society.

A word of caution regarding the usage of cognitive therapy techniques: Cognitive therapy is most effective with Black gay men when it is used to understand their perspective and to enhance the internal and external realities of their lives. Some multicultural thinkers have criticized cognitive therapy because it might ignore gender, diversity, and contextual issues (D'Andrea, 2000; Rigazio-DiGilio, Ivey, & Locke, 1997). However, there are multicultural theorists who argue that cognitive therapy is useful (Ivey, D'Andrea, Ivey, & Simek-Morgan, 2002) when cognitive strategies are employed to help clients change their thoughts, assume healthier behaviors, and interrupt constraining interactions that may exist in the wider sociopolitical context (Rigazio-DiGilio et al., 1997). Cognitive work on societal issues should be a part of the treatment process when working with minorities (Parham, 1999).

Third, competent multicultural counselors are familiar with and are willing to utilize community resources that provide support for Black gay males. One way in which counselors become credible and familiar with culturally sensitive resources is by being an active and visible part of the Black community, the gay community, or, to a smaller extent, the Black gay community. When I worked in the St. Louis area, I regularly encouraged my clients to participate in Umoja, an informal social organization that provides support to Black gay males and others.

Fourth, competent multicultural counselors are willing to use culturally appropriate value frameworks to help a Black gay male enhance his self-esteem by committing to a larger purpose in the community. The Nguzo Saba (Phillips, 1990), an Africentric model, connotes six basic principles of African communal living. These are *umoja* (unity), *kujichagulia* (self-determination), *ujima* (collective work and responsibility), *nia* (purpose), *kuumba* (creativity), and *imani* (faith). The Nguzo Saba can be used as a framework for understanding one's larger, spiritual purpose as consistent with Africentric values.

Fifth, competent multicultural counselors can be agents of social justice in the community. Culturally skilled counselors should work to eliminate biases, prejudices, and discriminatory practices, and develop sensitivity in people to issues of racism and oppression (Sue et al., 1998). Counselors can work at multiple levels on behalf of their Black gay male clients by educating the public and advocating for equal access to the basic services and privileges enjoyed by other groups. For example, I have worked with the American Psychological Association's Healthy Lesbian, Gay, and Bisexual Students Project to promote better treatment of these students during their K–12 student years. The project is designed to provide guidance in developing school policies sensitive to the needs of GLBT students. I have also developed relationship workshops designed to help Black gay men learn ways to validate and find satisfaction in committed long-term relationships.

Conclusion

This chapter emphasizes that U.S. society's prejudicial views with regard to race, ethnicity, and sexual orientation have contributed to unequal treatment, oppression, psychological distress, and perpetuation of shame in Black gay males. Tasks that Black gay men should master to deconstruct their shame and develop a healthy self that validates their Black and gay identities are proposed. Further, in order for a counselor to work successfully with and on behalf of Black gay males to deconstruct shame, the counselor must (a) develop multicultural competence by becoming aware of his or her own and a Black male client's worldviews and work on value biases, (b) have a theory-based rationale for counseling that is affirming to a Black gay male, (c) develop a multicultural therapeutic relationship, (d) have a flexible mode of operating services, (e) be skillful in using formal and informal tools to deconstruct shame, (f) be willing to use culturally sensitive community resources to help a Black gay male heal, find support, and find a larger spiritual purpose, and, finally, (g) have an action-oriented commitment to social justice.

References

D'Andrea, M. (2000). Postmodernism, social constructionism, and multiculturalism: Three forces that are shaping and expanding our thoughts about counseling. *Journal of Mental Health Counseling, 22*, 1-16.

de Monteflores, C. (1993). Notes on the management of difference. In L. D. Garnets & D. C. Kimmel (Eds.), *Psychological perspectives on lesbian and gay male experiences* (pp. 218-247). New York: Columbia University Press.

Everett, J. E., Chipungu, S. S., & Leashore, B. R. (1991). *Child welfare: An Africentric perspective.* New Brunswick, NJ: Rutgers University Press.

Gladding, S. T. (2001). *The counseling dictionary: Concise definitions of frequently used terms.* Upper Saddle River, NJ: Prentice Hall.

Herek, G. M. (1993). The context of antigay violence: Notes on cultural and psychological heterosexism. In L. D. Garnets & D. C. Kimmel (Eds.), *Psychological perspectives on lesbian and gay male experiences* (pp. 89-108). New York: Columbia University Press.

Isensee, R. (1997). *Reclaiming your life: The gay man's guide to love, self-acceptance, and trust.* Los Angeles: Alyson.

Ivey, A. E., D'Andrea, M., Ivey, M. B., & Simek-Morgan, L. (2002). *Theories of counseling and psychotherapy: A multicultural perspective* (5th ed.). Boston: Pearson.

Loiacano, D. K. (1993). Gay identity issues among Black Americans: Racism, homophobia, and the need for validation. In L. D. Garnets & D. C. Kimmel (Eds.), *Psychological perspectives on lesbian and gay male experiences* (pp. 364-375). New York: Columbia University Press.

Nugent, F. (2000). *Introduction to the profession of counseling* (3rd ed.). Upper Saddle River, NJ: Merrill/Prentice Hall.

Parham, T. A., White, J. L., & Ajamu, A. (1999). *The psychology of Blacks: An African-centered perspective* (3rd ed.). Upper Saddle River, NJ: Prentice Hall.

Pedersen, P. B. (1991). Counseling international students. *The Counseling Psychologist, 19*(1), 10-58.

Phillips, F. B. (1990). NTU psychotherapy: An Afrocentric approach. *Journal of Black Psychology, 17*(1), 55-74.

Pipes, R. B., & Davenport, D. S. (1999). *Introduction to psychotherapy: Common clinical wisdom* (2nd ed.). Boston: Allyn & Bacon.

Rigazio-DiGilio, S. A., Ivey, A. E., & Locke, D. C. (1997). Continuing the postmodern dialogue: Enhancing and contextualizing multiple voices. *Journal of Mental Health Counseling, 19,* 233-255.

Srebalus, D. J., & Brown, D. (2001). *A guide to the helping professions.* Boston: Allyn & Bacon.

Sue, D. W., Carter, R. T., Casas, J. M., Fouad, N. A., Ivey, A. E., Jensen, M., LaFromboise, T., Manese, J. E., Ponterotto, J. G., & Vazquez-Nutall, E. (1998). *Multicultural counseling competencies: Individual and organizational development.* Thousand Oaks, CA: Sage.

Chapter 10

Use of Narratives, Metaphor, and Relationship in the Assessment and Treatment of a Sexually Reactive Native American Youth

Lisa L. Frey

The case study describes the use of metaphors, personal narratives, and the therapeutic relationship in the assessment and treatment of a Native American youth who was referred for sexually reactive behavior. The multicultural counseling competency model is discussed in terms of the counselor's own personal and professional development as well as in terms of its contextual application in the relationship. Several of the youth's narratives, including those related to family relationships and to his identity development as a Native American, are presented and explored to provide a glimpse into the youth's personal meanings and experiences. The central role of these narratives in clarifying treatment interventions, identifying primary treatment modalities, and facilitating a healing experience is discussed.

This case study offers my understanding of the therapeutic relationship between a young Native American youth and his family, and myself. I do not offer this as a definitive work on therapeutic intervention with Native American youth, nor youth from a specific tribal group. That said, it is true that I have made a commitment to my own evolution as a multiculturally competent counselor, a process that informed my work with this youth. White counselors can fairly easily choose to live culturally encapsulated (Wrenn, 1962) lives, both professionally and personally. I know that I was never interested in that. I find myself energized by diversity in all its forms, but I realize in retrospect that my prior diversity interest was more as an observer than a participant. My perspective was given a major jolt, however, when I met a woman who was to become my mentor and friend. She not only challenged me to surpass the limits imposed by my monocultural socialization and cultural privilege, but she also helped me to realize that it is my responsibility, no one else's, to ensure that I am competent in my personal and professional cross-cultural relationships. Although I had long worked with clients who differed racially and ethnically from myself, it was not an issue that I directly addressed in our therapeutic relationship or even thought about much. Committing myself to a more pluralistic perspective meant making a number of changes, including taking the responsibility to become more knowledgeable about my clients' cultures of origin (instead of exercising my privilege by assuming it was their responsibility to educate me) and involving myself in educational opportunities and personal experiences in which I was forced to challenge my own culturally constricted beliefs and attitudes. Sodowsky, Kuo-Jackson, Richardson, and Corey (1998) have pointed out the importance of multicultural clinical experience, research, and training, including providing "trainee opportunities to reflect and work on their personal issues related to their socialization, power status, and worldview assumptions" (p. 261), in developing increased multicultural counseling competency. My journey has not always been comfortable, but being comfortable has become less important to me over time.

It must also be acknowledged that my conceptualizations and interventions with this youth were guided by my primary theoretical orientation, the Relational–Cultural Model. In general terms, this model focuses on the primary importance of meaningful and authentic human interconnections (in contrast to separation and individuation) as the path to healthy development and on an authentic, mutual, and "power with" orientation (in contrast to "power over" or oppressive orientation) to relationships (Miller & Stiver, 1997). In addition, my interventions were guided by narrative techniques. My orientation is evidenced by the thread that runs through the case study that follows, that of focusing on the voice of the youth, his family, and his community, and on deconstructing and honoring the meanings they attributed to words, events, feelings, thoughts, memories, and sensory experiences in their lives.

Case Study

In order to ensure the confidentiality of the strong and courageous youths that I work with, the case study in this chapter is based on a composite of several Native American youth that I have worked with through the years. In addition, it should be noted that the terms *Native*

American, *American Indian*, and *Indian* are used interchangeably in the case study.

> Jess was a 12-year-old youth, a member of the Lakota Sioux tribe. He had lived in a particular Midwest state all his life. He was referred to my office for a psychosexual assessment and ongoing counseling following an incident of sexually aggressive behavior, which included fondling of and forced oral intercourse with a 5-year-old child on the playground at his school. Jess was of high average intelligence and had no history of prior sexually inappropriate behaviors. He had not received previous counseling.
>
> Jess had lived with his biological parents on a reservation in the Midwest for several years as a young child. When he was about 8 years old, he was removed from their home for abuse and neglect, including intrafamilial physical abuse and extrafamilial sexual abuse. Since that time Jess had been in various urban foster homes. Although reunification had been attempted on numerous occasions, each attempt had reportedly been unsuccessful, and the legal authorities were in the process of terminating the parental rights of the mother and father. There had been no contact between Jess and his biological parents for 2 years.
>
> Jess's kinship history included strong relationships among Jess's seven siblings, three of whom were adults. Two of his adult siblings had been attempting to gain custodial guardianship of Jess for about 2 years. Although the adult siblings struggled with their own issues throughout their adolescence, as adults they were living productive lives. They were all involved in committed relationships, were employed, and had no adult criminal or substance abuse histories. Two of the three maintained consistent visitation with Jess. Jess's other siblings were living in various foster homes, and as foster home changes occurred over the years, visitation had become more infrequent. The kinship history included several biological family members with a history of substance abuse, including both of his parents. Jess's mother, however, had reportedly not used chemical substances during her pregnancy and fetal alcohol syndrome/effects had been ruled out. A history of generational trauma was present within his extended family and kinship network, including physical and sexual violence and multiple losses.
>
> Jess's older siblings were actively involved in tribal activities, but they had been unsuccessful in facilitating Jess' involvement. It was reported that this was due in large part to Jess's rejection of his tribal heritage and history.

Assessment

Guiding Orientation

Although the purpose of this chapter is not to provide an exhaustive review of the theory underlying my treatment interventions, I want to briefly highlight three aspects of my guiding orientation in order to provide the reader with a broader understanding of the specific assessment and treatment interventions that follow. I also want to note that my goal for the chapter is to explore culturally congruent aspects of the therapeutic relationship and intervention plan. It is beyond the scope of this chapter to provide a comprehensive review of assessment and treatment issues specific to children who engage in sexually aggressive behaviors. Clinicians working with youth engaging in such behavior are urged, however, to become familiar with the clinical and empirical literature on this topic.

The first aspect to highlight is my view of culture as the "grounding locus" (Dinicola, 1996, p. 409) in developing an understanding of Jess's experiences and the meanings he ascribed to those experiences. For example, I viewed one of my primary responsibilities to be attending to the culturally influenced meanings that Jess, his family, and his community attributed to his behaviors, his definition of self, and to the notions of therapeutic problems and solutions, both concepts based on Western-oriented, individualistic orientations to counseling. The second aspect is that my therapeutic orientation is based on a strength-based model from which I view symptoms as interrelated and only one aspect of the whole person. Therefore, my perspective was on Jess as a whole person, continually evolving and continually impacting and being impacted by relationships within his kinship network, peer group, community, and sociocultural context. The third aspect to highlight is that I believe it is possible to balance my own clinical training in primarily Western psychotherapeutic models with a respect for traditional Native American philosophies and practices. This does not, however, entail assuming a Native American persona. Wyse and Thomasson (1999) noted that non-Native counselors who attempt to assume such a persona fail to understand the disrespectful nature of that behavior. Such behavior is oppressive to American Indians in its attempt to coopt "yet another sacred sense of themselves" (Wyse & Thomasson, p. 90).

Assessment Interventions

Metaphors and story telling.
Because of my focus on clinical work with youth, I tend to be oriented toward the use of metaphor. In working with Jess, it quickly became apparent that metaphor was a comfortable communication tool for him. This style of communication prompted Jess to share some of the stories that he had been told as a child within his family and community.

In addition, it resulted in "critical moments of connection" (Sodowsky et al., 1998, p. 262) in our relationship as Jess gave voice to, and I was able to hear, his understanding of experiences and interpersonal relationships. During sessions many opportunities were provided for Jess to convey these meanings. One tool that aided in this process was the sand tray. With the sand tray Jess was able to visually represent a story or series of stories, which he then put words to. We also used drawings, cartoons, and oral story telling to facilitate the telling of Jess' story.

Over time, two primary themes, often interwoven with Jess's beliefs regarding spirituality, emerged from the assessment stories. The first of these themes was reflected in Jess's story about a boy who is in a coma. The family is told that the boy is not expected to improve. The boy's family members can't believe this and decide to consult a healer. The healer tries for hours to heal the boy, but to no avail. Just when he is ready to give up, the boy's sister begs him to try one more time and tells a story of how important the boy is to his family. The healer keeps trying. The story ends with a miracle: the boy becomes whole again and is able to rejoin his family. This story, and others like it, seemed to express Jess's connection to family, his profound sadness and longing related to the loss of this connection, his sense that healing would come about through reconnection, and his hope that those trying to help him would persevere.

Stories involving what we labeled *Indians* are reflected in the second recurring theme. These stories usually involved someone who engaged in bad behavior because of their *Indianness*. For example, a boy steals from his four best friends because "Indians are thieves" or a girl refuses to do her farm chores because "Indians are lazy." As this theme was explored further, Jess began to talk about his belief that he was abused by his parents because they were Native American and therefore innately abusive. This was a powerful belief in terms of Jess's own identity development as a Native American, and contributed to his own sexually aggressive behavior. His sexual aggression was further proof of his own badness and a reflection of his own self-hatred. From a broader sociocultural perspective, this belief also has its roots in the historical trauma and continuing institutionalized oppression experienced by Native Americans.

Holistic mapping of relationships.
An important part of the assessment process with Jess involved mapping kinship relationships. Similar to a genogram, the kinship network mapping that was done by Jess and me extended beyond the biological

123

family, encompassing the more intricate kinship networks of his child-hood. Jess's map included individuals who were not biologically related to Jess but were important individuals to him in childhood. For example, Jess identified an elderly neighbor woman who had taken Jess and his siblings to her home on many occasions when his mother was intoxi-cated and locked the children out of the house. He recalled this woman, whom he called grandmother, feeding and soothing him and his siblings. This mapping helped both Jess and me to better understand his sense of community and the meaning the loss of community had in his life. The process also facilitated exploration of the memories and experiences associated with various individuals in Jess's life.

Holistic mapping of experiences.

Mapping of life experiences was done as an offshoot of the kinship mapping. Jess and I sometimes moved between each map as, for exam-ple, his identification of a significant person in his life triggered memo-ries of life experiences. This map was conceptually similar to a time line or life graph (U.S. Department of Justice, 2000), although less linear and chronological in nature, and encompassed significant life ex-periences, including traumas, losses, sexual history information, and healing experiences (Wyse & Thomasson, 1999). The inclusion of healing experiences was considered to be an essential and culturally congruent aspect of the map for two reasons. First, it incorporated Jess's values regarding spirituality. Second, the realization that there were some positive, healing experiences intermingled with the ones of trauma and loss helped Jess to recognize that some people and experiences could still be trusted.

Family involvement.

Clearly, Jess's need for nurturing kinship and community relationships would be important to his healing. For this reason, I began to explore the possibility of family involvement in Jess's treatment. Although Jess's older siblings lived at some distance, they decided that Thomas and Susan, Jess's older brother and his wife, could begin to attend Jess's counseling sessions and serve as the representatives of the family. Thomas and Susan were also firmly committed to Jess coming to live with them.

During the assessment process, my primary focus with Thomas, Susan, and Jess was to gain a better understanding of the meanings they attributed to Jess's behavior and the family experiences. For exam-ple, Thomas and Susan were able to talk about the historical loss and trauma within the family and the influence that this had on all family members. While holding Jess responsible for his sexually aggressive behavior, they also communicated a sense of systemic or collective responsibility (Wyse & Thomasson, 1999) within the family for the circumstances culminating in Jess's behavior. In one session, Thomas told Jess a story of his belief in Jess's ability to heal his traumatic past. In the story, Thomas spoke of an event in Jess's childhood when two peers rejected him. Later the peers approached him to express an interest in a tree house that Jess had built. Although Jess was initially angry, he apparently decided that he was going to treat them more kindly than he had been treated, and invited the peers to play with him. Thomas's message was clear: Jess was capable of embracing the past, learning from it, and moving forward. These discussions helped me to better understand the connectedness between the older and younger members within the family.

Although the discussions took place in the assessment phase of intervention, they were clearly also healing interventions for Jess and are an example of the interrelatedness of components of counseling. Assessment, not just treatment, can provide powerful healing moments.

From Assessment to Intervention

The move from the assessment to the intervention phase was marked (somewhat artificially, to be sure) by a juvenile court hearing for the purpose of reviewing the assessment recommendations. For this hearing the family requested that a tribal legal advocate be assigned to the case in the juvenile court proceedings. I recommended that Jess be moved from his foster home into Thomas and Susan's home based on several factors. First, a home study had been completed with positive results. Second, Thomas, Susan, Jess, and I had explored the family's views of safety issues for the community and for Jess. A safety plan delineating appropriate supervision and monitoring, one that was both satisfactory to the juvenile court and involved contributions from all of his older siblings, had been developed. The plan included, for example, a supervision plan that cooperatively involved all three of the older siblings in ensuring full-day supervision for Jess. Last, I documented a therapeutic rationale for family placement in the assessment report. Shortly after the court hearing, Jess was moved into Thomas and Susan's home.

Once the move occurred, Thomas and Susan began to encourage Jess to become more involved in tribal activities. Their encouragement and Jess's resultant ambivalence brought his confusion about his identity as an American Indian to the forefront. He began to act out at activities he attended, in particular engaging in derisive and sarcastic name-calling toward other youth. After some discussion about the cause of this behavior, Thomas and Susan chose to deal with the behavior by involving Jess in activities in which he could learn more about his Native history. They made sure that he had contacts with older male members of the tribe and provided him with opportunities to participate in traditional healing rituals. In counseling sessions, we processed what he was learning about his history and wondered together what that meant about him and his family. Once again, story telling became a central focus of sessions as Jess struggled with what it meant to him to be Indian.

A story that Jess told during that time involved a young man who was given a guitar by a friend who said the young man was "born to play." However, the boy could not learn no matter how much he practiced. Even when he was given sheet music, he could not figure it out by himself. First he decided that he hated music and did not care to play guitar after all. Then, although frustrated and ready to give up, he forced himself to go to a music store and ask for lessons. The music store was what he needed, the musicians there understood exactly what to teach him, and eventually with lessons and lots of practice, he learned to play guitar beautifully. When Jess told such stories, we talked about the meaning the stories held for him but did not attempt to analyze and dissect components of the story. Jess's stories in their wholeness seemed to be what provided the healing experience. This particular story meant to Jess that he too could learn important lessons if he allowed those who were wiser to teach him.

Many of the cognitive interventions frequently used in working with sexually aggressive youth were also helpful for Jess. For example, together we worked on helping Jess identify the cognitive distortions that led to his sexually aggressive behavior. We discussed the cyclical nature of thoughts, behaviors, and feelings leading to sexual aggression (i.e., the sexual assault cycle; Isaac & Lane, 1990) and identified his personal cycle. Jess was receptive to learning ways to intervene in the cycle and to restructure distorted thoughts. He used this knowledge to develop a cycle of healing that counteracted each component of his assault cycle and included behavioral and cognitive interrupters. Jess understood these interventions as a way to prevent future sexually aggressive behavior by restoring balance in his patterns of thinking and behaving. Wyse and Thomasson (1999) noted that cognitive strategies may be culturally congruent for Native Americans, many of whom view thought as a vital aspect of health and illness.

Conclusion

All clinicians know that we learn as much from our clients as they ever learn from us. This was also true of my journey with Jess. Although reading and educating myself about Jess's culture was an important part of being multiculturally competent in the relationship, it was equally important to be open to Jess's subjective cultural experience (Sodowsky et al., 1998) and to communicate that talking about the differences between us was not only acceptable but essential.

As stated by Duran and Duran (1995), "the critical factor in cross-cultural psychology is a fundamentally different way of being in the world" (p. 17). Rigidly imposing a Western conceptualization of what comprises good therapy onto the therapeutic work with Jess would have been at least ineffective and, more likely, oppressive and traumatizing. Relying on culture as the "grounding locus" (Dinicola, 1996, p. 409) challenged me to attend to the meanings that Jess attributed to his experiences, relationships, and sense of self. This process resulted in the natural unfolding of the intervention plan. For example, the use of metaphor and story telling, initially employed as a culturally congruent means of communication, ultimately provided a path to increasing Jess's and my understandings of his experiences, relationships, and view of the world. Mapping Jess's life experiences and kinship relationships provided further opportunity for exploring and validating his experiences.

Through such interventions, it became clear that nurturing kinship and community relationships were important to Jess's healing. The involvement of family members in Jess's counseling provided Jess with a vital sense of connection to his family and community. This required a redefining of my role as the treatment modality shifted from a counselor-client dyad to a healing community. As members of the healing community, family members initiated Jess's involvement in traditional activities, which further extended the therapeutic process. For example, his increased involvement in tribal activities pushed him to deal more directly with his identity as a Native American.

Interventions specific to treating sexually aggressive youth were also incorporated into Jess's treatment. Cognitive strategies were useful in facilitating Jess's understanding of the thoughts, feelings, and behaviors leading to his sexual aggression.

On a more personal note, the challenge for me in working with Jess, as I have learned is often my challenge in my work with clients who are racially or ethnically different from myself, was tolerating my feelings of inadequacy and uncertainty, and forging ahead. So it was with Jess. Some of this we were able to talk about—what it was like for him and for his family to work with a White counselor, what it was like for us to know that they had struggles every day that I would never have to confront. Some of the uncertainty was mine to struggle with on my own. All in all, I believe that it is a good thing for me to not know. It allows me to continue to wonder with clients, to experience the intensity of a connection in a relationship with someone who seems (and in many ways is) very different from myself. Jess gave to me and, in the process, gave something of value to every individual that I will work with in the future. I gave to Jess and, hopefully, in that process also offered something of value.

Jess is doing well.

References

Dinicola, V. F. (1996). Ethnocultural aspects of PTSD and related disorders among children and adolescents. In A. J. Marsella, M. J. Friedman, E. T. Gerrity, & R. M. Scurfield (Eds.), *Ethnocultural aspects of posttraumatic stress disorder: Issues, research, and clinical applications* (pp. 389-414). Washington, DC: American Psychological Association.

Duran, E., & Duran, B. (1995). *Native American postcolonial psychology*. Albany, NY: State University of New York Press.

Isaac, C., & Lane, S. (1990). *The sexual abuse cycle in the treatment of adolescent sexual abusers* [Videotape with reference materials]. (Available from the Safer Society Press, P.O. Box 340, Brandon, VT 05733-0340)

Miller, J. B., & Stiver, I. P. (1997). *The healing connection: How women form relationships in therapy and in life*. Boston: Beacon Press.

Sodowsky, G. R., Kuo-Jackson, P., Richardson, L. F., & Corey, A. T. (1998). Correlates of self-reported multicultural competencies: Counselor multicultural social desirability, race, social inadequacy, locus of control racial ideology, and multicultural training. *Journal of Counseling Psychology, 45*, 256-264.

U.S. Department of Justice. (2000, March). *Abusers who were abused: Myths and misunderstandings*. Retrieved May 16, 2002, from http://w3.uokhsc.edu/ccan/Abusers%20who%20were%20Abused.doc

Wrenn, C. G. (1962). The culturally encapsulated counselor. *Harvard Educational Review, 32*, 444-449.

Wyse, M., & Thomasson, K. (1999). A perspective on sex offender treatment for Native Americans. In A. D. Lewis (Ed.), *Cultural diversity in sexual abuser treatment: Issues and approaches* (pp. 83-107). Brandon, VT: Safer Society Press.

Chapter 11

Multiculturalism and Immigrants

Jane Uchison

This chapter describes a semester-long multicultural interaction project for increasing cultural awareness and sensitivity. It was completed as part of doctoral training. The author met informally with a first-generation female immigrant from Poland; listening empathically was an integral part of the meetings. The project was mutually empowering and thus provided reciprocal learning.

This chapter is the result of a semester-long project completed as part of my doctoral training and as part of a course titled Diversity and its Clinical Enterprise. Its purpose was to increase our personal cultural awareness as well as sensitivity to the cultures and worldviews of others through a series of informal meetings with an individual from a different culture who lived in the local community. In these meetings, trainees were not expected to play the role of therapist, although empathic listening was an integral part of the relationship. Instead of the therapeutic relationship, the relationship in the multicultural interactions class project was meant to be mutually empowering in the sense that each trainee's offering of empathetic listening was returned through the interviewee's willingness to share with the trainee a part of his or her culture and personal stories related to this culture. In session process notes, the trainee reflected on the interviewee's stories by self-disclosing personal reactions that were framed within each trainee's own cultural and racial socialization and values. Thus this was a project of reciprocal learning.

The Case of Interviewee T

This is a case conceptualization of a first-generation female immigrant from Poland. The construct of multicultural counseling competencies, as articulated by Sue, Arredondo, and McDavis (1992), is utilized to provide

129

a framework for discussing a multicultural interviewing process. Berry's bidimensional model of acculturation (Kim & Abreu, 2001; Roysircar-Sodowsky & Maestas, 2000) is then utilized as a qualitative tool to examine this immigrant's acculturation process.

T is a 30-year-old female who is a first generation immigrant from Poland. She grew up in a suburb of Warsaw. T is from a middle-class family with two parents and one older sister. She described her mother as playing a prominent role in keeping the family intact while she saw her father as a dreamer and "someone who always had great ideas but lacked follow through." When T was young, her father made the decision to build a house so the family could move out of their apartment. This was an important event in T's family as it led to a major structural change within the family system. For instance, several years into the project, the family ran out of money to complete the house. In order to make the additional money needed, T's father was forced to find work in other cities and began to spend less and less time at home.

T's father later moved from Poland to America under the premise that he would continue to try to make money to finish the house and then return to live with the family. However, he did not return, and T and her sister continued to be raised by their mother. T's mother worked full-time as a secretary for a prosecutor's office and relinquished a great deal of the child-rearing responsibilities to her mother and father who lived in a nearby apartment.

T was brought up Polish Catholic, and her family adhered quite strongly to the traditions of this religion. They attended regular Sunday services and celebrated Polish-Catholic holidays. T described these holidays as a time when her family, friends, and neighbors came together to eat, drink, and honor the traditions of the church for that given holiday.

T attended a fine arts high school where she became increasingly interested in film production and the art of animation. She later went on to pursue a degree at a Polish film school. T received her master's degree in animation from this school. T struggled to find work in Poland with this new degree. She created several short animation videos and a longer claymation film in an effort to market her skills. However, there was little demand for her degree, and she determined that she was going to have difficulty supporting herself if she chose to stay in Poland. T spent the summer after her graduation with her older sister who had moved to Chicago to join their father. T was introduced to friends of her sister's who helped her to make a connection with individuals in a design school in Chicago. T attended some classes as a visitor and was asked to give a short presentation on her experiences in her Polish film school. Students and professors at the school took a great deal of interest in T and her work, and she was later offered a position as a part-time instructor. After a great deal of thought, T made the difficult decision to leave her home, mother, and friends in order to move to Chicago.

T moved in with her father who lived in a lower income area in south Chicago. She described feeling a sense of both culture and class shock coming into this neighborhood. She no longer felt safe to be out alone at night, and although there were other Polish individuals in the neighborhood, this did not add to her sense of security due to the high crime rate in the area. T described her experience of teaching as both exciting and disappointing. She stated that the students had a very different learning style from students in Poland, and this proved to be challenging at times. T soon was forced to gain other part-time employment in order to make ends meet. By this time her father had retired and had very little income, and she was helping out with rent and household expenses.

After teaching for a year at the school in Chicago, T decided to apply for full-time faculty positions in other institutions. She was offered an interview at a design school on the East Coast. Through the interview process T was introduced to other Polish faculty and community members. She attended a lunch with several of these individuals and described feeling welcomed and relieved to have discussions with individuals from her culture. Several weeks later, T was offered and accepted the position. This meant yet another difficult transition for T as she left her family, friends, and job in Chicago to move to a city where she knew no one except for the individuals who had been a part of her interview.

T presently continues to teach at the design school. She is in frequent contact with her other family members. Her sister and father remain in Chicago. Several years ago, her mother and father opted to sell the house that he had started building in T's childhood. T described the physical presence of the house as serving as a constant reminder to her mother of her father's shortcomings. She stated that she could not drive by the house without turning in the other direction. T said that the selling of the house also affected her father who was forced to give up the dream that he once had for his family. However, T's parents continue to remain married, and her mother speaks of immigrating to join her father once she retires.

Sue et al. (1992) targeted three different areas relevant to multicultural counseling competencies. Sodowsky, Kuo-Jackson, and Loya (1997) further clarified the Sue et al. model with tables and cases. Although the supervised interactional process I experienced with T was not a counseling relationship but rather a formal interactive learning component of the diversity course I was taking in my doctoral training, the multicultural competency areas are broad enough to incorporate into helping relationships with individuals from various cultures as well. I use three competency points—awareness of one's own assumptions, values, and bias; understanding the worldview of a culturally different client; and developing appropriate counselor interventions, strategies, and techniques—to discuss my process of learning throughout the time that I interacted with T.

Awareness of One's Own Assumptions, Values, and Bias

Roysircar (in press a) has pointed out that "The therapist's apparent similarities with an immigrant client can make the initial interviews confusing in that therapists may slip into assumptions that the client holds similar values and attitudes as they." T and I are similar ages, both involved in academic environments, and both from middle-class families. We also look and dress similarly. Although these things seem quite superficial, I recognized in myself a tendency to seek out and even possibly overemphasize these similarities because it provided me with both the groundwork and the comfort level to build our relationship upon. I do not think identifying common ground between two individuals is generally problematic when making a connection such as this. However, I do believe it initially hindered my abilities to encourage T to speak about her individual experiences.

I was made blatantly aware of an area of personal bias in an interaction that occurred between T and myself well into our process together. T told me early on that her mother was still residing in Poland while her father had lived in Chicago for several years. She rarely spoke of her father and mother in the same context, often excluding her father from conversations about her family altogether. It did not occur to me to ask if her parents were divorced, primarily because I assumed that any couple that had been physically separated for such a long period of time would not remain married. However, when T began to speak more about her family history, she mentioned that her mom often considered immigrating to the United States upon her retirement. This triggered me to ask if her parents were still together. "Oh yes," she responded, "my parents don't believe in divorce!" This put a completely different spin on my view of her family and the information that she had given me up to this point. Had I continued to operate on the basis of my assumptions and bias, a very important piece of T's family makeup would have been misunderstood.

Sue et al. (1992) encouraged counselors to be knowledgeable of how their own heritage affects the definition of normality and abnormality. I realized the importance of this through an interaction that T and I had around the issue of food. T and I both expressed an interest in preparing and eating good food from various cultures. We seemed to gravitate toward the topic of food in nearly every meeting that we had, perhaps because it was a topic that we both felt very safe discussing.

On several occasions, we spoke about preparing a Polish meal together. However, one day, T spontaneously invited me to her apartment for a meal that she stated she wanted to prepare for me. I accepted and when she asked if there was anything I couldn't eat, I told her that I don't eat red meat. T looked somewhat perplexed but said that she would find something to make that didn't include red meat. When I arrived at her apartment, she apologetically explained that most of the Polish dishes that she makes have some form of red meat in them so she instead had prepared a French dish. I recognized then that in all of our discussions about cooking, I had never asked her to describe typical Polish dishes for me. Instead, I had assumed that Polish cooking could be easily adapted to be vegetarian because this is such a common thing to do in my own middle-class, educated, White American culture. I quickly realized that what is seen as common or normal to me does not necessarily ring true in other cultures. After our dinner, I expressed to T that I wanted to become more familiar with traditional Polish cooking and asked her to share some of her favorite recipes out of her Polish cookbook with me.

Understanding the Worldview of a Culturally Different Client

Learning more about T's worldview greatly influenced my ability to recognize and correct for my own biases and assumptions. In asking questions about as many aspects of information that she was sharing with me as possible, I was able to develop a system of checks and balances by contrasting my own beliefs with T's in a nonjudgmental fashion. T and I had spoken a lot about our families and about some of the similarities between them. However, I also knew from our discussions that there were many ways in which our families functioned very differently, and I wanted to explore these differences more in an effort to understand how T's upbringing had affected her worldview. T shared with me the significant role that her grandparents played in her life growing up. She explained that the main role of grandparents after retirement is to take care of grandchildren. We discussed how this differed from my grandparents who, like many other retired individuals from my culture, use retirement as a time for travel or leisurely activities. T stated that her grandparents were very much a part of her upbringing and her everyday life. This role then reversed as they aged, and she, her sister, and her mother began to provide care for them. After her grandmother died, T's grandfather moved into their apartment where he lived out the remainder of his life. Although he became very sick and showed signs of

133

dementia prior to dying, the family did not consider alternative care, as care taking for elders is a role traditionally played by family members in the Polish culture.

T spoke about her mother and father very differently. She described her mother as being "the rock" of the family while often omitting mention of her father from conversations about her family unless I specifically asked. In a later discussion, she was able to share with me the story about the house he had started to build and the symbolism behind this for her family. She described her role in his life presently as prematurely turning into one of somewhat of a caretaker as he struggles both financially and physically.

Midway through our meetings, T loaned me a Polish film that she thought would give me some added insight into the culture. I found it interesting that, in many ways, the parental characters in this film mirrored the roles that T described her parents as playing. The mother in the film was very much viewed as the responsible one who kept the family running smoothly while the father was seen as somewhat of a disappointment. In speaking with T about this film, she stated that it is not uncommon for Polish women to play a more powerful role in families.

Learning more about T's family history helped me to gain perspective into the meaning that T places on her immigration experience. When T first told me the story of her immigration into the United States, I had very little background information about her or her family. Although she did discuss the hardships of immigration, her stories were overwhelmingly positive and very focused on her self-initiative and strength as an individual. She seemed almost surprised at times by how far she had come when she discussed her history as an immigrant. She emphasized her self-sufficiency and ability to make a new life for herself in a completely different country. Although these feelings seem fairly consistent with positive immigration experiences (Roysircar, in press a), the added insight that she gave me about her family allowed me to see that immigration has played a powerful role for T in validating her success as an individual, separate from both her mother and father.

Developing Appropriate Counselor Interventions, Strategies, and Techniques

As mentioned previously, I did not consider my role in this experience to be one of counselor. However, I learned several things from my time with T that I believe helped to make the relationship a successful one. I started out the first few meetings with T very informally. We spent several meetings getting to know one another, and I tried to allow her to set

134

the pace in terms of how much information she wanted to share with me. I recognized that asking her about the details of her life could seem somewhat invasive, and I wanted to provide opportunity for rapport to build. Surface-level conversations eventually turned into a more intimate interchange about her immigration experience and her family. I shared with T many of my own experiences of my recent relocation to a new city, resulting in fruitful and enlightening discussions about cultural and individual similarities and differences. T expressed both a willingness and an eagerness to share her stories with me. However, I feel that if I had not allowed for an initial level of trust to build between the two of us, or had not been willing to share part of myself with her, many of these very personal details about her life and experiences would have been left out.

Sodowsky, Kuo-Jackson, and Loya (1997) emphasized the importance of respecting the religious or spiritual beliefs and values of immigrant clients. Although T and I both were raised Catholic, our religious experiences were very different. One of the main religious holidays that T continues to value and celebrate is Easter. Shortly after Easter this year I met with T, and she shared stories with me about past Easter experiences in Poland. She discussed the importance of the holiday for her culture and taught me about the meaning behind several of the surrounding holidays. By listening to and respecting the information that T had to share with me about her beliefs and the beliefs of her culture, while not assuming that our experiences in this realm were parallel even though we are both Catholics, I was able to gain a better understanding of the importance that religion has played in T's life.

Conceptualization of the Case of T
From an Acculturation Model

Acculturation is defined as "the adaptation of minority groups to the culture of the dominant group" (Roysircar-Sodowsky & Maestas, 2000, p. 135). Berry's bidimensional acculturation model (Roysircar, in press b; Roysircar-Sodowsky & Maestas, 2000) focuses on the effects of two-way interactions between majority and minority groups in order to determine the level of acculturation of ethnic groups. The two issues that the ethnic minority must confront are "maintenance and development of one's ethnic distinctiveness by retaining one's cultural identity, and the desire to seek interethnic contact by valuing and maintaining positive relations with the dominant society" (Roysircar-Sodowsky & Maestas, 2000, p. 135). These two dimensions of acculturation are assessed by asking the questions: "Is it considered to be of value to maintain cultural identity and characteristics?" and "Is it considered to be of value to maintain relationships with other groups?" (Roysircar-Sodowsky & Maestas, 2000, p. 135). The answers result in the following acculturation attitudes (Kim & Abreu, 2001; Roysircar, in press b):

- *Integration* (yes/yes) occurs when an individual maintains connections with his or her culture while interacting on a daily basis with members of the dominant culture;
- *Assimilation* (no/yes) occurs when a person regularly interacts with members of the dominant culture but maintains no interest in remaining connected with his or her indigenous culture;
- *Separation* (yes/no) occurs when a person avoids contact with members of the dominant culture, emphasizing only connections with his or her culture of origin; and
- *Marginalization* (no/no) occurs when an individual has no interest in acquiring or maintaining connections or proficiency with either his or her host or native culture.

Although these terms are useful in providing a qualitative framework for viewing the acculturation process, using a bidimensional perspective does not account for individual differences in this process. Sodowsky, Kwan, and Pannu (1995) proposed a modified nonlinear version of the bidimensional model, taking into account that "individuals approach the acculturation process with their individual uniqueness, family history, cultural expectations and values, as well as life experiences prior to and after immigration" (p. 123).

This nonlinear model provides a useful approach of examining T's acculturation process. At first glance, it might seem that T fits neatly into the domain of Integration. She maintains solid connections to her Polish culture but is well acclimated to, and interacts regularly with, people from the host culture (the United States). However, by viewing T's process through the narrow lens of the bidimensional acculturation model, we miss out on several of T's individual differences. As mentioned earlier, T is a professor at a design school. In one of the conversations that we had, T mentioned that she feels that American students lack motivation and initiative because they are given too much structure by their professors. T further stated that she feels she was taught to think creatively by her Polish teachers and professors who did not provide students with this level of structure. She discussed how, as a professor, she is trying to break American students from their need for structure. This is an example of where T fits more into the Separation stage.

Although T is not avoiding contact with individuals from the dominant group, she is placing more worth on her own cultural values while not perceiving the fact that there may be more than one correct way of teaching and learning creativity.

T shared how religion and Polish-Catholic holidays were a major part of her upbringing. She spoke fondly about Easter celebrations and talked about the importance placed on attending mass each Sunday. However, when I asked her to tell me about some of the additional Polish holidays, she recognized that she had forgotten many of them and stated that she had not been to church for several months. This is an example of where T might fall more into the category of Assimilation. Although her attitude toward her original culture's emphasis on these issues is not one of rejection, the U.S. White dominant culture has clearly affected the amount of emphasis she places on rituals and customs that used to be an important part of her identity.

In her poem "For the White Person Who Wants to Know How to Be My Friend," Pat Parker (1990) wrote, "The first thing you do is to forget that I'm Black. Second, you must never forget that I'm Black." This same philosophy can be applied to working with other minority groups by substituting their cultural difference for the term *Black*. The assumptions that I made throughout my interactional process with T were a result of my sometimes forgetting that she has had a unique experience, influenced by her history and culture. However, if I had only been able to see T as a product of her culture, I would have overlooked the many ways that we are more alike than different.

T's acculturation process is one that is clearly ongoing. Taking the time to sit with her as she reflected back on her journey provided me with more insight than I could ever gain from books or journal articles. For T, I believe that our interactional process provided a welcoming environment in which to share her very rich and powerful experiences.

Conclusion

By challenging ourselves to take a more critical look at our own assumptions in relation to individuals with various backgrounds, we benefit by gaining privileged insight into the worldview of culturally diverse individuals. The multicultural counseling competencies of Sue et al. (1992) and Berry's bidimensional model of acculturation (see Kim & Abreu, 2001; Roysircar-Sodowsky & Maestas, 2000), both having been applied (Sodowsky et al., 1997) to illustrate how effective relationships may be formed with immigrants, give us helpful tools to gain an understanding and greater compassion in our work with immigrants.

Taking the time to simply sit with individuals who have various stories to relate about their acculturation process can provide us with perhaps the richest experience in terms of expanding our own levels of knowledge, cultural awareness of others, and, consequently, perspective-taking or empathy. In addition, this experience gives us the opportunity to take a closer look at our own worldview and, further, challenges us to replace value-based assumptions with inquiry and understanding.

References

Kim, B. S. K., & Abreu, J. M. (2001). Acculturation measurement: Theory, current instruments, and future directions. In J. G. Ponterotto, J. M. Casas, L. A. Suzuki, & C. M. Alexander (Eds.), *Handbook of multicultural counseling* (2nd ed., pp. 394–424). Thousand Oaks, CA: Sage.

Parker, P. (1990). For the white person who wants to know how to be my friend. In G. Anzaldua (Ed.), *Making face, make soul*. San Francisco: Aunt Lute Foundation Books. Retrieved from http://orion.neiu.edu/~lsfuller/poems/white.htm

Roysircar, G. (in press a). Therapy for acculturation and ethnic identity concerns: Immigrants from South Asia and international students. In T. Smith & P. S. Richards (Eds.), *Practicing multiculturalism*. Boston: Allyn & Bacon.

Roysircar, G. (in press b). Understanding immigrants: Acculturation theory and research. In F. D. Harper & J. McFadden (Eds.), *Culture and counseling: New approaches*. Boston: Allyn & Bacon.

Roysircar-Sodowsky, G., & Maestas, M.V. (2000). Acculturation, ethnic identity, and acculturative stress: Evidence and measurement. In R. H. Dana (Ed.), *Handbook of cross-cultural and multicultural personality assessment* (pp. 131–172). Mahwah, NJ: Erlbaum.

Sodowsky, G. R., Kuo-Jackson, Y. P., & Loya, G. J. (1997). Outcome of training in the philosophy of assessment. Multicultural counseling competencies. In D. Pope-Davis & H. Coleman (Eds.), *Multicultural counseling competencies: Assessment, education and training, and supervision* (pp. 3–42). Thousand Oaks, CA: Sage.

Sodowsky, G. R., Kwan, K. L., & Pannu, R. (1995). Ethnic identity of Asians in the United States. In J. G. Ponterotto, J. M. Casas, L. A. Suzuki, & C. M. Alexander (Eds.), *Handbook of multicultural counseling* (pp. 123–154). Thousand Oaks, CA: Sage.

Sue, D. W., Arredondo, P., & McDavis, R. J. (1992). Multicultural counseling competencies and standards: A call to the profession. *Journal of Multicultural Counseling and Development, 20*, 477–486.

Part Three

Multicultural Practices Applied to Theory and Setting

Chapter 12

Multicultural Competencies and Group Work: A Collectivistic View

Tarrell Awe Agahe Portman

This chapter is a qualitative, experiential perspective of an American Indian female group participant and the facilitator. Incorporation of Native American values as applied to group work practices are shared. A collectivistic perspective that embraces group processes and mutual respect as a part of group processes is provided.

G roup work is by nature collectivistic in that norms and attitudes of others in the group facilitate change among the members. Therefore, group work as a multicultural counseling intervention may connect with basic underlying cultural principles found in members from certain collectivistic cultures. The following statement of a Native American chief highlights the group orientation of a cultural group:

> Watch the birds in the winter, how they flock together for comfort and survival. Watch the fish in the stream, how they must move together against the current to feed, so they can survive. Watch the cattle in the field, how they stand together in preparation for the storm. Watch the Earth, how the seeds fall together to the soil, so the plant will pass on from one generation to another. By watching our brothers and sisters in the circle, humans learn to survive in the circle of life through being aware of the power in groups. (Chief Charlie Dawes of the Ottawa [Adawe] Nation of Oklahoma, personal communication, September 7, 1997)

These words are just a few from the American Indian teachings I have received from elders throughout my life. These teachings have provided a framework for my experiences as a group facilitator in my career. People can learn to survive and function in their daily lives

141

through group work. American Indian people have been functioning in groups for therapeutic purposes for many years (Garrett, Garrett, & Brotherton, 2001). In fact, we have embedded group work into our daily existence to the point that it permeates our lives, thoughts, and healing practices. As a collectivistic culture, individual decisions are influenced by collective consequences to our families, communities, and nations. In essence, the words "the joy of one is the joy of all, and the hurt of one is the hurt of all" serve as a summation of collectivism. My people live in a collectivistic culture dedicated to the good of the group. This chapter serves as a self-evaluation of my experiences as a group worker over the past 20 years with multicultural group work.

The aim of this chapter is to offer a qualitative self-report of professional application and counseling strategies used in implementing multicultural competencies in group work and to report on outcomes, which may prove beneficial to the reader. My socialization in Native American collectivism shapes my worldview, which, in turn, impacts my professional counseling practices and affects my underlying philosophy of group work. For further understanding of Native American values and perspectives, the reader is referred to the counseling literature (Garrett, 1999; Garrett & Garrett, 1994; Herring, 1997; Portman, 2001).

Overview of Group Work

Much has been written about group work as a specialty and as an intervention in the counseling profession. Recent group work literature provides multiple examples of effective interventions and group methods targeting the needs of culturally diverse groups (Colmant & Merta, 1999; Garrett et al., 2001; Gloria, 1999; Kim, Omizo, & D'Andrea, 1998; Merta, 1995; Salvendy, 1999; Torres-Rivera, Wilbur, Roberts-Wilbur, & Phan, 1999; Williams, Frame, & Green, 1999). The primary mode for disseminating this knowledge to counseling professionals is the *Journal for Specialists in Group Work*, a publication of the Association for Specialists in Group Work (ASGW), a division of the American Counseling Association. ASGW offers a home base for counseling professionals dedicated to a focus on group work theory, interventions, training, current issues, and research. The *Journal for Specialists in Group Work* has a regular section dedicated to practice issues, which provides applicable information for practitioners.

ASGW leads the profession in ethical training and competent practice standards for group work. The organization endorsed a specific living document on August 1, 1998, entitled *Principles for Diversity— Competent Group Workers* (Haley-Banez, Brown, & Molina, 1999). The value ASGW places on multiculturalism in group work is clearly expressed in the following statements in the document's preamble:

> The Association for Specialists in Group Work (ASGW) is committed to understanding how issues of diversity affect all aspects of group work. This includes but is not limited to: training diversity-competent group workers; conducting research that will add to the literature on group work with diverse populations; understanding how diversity affects group process and dynamics; and assisting group facilitators in various settings to increase their awareness, knowledge, and skills as they relate to facilitating groups with diverse memberships.
>
> As an organization, ASGW has endorsed this document with the recognition that issues of diversity affect group process and dynamics, group facilitation, training, and research. As an organization, we recognize that racism, classism, sexism, heterosexism, ableism, and so forth, affect everyone. Our personal responsibility as individual members of this organization is to address these issues through awareness, knowledge, and skills. As members of ASGW, we need to increase our awareness of our own biases, values, and beliefs and how they impact the groups we run. We need to increase our awareness of our group members' biases, values, and beliefs and how they also impact and influence group process and dynamics. Finally, we need to increase our knowledge in facilitating, with confidence, competence, and integrity, groups that are diverse on many dimensions. (p. 1)

This document is an excellent, practical resource for every counselor practicing group work. The overarching framework for becoming diversity-competent group workers is grounded within the principal domain areas of the multicultural competencies (knowledge, awareness, and skills). ASGW provides innovative structures within these domains, which, in turn, add insight into the dynamics of multicultural competencies. These dynamic structures within the basic multicultural competencies, as implied in the preamble, are commitment, recognition, personal responsibility, and professional action.

Skills in each of these four structures become necessary. ASGW provides examples of skills for group workers such as (1) actively seeking opportunities for experiences with members of various cultural groups, (2) seeking to understand yourself and your own multiculturalism, (3) active participation with cultural group members in their own cultural events away from the counseling setting, (4) ability to exercise institutional intervention skills on behalf of their group members, and (5) taking responsibility in educating group members to the processes of group work. These counseling skills may empower group participants within groups. Group member empowerment is exemplified in three practical group work interventions, described in the next section, which have proven to be successful during my counseling career.

Successful Multicultural Methods
Implemented in Group Work

I fully agree with the assertion that "Group leaders must experience the power of group dynamics both as a member and a leader to truly understand them" (DeLucia-Waack, 2000, p. 325). My first experiences in groups were in a cultural setting, primarily with relatives and extended family. These were positive experiences that I cherish. In subsequent years, I entered my counselor preparation program and began my training in group work. However, my early experiences in counseling groups may not be described as positive. My cultural perspective became pronounced in these professional groups, and I realized my Native American beliefs, values, and perspectives were very different from those of the majority of my cohort group. Thankfully, I had a group leader who recognized the difference and encouraged my growth. These experiences of being different and group members' responses to my difference enhanced my concept of group work as a social microcosm (Yalom, 1995).

Reflecting upon my experiences as a group member from a culturally diverse background, I consider my progress as developmental after considering Yalom's 11 therapeutic factors. These factors are listed, in the order that I feel were most salient to me as a minority group member and as I became more comfortable with the professional group process, are existential dimensions, development of socializing techniques, imitative behavior, interpersonal learning, group cohesiveness, altruism, universality, imparting of information, catharsis, instillation of hope, and recapitulation of family experiences (Yalom, 1995). First, I learned to understand the meaning behind the group work and its prerequisite skills before I learned to trust other group members. In hindsight, these experiences helped me to formulate my underlying philosophy of multicultural group work, which unbeknownst to me then embraced the multicultural competency domains of awareness, knowledge, and skills.

As a group leader, I have led groups both in K–12 school settings and in hospital outpatient settings with children and adolescents. I soon began to realize my cultural experiences and beliefs were interwoven with my professional skills training. Group work interventions began to emerge for me, incorporating Native American perspectives in the group process. Incorporation of these perspectives, these concepts, as therapeutic interventions have proved helpful to me in conducting group work. It is my belief that these perspectives align with ASGW's principles for diversity-competent group workers and the multicultural competencies. Three of these—immediacy of time, noninterference, and harmony and balance—are presented here.

Immediacy of Time

The Native American value of immediacy of time continues to guide the effectiveness of my group work (Garrett et al., 2001). In the counseling profession we call this working in the here-and-now. A present-time orientation is embedded in my worldview, and therefore, as a group leader it is my unconscious frame of reference. Early in the group process, group members are introduced to this concept in a manner that helps them distinguish between a futuristic orientation and a present orientation to time. In my experience, immediacy of time is introduced first when I begin group by discussing my worldview and theoretical orientation.

Noninterference

The concept of noninterference as a practice within group work can be effective. In my opinion, the closest translation of this value is the concept of mutual respect. Native Americans live and celebrate in an atmosphere that is primarily intertribal (many different nations and peoples coming together). Intertribal group events require high levels of mutual respect due to various tribal or familial beliefs and traditions (for example, underlying views of sex roles as matrilocal vs. patrilocal). Nonverbally, regalia (dress), symbols, or demeanor distinguishes the individual tribal affiliation and communicates these differences at intertribal group meetings. When nonverbal signs are unavailable, a verbally appropriate greeting is given—the person's name and tribal affiliation. Transferring this concept to group work has helped to enrich group member experiences in groups. The early identification of cultural background and perspectives at the beginning of the group increases understanding between group members and personal awareness of one's own cultural identification. Cultural identification, occurring early within group work, is one component of noninterference or mutual respect.

A second component is one in which group members are respected for making their own choices and decisions about their thoughts, feelings, and actions. In counseling we may refer to this as validation. Integrating this perspective into group work enables group members to be

145

respectful of others' choices and decision making. This does not mean group members are unable to challenge each other, but it does help to decrease overt imposition of biases and prejudicial statements when noninterference is incorporated.

Harmony and Balance

The Native American value I incorporate most into group work is the concept of harmony and balance. Harmony as a concept does not eliminate conflict with others. Harmony is a frame of reference equivalent to being at peace with the universe, others, and yourself. It may be viewed as agreeing to disagree in the process of understanding the perspective of another person. Balance is more of an intrapersonal experience involving physical, emotional, intellectual, and spiritual well-being. Being comfortable with who you are in the circle of life is important in maintaining balance. I have found that defining and using the terms balance and harmony within group work have been very beneficial in giving group members a common language.

Implications/Conclusion

Incorporating Native American perspectives into group work as a method of moving toward multicultural competency implies that counseling professionals must engage in paradigm shifts concerning their own awareness of multiculturalism. Each group member's worldview or value-based assumptions must be recognized early in every group because the process of the group will be affected by individual members' cultural influences. Creating an atmosphere of mutual respect by acknowledging multicultural issues initially in the group may help to establish existential meaning in differences, and subsequently integration of differences, dualities, and polarities. This creates movement toward group cohesiveness. Group leaders may wish to build community as a social microcosm, utilizing the intertribal gathering concept.

Incorporating collectivistic Native American values, such as sharing, cooperation, noninterference, importance of community contribution, acceptance, harmony and balance, extended family, attention to nature, immediacy of time, awareness of the relationship, and a deep respect for elders, into group work may help increase opportunities of group member growth. Helping professionals are encouraged to explore and incorporate into their group work practices the collectivistic methods of many nonmajority cultural groups whose members practice group work as a way of life.

References

Colmant, S. A., & Merta, R. J. (1999). Using sweat lodge ceremony as group therapy for Navajo youth. *Journal for Specialists in Group Work, 24*, 55-73.

DeLucia-Waack, J. L. (2000). The field of group work: Past, present, and future. *Journal for Specialists in Group Work, 25*, 323-326.

Garrett, M.T. (1999). Understanding the "medicine" of Native American traditional values: An integrative review. *Counseling and Values, 43*, 84-98.

Garrett, J. T., & Garrett, M. T. (1994). The path of good medicine: Understanding and counseling Native Americans. *Journal of Multicultural Counseling and Development, 22*, 134-144.

Garrett, M., Garrett, J. T., & Brotherton, D. (2001). Inner circle/outer circle: A group technique based on Native American healing circles. *Journal for Specialists in Group Work, 26*, 17-30.

Gloria, A. M. (1999). Apoyando estudiantes Chicanas: Therapeutic factors in Chicana college student support groups. *Journal for Specialists in Group Work, 24*, 246-259.

Haley-Banez, L., Brown, S., & Molina, B. (1999). Association for Specialists in Group Work principles for diversity-competent group workers. *Journal for Specialists in Group Work, 24*, 7-14.

Herring, R. D. (1997). Counseling Native American youth. In C. C. Lee (Ed.), *Multicultural issues in counseling: New approaches to diversity* (2nd ed., pp. 37-47). Alexandria, VA: American Counseling Association.

Kim, B. S., Omizo, M. M., & D'Andrea, M. J. (1998). The effects of culturally consonant group counseling on the self-esteem and internal locus of control orientation among Native American adolescents. *Journal for Specialists in Group Work, 23*, 145-163.

Merta, R. (1995). Group work: Multicultural perspectives. In J. G. Ponterotto, J. M. Casas, L. A. Suzuki, & C. M. Alexander (Eds.), *Handbook of multicultural counseling* (pp. 567-585). Thousand Oaks, CA: Sage.

Portman, T. A. (2001). Sex role attributions of American Indian women. *Journal of Mental Health Counseling, 23*, 72-84.

Salvendy, J. T. (1999). Ethnocultural considerations in group psychotherapy. *International Journal of Group Psychotherapy, 49*, 429-464.

Torres-Rivera, E., Wilbur, M. P., Roberts-Wilbur, J., & Phan, L. (1999). Group work with Latino clients: A psychoeducational model. *Journal for Specialists in Group Work, 24*, 383-404.

Williams, C. B., Frame, M. W., & Green, E. (1999). Counseling groups for African American women: A focus on spirituality. *Journal for Specialists in Group Work, 24*, 260-273.

Yalom, I. D. (1995). *The theory and practice of group psychotherapy* (4th ed.). New York: Basic Books.

Chapter 13

Culture-Centered Counseling From an Existential Perspective: What Does It Look Like and How Does It Work for an African American Woman Client?

Marcheta P. Evans and Albert A. Valadez

This chapter focuses on culture-centered counseling from an existential perspective while also emphasizing the needs of the client from a culturally specific orientation. This theoretical approach is based on the premise that all cultures experience universal issues of love, death, anxiety, and crisis. This framework of existential theory is made culturally relevant through the lens of an African American woman undergoing life transition and grief issues.

Culture-centered counseling from an existential perspective: What is this concept and how is it manifested? To answer these questions, individuals within the field of counseling must develop a clear understanding of both concepts: culture-centeredness and existentialism. According to Pedersen (personal communication, May 2, 2001), culture-centered counseling involves making the client's culture central to the goals, objectives, and services being provided by the counselor. The term *culture* we apply in the broadest sense, incorporating many significant aspects of the individual, such as age, gender, race, ethnicity, and religion and his or her experiences in various contexts of life.

Existentialism is potentially the most suitable theory for application within a multicultural or cross-cultural context (Epp, 1998; Ibrahim, Roysircar-Sodowsky, & Ohnishi, 2001). According to Vontress, Johnson, and Epp (1999), existentialism fills the void left by person-centered counseling. Person-centered counseling emphasizes the importance of the relationship between the client and the counselor and the counselor's ability to relate to the client's worldview. Existentialism integrates these important considerations within its concept of relatedness with the philosophy that all humans are viewed as products of their unique cultures and grounding. Further, existentialism allows the counselor to focus on some of the most gripping issues human beings encounter: anxiety, suffering, death, and love (Seligman, 2001). These issues are pervasive and ubiquitous across cultures. They transcend and imbue all aspects of living, not being unique to a certain culture. But how people give meaning and interpretation to these issues depends on a society's way of looking at life, or worldview. It is for the counselor to get to the client's culture-based meanings. Thus a relationship between the tenets of existentialism and culture-centered counseling, based on the theoretical underpinnings of these two concepts, is apparent.

The purpose of this chapter is to assist the counselor in the utilization of culturally appropriate intervention strategies from an existential perspective. Again, it is our intention to reiterate the importance of counselors being knowledgeable about their client's culture. This knowledge essentially leads to effective existential practice.

Application of Culture-Centered
Existential Theory to Practice

When clients visit their counselors seeking help, they are indirectly and nonverbally saying to the counselor, "I need to believe and trust that you can help me. I need assistance in working through my life problems. Can you and will you help me?" The pleas behind the questions represent basic help-seeking attitudes revealed to the counselor. How we respond to them is critical.

First, it is important that we assess our qualifications and competencies to meet our client's needs. Included in this self-assessment should be questions regarding our attitudes, beliefs, and knowledge about the respective cultures our clients represent. This introspective process will be central to the interventions subsequently presented to the client. This form of counselor self-exploration is essential before the counselor decides to move further in the relationship with the client. It does not imply that the counselor has to be culturally omniscient to be effective. However, it does imply that the counselor needs to be knowledgeable and sensitive to the needs of the client, particularly if these needs have cultural implications (Sodowsky, 1996).

Existentialism presents the notion that people are constantly changing, evolving, and emerging from the givens of life. Culturally speaking, we are products of our past and of our present. These temporal influences shape the counselor's decision-making processes and worldviews

150

(Ihle, Sodowsky, & Kwan, 1996). When the client sits down in the counselor's office, he or she brings the history of countless interactions and encounters that have been experienced with individuals throughout his or her life context (P. Pedersen, personal communication, May 2, 2001). The counselor connects this history into the here-and-now circumstances of the client, throwing light on the client's current dilemmas.

At the core of the existential approach is the belief that every client has the freedom to make individual life choices, despite oppressions, the existence of evil, and the vagaries of life. In essence, clients have a choice as to how they view their lives and sufferings, whether that view is positive or negative. Ultimately, clients must realize that they are the architect and author of their designs and stories. They need to empower themselves in order not to be reactors to or victims of circumstances (Corey, 2001). However, in empowering the client, the counselor first listens to the client's experiences of oppression, prejudice, and abuse, and affirms the client's challenges of survival. By taking the perspective of the client's expressions and affectively reaching out to him or her, the counselor leads the way for the client to make choices.

A cursory glance at the principles of existentialism might lead the reader to believe that life is sated with unhappiness and loss. For instance, when addressing the emotional difficulties that life presents, there are central aspects universal to all people: the inescapability of death, existential alienation or isolation, meaninglessness, anxiety as a condition of living, and guilt (Seligman, 2001). The client can often feel helpless and overwhelmed. These propositions potentially paint a dismal and bleak picture of life. However, it is also existentialism that points to a life that is filled with the promise of hope and optimism, making the difference in a client's future possibilities. Even though the aforementioned painful conditions are manifest in the human condition, individuals have the potential to confront and persevere through these difficulties to ultimately find meaning. To further demonstrate this notion, Seligman (2001) addressed several areas that provide the promise of peace. These include hope and awareness, authenticity and intimacy, freedom and responsibility, self-actualization and meaning. The ability to integrate the dualities of life gives meaning to issues which, when seen alone, seem meaningless.

Goals, Strategies, and the Counseling Relationship

The primary goal of existential counseling is assisting clients in seeing the value, meaning, and purpose of their lives. The existential therapist emphasizes the client's power, responsibility, and freedom to make

151

choices about how they view their lives and the changes they might consider to improve their lives. During this process, it is the counselor's objective to assist clients in realizing that they are in control of their reactions to and the decisions they make about their lives. When clients realize that actions must be taken to facilitate their desired life changes, their progress is subsequently accelerated. The therapist must then assist each client in realizing that even nonaction is a form of action. In turn, the clients must be able to release the crippling fear that often immobilizes their actions (May, 1990; Seligman, 2001). Ultimately, the goal of therapy is for the clients to be able to identify the barriers that preclude them from feelings that grant power and freedom over their life.

In the therapeutic relationship, the counselor must be able to appreciate the client's phenomenological world. The alliance between practitioner and client is critical to therapeutic effectiveness. Additionally, the therapist's ability to gain entrance into the client's world in order to understand what the client is experiencing culturally will directly impact the client's growth (Assay & Lambert, 1999). The role of the therapist in this process is critical; the use of "self as a tool" by the counselor is a core to successful therapy (Baldwin, 1987). With this approach to counseling, therapists are encouraged to share their own values and beliefs (Bugenthal, 1987; Seligman, 2001).

This sharing approach approximates Buber's (1970) I/Thou philosophy in that it allows for various levels of client/counselor interactions. According to Buber, in the existential approach, the most profound and meaningful level of interaction is this I-to-thou relationship. In this shared alliance, the counselor and client have the sincerest respect for each other and a high sense of relatedness (Bugenthal, 1978).

In reference to specific techniques or strategies utilized with culture-centered existentialism, there is a deemphasis on a cookbook or standardized method (Van Deurzen-Smith, 1990). The client–counselor relationship is typically the primary intervention technique utilized. This gives the counselor the flexibility to be more culture focused, enabling the counselor to see the self in relationship to an individual's context. Any strategy that may be employed is implemented with the intention of assisting the client in understanding their choices and options for action within context (Corey, 2001). Further, in the applications of the culture-centered framework, counselors become cognizant of the intervention appropriate for the client's cultural needs.

Even though specific techniques are not emphasized, some existential interventions have been highlighted in the literature: Being in the World (May, Angel, and Ellenberger, 1958); Symbolic Growth Experience (Frankl, 1963; Frick, 1987; Maslow, 1968); Logotherapy and paradoxical intention (Frankl, 1978); and dereflection (Yalom, 1980). In addition, there are numerous inventories, such as the Life Attitude Profile—Revised (LAP-R; Reker, 1992) and Sources of Meaning Profile (SOMP) (Reker, 1992, 1996), that explore individual value systems within an existential frame of reference. However, not enough research or data have been generated to validate the accuracy of these inventories (Frank, 1995; Seligman, 2001).

Content Versus Context and Existentialism

Many individuals come to therapy with existential-type crises that are rooted in an underlying search for meaning. Depression allows an individual, with the help of a therapist, to begin to see through the window to his or her own soul and potentially discover a meaning yielding insight and personal growth. When taking into account the cultural imperatives that might influence the process to this discovery, the question of content versus context must be considered. In Western culture, the process of gaining knowledge is predicated on order, form, and utility. This emphasis on content often comes at the sacrifice of the ability to see the greater context. The worldviews of African American and Hispanic cultures tend to incorporate, more often than the White dominant culture, the greater context or the external/situational factors that might influence the condition of being.

An examination of the concept of pain through an African American lens will illustrate. A personal story is shared to emphasize the content versus context concept. Generally speaking, most of the second author's clients want to eradicate pain in their lives. With any existential struggle comes pain; from this pain might come messages from the soul. In African American culture, pain might be celebrated rather than denied. For example, musical blues are an art form in which the soul manifests itself from a place of pain. When working late in my office one night, two custodians approached me: one African American and the other White. They were having an ongoing argument as to the origin of the hymn "Amazing Grace." The African American custodian insisted that it was a slave song that men and women sang while they were in the hot sun picking cotton in the fields. The White custodian proclaimed that it was a song of English origin. Seeing several books on my shelves on word origins, they sought me out to resolve the conflict. It is true that "Amazing Grace" has words in its text that are English, thus suggesting an English origin. This is an example of answering the question via an examination of content. Equally true, however, is the song's use during backbreaking work by slaves in the fields. They were both correct. The African American custodian was more concerned with its origination in the *context* of painful occurrences. For him, this was meaning. The White custodian wanted to identify words and structure (form) of the lyric of the song that could confirm its English origin. For him, this was meaningful. To the extent to which a therapist can see problems and issues from a contextual perspective, outside of contents, will determine his or her efficacy in addressing existential issues from a multicultural perspective.

Case Example

A review of the literature reveals that existential counseling works very well with certain populations and situations:

- individuals dealing with life-threatening and chronic illnesses,
- those who have suffered loss of all kinds,
- those whose lives have challenging limitations, and
- individuals at crossroads who need some form of direction in their lives (Seligman, 2001).

To illustrate this culture-centered approach to counseling from an existential frame, excerpts from a case study are presented. Michelle is the name given to this client. Highlights of the intake session, Michelle's views of religion, her relationship with her mother, father, and siblings, and her views of personal worth are explored and discussed.

Client Background Information

Michelle is a 52-year-old African American female. She is single, has no children, and at the time of intake was unemployed. She is the youngest of five children. She has an older sister and three older brothers. Michelle lives in a suburb of a major city in a southern state. She graduated from Howard University, a prominent historically Black university, with an undergraduate degree in music-voice concentration and continued her education to obtain a professional degree in pharmacy. She had previously worked for many years as a pharmacist in a northern urban city. She quit her job and returned to care for her mother, who recently died of complications related to a stroke suffered 3 years prior to this study.

In the initial sessions, Michelle stated that her reason for coming to counseling is to deal with the emptiness in her life and the lack of direction since her mother's death. In addition to the death of her mother, her father died in May of the same year. A friend of the family referred Michelle to counseling. Michelle also said

> You know, I have been in counseling before and it really seems to help. I just need to talk to someone to help me get focused. I am feeling completely lost since my mother died. I have been to see a psychiatrist before, but I don't know what to do. I was hoping to find a counselor here in town. The other one was in a nearby town, but the traveling every week was difficult. I am really concerned about someone in the community knowing that I am in counseling. I really wish I could go to see someone out of town. Unfortunately, there are not a lot of African American counselors around. I am kind of worried that someone in the community will know that I am seeing a counselor. This may impact their trust in me as a pharmacist. I don't know! I have not been able to do much lately. I don't want to go out of the house, and I just spend a lot of time with my plants. They [the plants] are my release and joy.

Michelle's self-description:

> I really don't know who I am. I have tried so many different things. I like doing so many different things. I have owned a house-moving company, dug wells, owned a construction company, gotten my license for asbestos removal, and joined about every money scheme available. . . .
>
> You know, I just want some peace. I feel as if my soul is trapped at times. I want to be loved for me, but there are seemingly so few people that could handle my needs. Also, I get tired of people that don't have any ambition or drive. . . . I need to lose weight and I have tried. I really believe this is due to my depression and how I was raised in my Black culture. As kids we were taught to eat when you are happy, sad, or whatever. It didn't make a difference. Everything always centered around food. It still does. There are times when I just gorge myself with food. It is as if I am trying to fill a hole inside of me.

Michelle's description of her relationship with her mother:

> My mother was a very special woman. She had some college education, which was almost unheard of during her time for a Black woman. She constantly pushed education for all her children. Even though my father had no formal education, she felt this was the key to a better life. She and my dad were married over 50 years. Truly, she was a needy woman. She wanted her children to be around her all the time. My mother would manipulate or do whatever to get her children home. She gave my older sister fits. She would say very hurtful things to all of us, but deep down we knew she loved us. As long as she controlled us, she was happy. Ours was a family that was run around her wishes.

155

Michelle's description of her relationship with her father:

> I had no real relationship with my daddy. He was a hard man. I was afraid of him
> as a child and really never became very close to him. He only had a third grade
> education, but he could do just about anything. He was a jack of all trades. I think
> my mother only married him to get out of her family and be on her own. He
> owned his own garage and did ornamental ironwork. Near the end, at times, I
> almost felt as if I hated him and especially when I thought about how he treated
> me as a child.

Michelle's description of her siblings:

> My sister and brothers all have degrees in education or nursing. It was important
> to my mother that we were all educated. As educated as we are, we all have
> problems getting along with each other. When we come together, it usually ends
> up in someone getting mad about something that happened 20 years ago or who
> was the favorite child. I am just so tired of this. I wish we could get along better.
> We have so much potential as a family, but at times I feel as if we are cursed.
> We just can't seem to move beyond petty stuff.

Michelle's description of religion:

> I am a Seventh-Day Adventist. I am not sure how much you know about this reli-
> gion, but it is a very conservative Christian theology that is similar to Orthodox
> Jewish theology in regards to the Sabbath and dietary habits. Religion has caused
> a lot of pain in my life. Right now I am not sure what I believe. I have been dab-
> bling in astrology, numerology, and other alternative thoughts. My mother would
> have a duck if she knew, but she is gone! I still can see her face and how she
> would be disapproving. She still has such a hold on all of us. It is as if we can't go
> on yet. She is still here over us. It is stifling and I just don't know what to do now!!

Culture-Centered Therapeutic Paradigm

The existential culture-centered paradigm was used in working with
Michelle. During the initial phase of therapy, I assisted Michelle in identifying and clarifying her assumptions about her interpersonal relationships, as related to her mother, father, and siblings, and about other
aspects of her life, such as her religion and her multitalented vocational
life. We examined her values and beliefs through her own cultural lens,
some African American and some her individualized views, and defined
how she questioned and perceived her existence within this context.
Throwing light on her internal life and what was implicit to her was ini-

tially difficult because Michelle repeatedly presented her problems as resulting from external causes. She dwelled extensively on how "others made her feel." Knowing that many ethnic minority groups have a collectivistic orientation and an external locus of control helped the counselor to accept Michelle's "other" orientation.

During the next phase, Michelle was encouraged to look at the source and authority of her present value and belief system. This self-exploration led to new insight and some restructuring of her values, beliefs, and attitudes. This process essentially provided her with the power to choose what type of life she wanted to live.

She was then encouraged to use the information gleaned from the counseling sessions and put it into action. For Michelle, this entailed a process of implementing her new internalized values in a concrete form. She was admonished that finding meaning is a lifelong process; that the search for meaning is as long as life; that how life is lived is a choice made during the journey.

Initial Assessment and Counseling Sessions Overview: From a Cultural Perspective

After Michelle talked about herself and discussed her reasons for coming to counseling, conversation ensued regarding a number of the symptoms she had been experiencing. She reported feelings of emptiness, loneliness, depression, reactions of agoraphobia, inadequacy, and an overall feeling of hopelessness.

After reviewing her life story, which included a discussion of her family and their African American beliefs and practices, a decision was made to employ some of the tenets of existentialism: death, loss, grief, and finding meaning. As noted, Michelle had experienced some significant losses in her life over the past 3 years: the death of her strong mother, the death of her father with whom she had unresolved issues, changes in her professional career due to relocation, and her current unemployment. In addition, she was in an existential crisis and was pleading for direction, hope, and peace. She was at a major crossroad in her life.

The primary goals of the interventions planned for Michelle were geared to assist her in living a more fulfilling and genuine existence. During the numerous counseling sessions, Michelle was assisted in clarifying her values and the directions she wanted to take in her life. It was important for her to look at her life from a cultural perspective: her religion, siblings, community, and parents. The sessions covered everything from her family eating styles, skin color (her mother was very light skinned, her father dark skinned) to absence of children in her life and her job concerns. These discussions were characterized by a mixture of cultural and universal concerns.

The treatment employed covered a broad spectrum of counseling approaches. The intent was to see what could better assist Michelle in meeting goals that were of her choice in how she viewed herself in relationships to her context. Primary to the accomplishment of this goal was establishing a therapeutic relationship between Michelle and the counselor. Michelle stated that working with an African American counselor made it much easier for her to talk about her concerns. She also repeatedly stated how comfortable it was to have an educated, African American female that she could converse with without the worry of censoring herself. Additionally, there were discussions concerning the pros and cons of having someone of the same gender and race as a counselor. These discussions set the groundwork for building trust and safety with the counselor, allowing her to proceed. Throughout the sessions, techniques such as imaginative re-creations were employed. At times, the counselor had to hold back from moving too quickly and not overidentifying with the client's issues. Potentially, this overidentification could have exerted a harmful impact on Michelle's growth and her ability to author her own existence, totally contrary to the basic premise of existentialism, which emphasizes personal choice and responsibility. This was a concern that the counselor constantly revisited throughout the sessions together. She sought consultation on this case through peer debriefing to make sure she was not allowing her biases to interfere with their work.

Michelle had previously been prescribed medication to deal with her agoraphobia and general anxiety. At the time of these sessions, she was no longer taking any medications. She felt as if she could handle these issues on her own without the medication, and after hearing her story, the counselor proceeded with their work cautiously, always monitoring the client's anxiety responses.

Over the next year, Michelle worked very diligently in the counseling process. Some of the existential issues explored dealt with her loneliness (no children or spouse), fear of death (following her parent's death), meaninglessness (searching for peace and contentment), and freedom (her desire and need to author her own existence within and outside her culture). She came to the conclusion that she did have the freedom to choose her life's direction. She discovered that it would not be an easy process, based on the nature of her relationships with her siblings and the internalization of her cultural dictates. However, clearly listing and following her values and beliefs, and not the values and beliefs of her parents, siblings, or others, was the choice she made for her life direction. Although some of these continued to be culturally oriented, she expressed her personal ownership and commitment to them.

At the end of the sessions, she displayed an inner peace that gave her hope to tackle life from a different and more powerful perspective. She had more energy and a more positive outlook on the future. Of course she knew that some rain was sure to fall at certain times in her life, but it was her view that was going make the difference in how she viewed the downpour.

Conclusion

As demonstrated through the case study, the counselor must be conscious of and skilled in understanding the client's culture. Counselors must move away from the one-size-fits-all approach to counseling. Counseling must not be a process of making the client fit the theory, but for the counselor to mold the theory to meet the cultural and contextual needs of the individual client. The theoretical approach and application must take into account the culture of the client, particularly as it manifests in values and beliefs. As effective multicultural counselors, we must continue to grow and develop our awareness and appreciation of differences. This is the only way we will meet the needs of those we are serving.

References

Assay, T. P., & Lambert, M. J. (1999). The empirical case for the common factors in therapy: Qualitative findings. In M. A. Hubble, B. Duncan, & S. D. Miller (Eds.), *The heart and soul of change: What works in therapy* (pp. 23–55). Washington, DC: American Psychological Association.

Baldwin, D. C., Jr. (1987). Some philosophical and psychological contributions to the use of self in therapy. In M. Baldwin & V. Satir (Eds.), *The use of self in therapy* (pp. 27–44). Palo Alto, CA: Science and Behavior Books.

Buber, M. (1970). *I and thou*. New York: Scribner.

Bugenthal, J. F. T. (1978). *Psychotherapy and process: The fundamentals of an existential humanistic approach*. Reading, MA: Addison-Wesley.

Bugenthal, J. F. T. (1987). *The art of the psychotherapist*. New York: Norton.

Corey, G. (2001). *Theory and practice of counseling and psychotherapy* (6th ed.). Pacific Grove, CA: Brooks-Cole/Wadsworth.

Epp, L. R. (1998). The courage to be an existential counselor: An interview of Clemmont E. Vontress. *Journal of Mental Health Counseling, 20*, 1-12.

Frank, M. L. (1995). Existential theory. In D. Capuzzi & D. R. Gross (Eds.), *Counseling and psychotherapy: Theories and interventions* (pp. 207-235). Upper Saddle River, NJ: Prentice Hall.

Frankl, V. E. (1963). *Man's search for meaning.* Boston: Beacon Press.

Frankl, V. E. (1978). *The unheard cry for meaning.* New York: Simon & Schuster.

Frick, W. B. (1987). The symbolic growth experience and creation of meaning. *International Forum for Logotherapy, 10,* 35-41.

Ibrahim, F. A., Roysircar-Sodowsky, G., & Ohnishi, H. (2001). Worldview: Recent developments and needed directions. In J. G. Ponterotto, M. C. Casas, L. A. Suzuki, & C. M. Alexander (Eds.), *The handbook of multicultural counseling* (2nd ed., pp. 425-456). Thousand Oaks, CA: Sage.

Ihle, G. M., Sodowsky, G. R., & Kwan, K. (1996). Worldviews of women: Comparisons between White American clients, White American counselors, and Chinese international students. *Journal of Counseling & Development, 74,* 306-312.

Maslow, A. (1968). *Toward a psychology of being* (2nd ed.). New York: Van Nostrand.

May, R. (1990). Will, decision, and responsibility. *Review of Existential Psychology and Psychiatry, 20,* 269-278.

May R., Angel, E., & Ellenberger, H. F. (Eds.). (1958). *Existence: A new dimension in psychiatry and psychology.* New York: Simon & Schuster.

Reker, G. T. (1992). *Manual of the Life Attitude Profile—Revised (LAP-R) and Sources of Meaning Profile (SOMP).* Peterborough, Ontario, Canada: Student Psychologists Press.

Reker, G. T. (1996). *Manual of the Sources of Meaning Profile—Revised (SOMP-R).* Peterborough, Ontario, Canada: Student Psychologists Press.

Seligman, L. (2001). Existential therapy. In *Systems, strategies, and skills of counseling and psychotherapy* (pp. 233-255). Upper Saddle River, NJ: Prentice Hall.

Sodowsky, G. R. (1996). The Multicultural Counseling Inventory: Validity and applications in multicultural training. In G. R. Sodowsky & J. Impara (Eds.), *Multicultural assessment in counseling and clinical psychology* (pp. 283-324). Lincoln, NE: Buros Institute of Mental Measurements.

Van Deurzen-Smith, E. (1990). *Existential therapy.* London: Society for Existential Analysis.

Vontress, C. E., Johnson, J. A., & Epp, L. R. (1999). *Cross-cultural counseling: A casebook.* Alexandria, VA: American Counseling Association.

Yalom, I. D. (1980). *Existential psychotherapy.* New York: Basic Books.

Chapter 14

Including Spirituality in Multicultural Counseling: Overcoming Counselor Resistance

Kathy M. Evans

Increasingly counselors are encouraged to address the whole client—mind, body, and spirit—and to do so within the context of the client's culture. Competent multicultural counselors are knowledgeable and accepting of the spiritual differences between themselves and their clients, but many counselors are working toward multicultural competence and may experience difficulties in this area. Some of these counselors may be enthusiastic about the prospect of including a spiritual dimension in their practice while others may be reluctant or may lack the knowledge and skill they need to do so. Nowhere is it more important than in multicultural counseling to be able to include spirituality in counseling, and nowhere is it more important to be open and accepting of diversity. This chapter provides strategies for including spirituality in multicultural counseling to those who are reluctant and unsure of how to proceed and to those who completely embrace this concept.

Although counselors are increasingly encouraged to focus on the whole client—mind, body, spirit, and culture—many counselors have neither the expertise nor the inclination to do so. Multicultural courses are required so that counselors possess knowledge of different religious and cultural groups and explore their biases and prejudices. It is quite a different phenomenon, however, to engage clients in an exploration of their spirituality. Unfortunately, counselor education programs rarely require courses on spirituality. As a result, counselors are unprepared and may be reluctant to discuss spiritual issues. Counselors may (a) feel uncomfortable addressing spiritual issues at all, (b) be unaware that there is a spiritual issue or that spirituality is a prominent factor in their client's life, (c) hold beliefs that are diametrically opposed to their clients, (d) feel disloyal to their own religious or spiritual convictions, or (e) have other equally compelling reasons to avoid the topic.

This chapter first defines spirituality and religion and reviews the rationale for including spirituality in multicultural counseling. The chapter next reviews spiritual identity development models to explain the resistance to including spirituality in multicultural counseling, uses one model of spiritual identity development to suggest strategies for overcoming resistance and gaining competence, and then presents good practices for bringing spirituality and religion into multicultural counseling.

Definitions of Spirituality and Religion

Spirituality and religion are often confused because the two are interrelated but not interchangeable. Of the two, spirituality is the most difficult to define. This chapter uses the definition of spirituality developed by the leaders of the Association for Spiritual, Ethical, and Religious Values in Counseling (ASERVIC): Spirituality is

> the animating force in life, represented by such images as breath, wind, vigor, and courage. Spirituality is the infusion and drawing out of spirit in one's life. It is experienced as an active and passive process. It is an innate capacity and tendency to move towards knowledge, love, meaning, hope, transcendence, connectedness, and compassion. It includes one's capacity for creativity, growth, and the development of a values system. Spirituality encompasses the religious, spiritual, and transpersonal. ("Summit Results," 1995, p. 30)

Religion is a form of spirituality but more easily defined: Religion is an institutionalized expression of faith, beliefs, values, emotions, rituals, and traditions.

Richards and Bergin (1997) stated that individuals may be spiritual but not religious, and that they can be religious without being spiritual. For example, I worked with a depressed 20-year-old White female client who very tentatively brought up meditation, altered states of consciousness, and holistic medicine in her search for spiritual meaning in her life. She felt guilty about her own spirituality when she spoke with her parents and other relatives who condemned her for abandoning church, God, and her Methodist upbringing. Here was a young woman who was very spiritual, yet she did not observe an organized religion.

It is equally likely that counselors will encounter clients who participate in religion but are not spiritual. As a college counselor, I often encountered students who faithfully attended church and participated in its rituals. However, many did so more from habit than because they had internalized spirituality.

Why Include Spirituality in Multicultural Counseling?

The Association for Multicultural Counseling and Development has specifically stated that the culturally competent counselor is one who "respects clients' religious and/or spiritual beliefs and values, including attributions and taboos" (Arredondo et al., 1996, p. 52) and who not only respects indigenous helping practices but also is not averse to seeking consultation with spiritual healers. This statement makes the case for the inclusion of spirituality in multicultural counseling. Moreover, ASERVIC's competencies for effective use of spirituality in counseling require that counselors have the capacity to "describe religious, spiritual, and transpersonal beliefs and practices from the perspective of diversity" and "demonstrate empathy for understanding a variety of religious, spiritual, and transpersonal communication" ("Summit Results," 1995, p. 30). It is reasonable to assume, therefore, that a counselor should be spiritually competent in practice to be multiculturally competent and vice versa.

Spirituality and religion stand out as defining characteristics among many ethnic minority groups in the United States. It is virtually impossible to effectively counsel individuals across cultures without an understanding of the various religious beliefs of ethnic minority groups. Moreover, Fukuyama and Sevig (1999) suggested that with the increasing religious diversity within families (interfaith, interracial, and intercultural marriages), there will be an even greater need to combine competence in spirituality and multicultural counseling. According to Fukuyama and Sevig, the values in spirituality and multiculturalism can be integrated to promote effectiveness in counseling diverse families. For example, a client's spiritual values of love, compassion, and connectedness are useful in helping him or her deal with oppression.

Spirituality Identity Development Models and Multicultural Counseling

Developing multicultural competence is difficult and painful (Fukuyama & Sevig, 1999). It involves unlearning those ideas, attitudes, and behaviors that promote misunderstanding and bias. The goal is to relearn ways to value differences between self and others. Fukuyama and Sevig specifically referred to the resistance counselors feel about making the transition from monoculturalism to multiculturalism. They liken this journey to that of those seeking to develop spiritually. Counselors need to have attained significant spiritual maturity to effectively assist clients in their own spiritual journeys. Understanding spiritual identity development is an important part of spiritual maturity.

Several models of racial and cultural identity development explain how a person can move from a negative perception of his or her race or culture to an acceptance not only of his or her race and culture but also of other groups (Atkinson, Morton, & Sue, 1989; Casas & Pytluk, 1995; Cross, 1971; Helms, 1984; Sue & Sue, 1990). The spiritual identity development models explain how a person grows from a very narrow perspective of spirituality to a broad universal perspective. Using developmental models assists in developing counselor competence in multicultural spiritual counseling and in planning treatment for clients' spiritual issues.

Developmental models were originally hierarchical and linear. Individuals were expected to complete tasks in one stage before moving on to the next. However, over the years, these models have evolved to allow for overlapping of stages and, in some cases, a completely nonlinear sequence. Nevertheless, the models are helpful in understanding the spiritual dilemmas of clients and counselors alike. A brief review of a small sample of spiritual identity development models follows. Readers are encouraged to explore these and others more thoroughly.

Peck's (1978) model of spiritual identity describes how a person develops through four different stages: nonspiritual and unprincipled; following a moral code; gaining personal meaning with no institutional affiliation; and gaining connectedness and unity with life. Unlike many stage models, the Peck model allows for overlapping stages simultaneously, and for frequent movement from one stage to another.

Kahn's (1988) mystical awakening model includes both Eastern and Western mysticism. People move from an awareness of a yearning for spirituality to confusion and bewilderment over spirituality, to understanding, to sympathy and compassion, and finally to communication and connection with all beings. Kahn's model may seem hierarchical and linear, but in fact it can be cyclical as well.

Myers et al. (1991) developed the OTAID—Optimal Theory Applied to Identity Development—model. OTAID integrates many worldviews, recognizes multiple oppressions, and emphasizes the inseparability of the spiritual and material worlds. It is neither linear nor hierarchical, and each phase is distinct. The three underlying tenets of OTAID are (1) identity broadens and deepens one's worldview; (2) the self is multidimensional; and (3) spirituality is part of being. The phases of OTAID resemble those of the racial and cultural identity models with the addition of the It-is-I phase. In this phase an individual defines self to include ancestors, the yet unborn, nature, and community. The worldview held in the It-is-I phase is that all things are interdependent and their reality is defined based on spiritual awareness rather than external circumstance.

Fowler, who was influenced by Piaget and Kohlberg (Gathman & Nessan, 1997), developed a theory of stages of faith or spiritual development based on a study of over 350 individuals (Lownsdale, 1997). His model has seven stages that are numbered 0 to 6. Although the stages are sequential and cannot be skipped, Fowler's model does allow for some beliefs and ideas to overlap from one stage to the next. Growth, however, is not inevitable. Some people get stuck at one stage and progress no further. Stage 0 is Primal faith, which is undifferentiated and refers to the prelanguage period of cognitive development. The child learns to have trust and faith in his or her caregivers. Stage 1 is Intuitive-Projective Faith, in which the individual learns about faith from the parents' formal religion and makes meaning out of the world through stories and rituals. In Stage 2, Mythical-Literal Faith, the person is able to separate reality from fantasy but takes a literal approach to his or her faith. The individual learns the beliefs and symbols that indicate he or she belongs but has not internalized the meaning of faith. In Stage 3, Synthetic-Conventional Faith, individuals understand more complexities of faith and conform to the expectations of parents and other significant people, but their beliefs and values have not truly been examined. Stage 4 is Individuative-Reflective Faith, which occurs when individuals begin to question and critically reflect on the stories, rituals, and symbols of their faith. In this stage individuals begin to internalize beliefs and values and develop their own worldview. Stage 5 is Conjunctive Faith (which eludes most of us), also known as Paradoxical-Consolidative Faith because individuals integrate polar opposites in their lives and begin to acknowledge multiple perspectives of faith. They start to own those aspects of self they have previously denied or devalued. Finally, Stage 6, Universality of Faith, occurs in only a rare few (e.g., Mother Teresa). In this stage, the individual is committed to universal values and is grounded in oneness and power of being or god (Fowler, 1991).

Using Fowler's Spirituality Development Model

Given this chapter's limited space, I have chosen Fowler's as the one model to illustrate how to develop competence and address resistance to including spirituality and religion in multicultural counseling. Note, however, that although the Fowler model is the one used, spiritual identity models in general can be helpful to counselors and clients alike. In all the models discussed, lower levels of spiritual development define individuals who are confused or unaware of their spirituality. Clients with such characteristics will find spiritual counseling helpful, but counselors with such characteristics will be unable to assist such clients. Counselors, therefore, are encouraged to explore their own spiritual development and work toward achieving spiritual maturity. Only at the upper levels of the spiritual development models do individuals accept their own and other's spiritual beliefs. Counselors who have achieved these upper levels can effectively use spiritual identity development models to help clients understand and resolve their spiritual issues.

Using Fowler's Model to Overcome Resistance

The following is a case example of how I have used Fowler's model to assist a supervisee in addressing the issues of spirituality and multiculturalism.

Fatima was a 25-year-old Arab American school counselor-in-training whose religious background is Islam. Because of several tragedies in the school, Fatima's onsite supervisor asked her to lead a ninth grade grief group as part of her internship. Although the school was racially and culturally diverse, Christianity was the primary religion of most students. Growing up Muslim in a Christian community had been a challenge for Fatima, but she seemed to have reconciled any issues she may have had with it. The grief group went well at first, but then Fatima became uncomfortable when a student brought up religion in one of the sessions. Fatima's worry was that she was in a school setting, and she did not know if they could even talk about religion. She was afraid that if she allowed discussion of spirituality, parents might accuse her of trying to convert their children to her religion. Most importantly, Fatima did not know how to approach a discussion of spirituality and religion with clients and was afraid of doing something wrong. Although she had legitimate concerns about addressing spirituality and religion in the school, most of Fatima's resistance stemmed from the fact that she was unprepared to address spiritual and religious issues with her clients. I took an opportunity during Fatima's supervision group to cover some information about including spirituality in counseling. Following the directions of Fukuyama and Sevig (1999) and Ingersoll (1997), I encouraged my students to spend some time exploring and understanding their own spiritual development, their biases and prejudices concerning other religious groups, and cultural issues surrounding clients' spirituality. In our individual sessions, Fatima stated that she was solidly in Stage 4 of Fowler's model (Individuative-Reflective Faith). She had satisfied her own questions about her faith and she truly embraced it. She did not believe that letting her Christian clients discuss their religion would be a threat to her, and she did not believe that she would be a threat to them. She realized, however, that she held some prejudices about Christian groups and that these biases probably have prevented her from moving on to Fowler's Stage 5—Conjunctive Faith. At that stage, the individual becomes open to alternative approaches to faith but is able to stay well grounded in his or her own faith. Fatima wanted to work on Stage 5 so as to work on her biases. To facilitate this growth, Fatima began by expanding her knowledge of Christianity, its denominations, and the ways the different cultural groups in her school observed their religion. She explored the worship methods practiced by various denominations of the Christian faith and the use of music, metaphor, narrative, and movement to develop a greater acceptance of Christianity.

Using Fowler's Model to Develop Competence

Here is an illustration of how I used Fowler's model to assist a woman with spiritual issues.

I was seeing Suzie, a 29-year-old African American woman, for career counseling when she came to a session extremely angry with one of her coworkers. She stated emphatically, "I just cannot work with this woman. She's a walking Bible—just walking around citing scriptures to every one all of the time." Suzie stated also that the woman was a complete hypocrite who says that she is a Christian but who is a complete racist. This outburst initiated our discussion of Suzie's race and spirituality. She, like me, was raised in the African Methodist Episcopal (AME) church where she learned a lot about her culture and about Christianity. As an adult, she considered that church to be dogmatic, sexist, and full of hypocrites. Suzie had many questions about Christianity, in general, and was playing with the idea of getting involved in spiritual groups that were not affiliated with any specific religion.

I introduced Suzie to Fowler's stages of spiritual development and asked her to identify where she thought she was on that continuum. I asked her to talk about how these developmental stages (previous and current) have affected her personally. She said that she was glad that she had experienced Stages 1 through 3 while she was growing up. These experiences gave her a solid background and enabled her to be a good person. However, when she got out on her own, she saw many problems not only with her denomination of Christianity but with Christianity as a whole. Suzie was currently working on Stage 4 (Individuative/ Reflective Faith). She had questions about her faith and had not resolved them. She also had some ideas that resembled Stage 5 in that she was open to looking at other religions. Because Suzie had not completed the tasks of Stage 4, she decided that she needed to explore her own faith further. When we talked about how her beliefs affected her relationships with others, Suzie admitted that her questions regarding her faith made her less tolerant of others who seemed to be so sure of their own.

As we continued to work together, Suzie began to read books on Christianity, Eastern religions, and feminist faith. She attended non-Christian and nondenominational spiritual services. In addition, I suggested that Suzie talk to women leaders in the AME Church to discuss her issues with church practices. Suzie soon found that meditation and prayer helped her and that she was beginning to get a better idea of her own spirituality. She admitted that it felt better when she went back to the AME Church, heard the congregation call and response, and the choir sing. She believed that these will always be a part of her spirituality. However, Suzie said that she needed something else to be spiritually fulfilled. Interestingly, Suzie found that understanding Fowler's stages helped her to understand where her coworker was coming from, and this also facilitated the development of a better collegial relationship

Good Practices

The developmental models may help with assessment and treatment planning but they are only part of the puzzle for effective multicultural spirituality counseling. To be multiculturally effective, counselors must address spiritual issues in the context of culture. Suggestions for good practices in multicultural spiritual counseling include the following.

Culturally and spiritually sensitive counselors

1. examine and overcome their own biases about spirituality and the varying ways that clients observe their beliefs. As with other multicultural issues, counselors who have biases risk harming their diverse clients.
2. explore the client's religious and spiritual background especially in context of his or her culture. For example, in the United States, Christianity is observed differently by African Americans, Latinos/as, and Native American Indians (Falicov, 1999; Hammerschlag, 1988; Jones, 1993; Wimberly, 1991). Counselors need to be knowledgeable about these cultural differences when they work with clients on spiritual issues.
3. have the client give consent to use spirituality.
4. assess the client's religious and spiritual background or religion in the counseling sessions (Richards & Bergin, 1997). Some clients may have spiritual issues but may not want to work on them with a counselor. Such clients may be referred to clergy or

other religious leaders to deal with these issues. I use Fowler's (1991) spiritual identity development model to assess clients and to develop treatment strategies.

5. help clients clarify spiritual values, but the counselor should be careful not to insert any of his or her own values (Richards & Bergin, 1997). This is a basic counseling skill; however, the counselor who sees clients that practice the same religious faith as the counselor bears reminding. It is not the counselor's job to be a spiritual advisor but to facilitate the client's exploration of his or her own beliefs.

6. recommend spiritual programs. It is important for counselors to keep a referral list of the culturally appropriate programs in their geographic area.

7. pray with clients, if they use prayer themselves. It is better to let clients lead the prayer in most cases for ethical and legal reasons. Few counselors have the educational background to be religious advisors or religious leaders. Therefore, counselors can support and encourage spiritual discussion by a willingness to participate in prayer without leading the prayer themselves.

8. consult with indigenous spiritual healers and other religious authorities when working with clients who raise spiritual or religious concerns (Falicov, 1999; Lee, 1996). Acceptance of spiritual healers demonstrates acceptance of a client's spiritual beliefs.

9. seek supervision when using spiritual or religious interventions (Fukuyama & Sevig, 1999). Supervision provides counselors with the support and guidance they need to be effective in spirituality counseling as well as multicultural counseling. This is true for the counselor who is new to spirituality counseling, and it is also important for counselors with experience. The different perspective that supervisors can provide may be just what is needed to help the client to progress.

Conclusion

This chapter has discussed resistance to using spirituality in counseling and suggested ways of overcoming that resistance. Also discussed were the reasons that counselors use for avoiding spiritual issues in counseling; a primary cause might be that counselors need to work on their own spiritual development. Several models of spiritual development were presented and some examples given of how counselors may use these models in their own development and with their clients.

It is difficult for counselors to be multiculturally competent if they resist addressing the client's spiritual issues. I hope that counselors will use these models to help them grow spiritually and, in turn, help their clients grow. Counselors who have explored their own spirituality are apt to be more comfortable with client's spiritual issues. If counselors know about spiritual development models, they can recognize when clients need to and want to work on these concerns. Finally, counselors who are generally multiculturally competent are able to be sensitive to cultural differences in spiritual practices and are accepting of beliefs that differ from their own. I believe that counselors who are spiritually mature and include spirituality in their work with clients epitomize the culturally competent counselor.

References

Arredondo, P., Toporek, R., Brown, S. P., Jones, J., Locke, D., Sanchez, J., & Stadler, H. (1996). Operationalization of the multicultural counseling competencies. *Journal of Multicultural Counseling and Development, 24*, 42-78.

Atkinson, D. R., Morton, G., & Sue, D. W. (Eds.). (1989). *Counseling American minorities: A cross-cultural perspective* (3rd ed.). Dubuque, IA: William C. Brown.

Casas, M., & Pytluk, S. (1995). Hispanic identity development: Implications for research and practice. In J. Ponterotto, M. Casas, L. Suzuki, & C. Alexander (Eds.), *Handbook of multicultural counseling* (pp. 155-180). Thousand Oaks, CA: Sage.

Cross, W. E. (1971). Negro-to-Black conversion experience. *Black World, 20*, 13-27.

Falicov, C. J. (1999). Religion and spiritual folk traditions in immigrant families: Therapeutic resources with Latinos. In F. Walsh (Ed.), *Spiritual resources in family therapy* (pp. 104-120). New York: Guildford Press.

Fowler, J. W. (1991). Stages in faith consciousness. *New Directions for Child Development, 52*, 27-45.

Fukuyama, M.A., & Sevig, T. D. (1999). *Integrating spirituality into multicultural counseling*. Thousand Oaks, CA: Sage.

Gathman, A. C., & Nessan, C. L. (1997). Fowler's stages of faith development in an honors science and religion seminar. *Zygon, 32*, 407-414.

Hammerschlag, C. (1988). *The dancing healers: A doctor's journey of healing with Native Americans*. New York: Harper Collins.

Helms, J. E. (1984). Toward a theoretical explanation of the effect of race on counseling: A Black and White model. *The Counseling Psychologist, 12*, 153-165.

Ingersoll, R. E. (1997). Teaching a course on counseling and spirituality. *Counseling and Values, 36*, 192-200.

Jones, S. L. (1993). *Wade in the water: The wisdom of the spirituals.* Maryknoll, NY: Orbis.

Kahn, H. I. (1988). *The awakening of the human spirit.* New Lebanon, NY: Omega.

Lee, E. (1996). Asian American families: An overview. In M. McGoldrick, J. Giordano, & J. Pearce (Eds.), *Ethnicity and family therapy* (2nd ed., pp. 227-248). New York: Guilford Press.

Lownsdale, S. (1997). Faith development across the life span: Fowler's integrative work. *Journal of Psychology and Theology, 25,* 49-63.

Myers, L. J., Speight, S. L., Highlen, P. S., Cox, C. I., Reynolds, A. L., Adams, E. M., & Hanley, C. P. (1991). Identity development and worldview: Toward an optimal conceptualization *Journal of Counseling & Development, 70,* 54-63.

Peck, M. S. (1978). *The road less traveled: The unending journey toward spiritual growth.* New York: Simon & Schuster.

Richards, P. S., & Bergin, A. E. (1997). *A spiritual strategy for counseling and psychotherapy.* Washington, DC: American Psychological Association.

Sue, D. W., & Sue, D. (1990). *Counseling the culturally different: Theory and practice* (2nd ed.). New York: Wiley.

Summit results in information of spirituality competencies. (1995). *Counseling Today, 38*(6), 30.

Wimberly, E. P. (1991). *African American pastoral care.* Nashville, TN: Abingdon.

Chapter 15

Applying Multicultural Competencies in the School Setting: Sexual Identity of an African American Adolescent

Canary C. Hogan

The goal of this chapter is to share a situation I encountered that is becoming more noticeable and requires more education and empathy on the part of the school community—counseling adolescents regarding sexual identities. Clearly, school settings are areas in which more education and training are needed to address the needs of diverse students.

Professional school counselors have an increasingly difficult job navigating the minefield of today's youth. Counselors frequently deal with puberty, peer pressure, drugs, gangs, teen pregnancy, sexuality issues, abuse, and violence. The issues adolescents must navigate today are larger and more dangerous than they have ever been. In addition, consider a counselor:student ratio of 1:585, which makes clear the true meaning of the slogan, "I am counseling as fast as I can."

School settings today are focused on being a safe place for students to learn and grow socially. However, there exists great physical, psychosocial, cognitive, cultural, and ethnic diversity among students (Voltz, 1999). In addition, adolescence is an inherently diverse stage of development in which differences abound in the areas of religion, gender, and sexuality. Providing safety to such a diverse student body can be a challenge for school personnel.

Professional school counselors have the greatest opportunity for making a positive difference in the acceptance of diversity in the school setting. They are advocates and role models for all students, and they understand the developmental stages of adolescence and recognize their challenges. Professional school counselors must be willing to explore developmental concerns and other issues that have a major impact on healthy student development. They should lead the way in promoting a safe school environment and acceptance of the diversity that exists within the walls of the school.

Caseloads for school counselors, as previously described, are frequently higher than they should be. With 585 students, counselors learn to address the issues that require top priority: a student bringing a gun to school and the aftermath associated with that incident; child physical and/or sexual abuse; and physical and verbal conflict/violence. There are many fires to put out and only 6.5 hours in a day. Nevertheless, professional school counselors must juggle their schedules to meet the more pressing needs of fragile/needy students, and also provide preventive developmental education to the student body at large. They must also serve as advocates for students while working with teachers, administrators, and parents. How school counselors have to face psychological concerns of students and provide support services is illustrated through the following case study.

Case Study

Johnny, during his seventh grade year, was a quiet African American student who was very rarely noticed unless you looked really hard at his mannerisms or sharp, pointed fingernails. During the middle school years, developmental growth is different and uneven for everyone, so much so that the differences from my eyes look normal. However, when Johnny got to eighth grade, it was obvious that he had developed in ways very different from other students. Physically, he was larger than he was in the seventh grade; his hair had grown longer; and his fingernails were still long, well manicured, and beautifully painted like flags with red, white, and blue. He began to walk with a twist that caused others to notice him. A few months into the school year, Johnny started wearing a wig, and if I hadn't known him, I would have thought he was a girl. Actually, in retrospect, when he mingled in the crowd, anyone could have very easily mistaken him for a girl. Was this what he wanted? Or was this my imagination?

It wasn't long before some teachers began to make comments about Johnny wanting to be a girl. A male student told me that he heard from other students that Johnny really liked him. A teacher came to me and said, "Don't put that faggot in my RA class!" Comments like these ruffled my ears and made me take note of Johnny. He was different. Even though I have had other students with feminine tendencies, I've never had one come out as Johnny did. Johnny started wearing bras and female blouses to school. He wore several different wigs—Jeri curl, long straight shoulder length hair, and/or pony tails. Soon he was wearing women's Capri pants. The principal met with Johnny and told him that he could not continue to dress like a female because it was disruptive to the learning environment.

He gave him a copy of the *Student Code of Behavior Handbook*. In addition, he explained to me what he had done and referred Johnny for counseling. I was not quite sure how I was going to handle this situation, but I knew I had to be prepared to meet with Johnny. I began with a review of the literature.

Review of the Literature

The review revealed that the exact number of transsexuals in any given population will probably never be accurately known. The best current estimate is 1 per 50,000 (Bullough & Bullough, 1993). Transsexuals are defined as individuals who are born into one gender but identify psychologically and emotionally as the other gender. There is disagreement on what causes this behavior. On one hand, some scientists believe that a chemical imbalance that affects sexual difference occurs when the developing fetus is in the womb. On the other hand, medical research currently being done appears to support the theory that transsexualism is related to genetic influence or mutation (McIntosh, 1991). There is agreement, however, that gender identity is developed by age 3. Gender identity refers to a person's actual or perceived sex, and includes a person's identity, appearance, or behavior, which may be different from the person's sex at birth (Goodrum, 2001).

Many people use the terms *transsexual* and *transgender* interchangeably. However, transgender is a broad term used to encompass all manifestations of crossing gender barriers. Transgender refers to people whose anatomies and/or appearances do not conform to those considered appropriate for culturally predominant gender roles. When transgender is used in the case of a sexual minority, it refers to one of the following five categories: transsexual (a person whose gender identity does not match his or her anatomical sex); intersexed (people who were born exhibiting some combination of both male and female genitalia); cross dressers (those who identify as, and are completely comfortable with, their physical gender at birth, but will occasionally dress and take on the mannerisms of the opposite gender); drag performers (performers who dress and act like the opposite sex for the entertainment of an audience); and gender blenders (people who may or may not identify as one or the other in a binary gender system, and many times will assume a mixture of male and female dress and characteristics, combining elements of both (Nangeroni, 2001).

Although some people believe transgendered individuals have particular maladjustments, none are listed in the diagnostic criteria in the fourth edition of the *Diagnostic and Statistical Manual of Mental*

Disorders (DSM-IV; American Psychiatric Association [APA], 1994). There is, however, information on gender identity disorders in the *DSM-IV.* It is important to note that the American Psychiatric Association Board of Trustees in 1973 deleted homosexuality from its official nomenclature of mental disorders in the second edition (*DSM-II*). For a mental condition to be considered a psychiatric disorder, it must constitute dysfunction within an individual, cause present distress, disability, or a significant increased risk of suffering death, pain, disability, or an important loss of freedom. A transgendered person may experience conflict with a homophobic society; however, such conflict is not a symptom of dysfunction in the individual (APA, 1998). Sex is in the brain and not in the body; thus transsexuals seek to change the erroneous sex labels that were assigned to them at birth. The only way to change those labels is to change the basis upon which those sexual labels were applied, namely the outward expression of sex. This means that to change a sexual label, individuals must change their gender identity.

Transsexuals suffer many hurdles in changing their gender identity: loss of family and friends, social oppression, inner turmoil, culturally indoctrinated shame, open ridicule, and punishment from individuals in authority positions who seek to discourage such behaviors. Also, it is important to note that controversy exists over the treatment for transsexuals. Medical doctors recommend gender reassignment surgery.

However, many national associations have joined together opposing such surgery and/or reparative or conversion therapy intended to change the sexual homosexual orientation. These organizations include the American Psychiatric Association, American Academy of Pediatrics, American Medical Association, American Psychological Association, American Counseling Association, and the National Association of Social Workers (APA, 1998). These associations recommend sensitive affirmative therapy by a therapist who is positive and supportive about accepting an individual's homosexual or bisexual orientation.

Interventions

In the case of Johnny, the first counseling session was an information-gathering session to determine his knowledge and awareness of self and to develop goals for future sessions. Many probing questions were asked. At this stage, interventions were based on four specific dimensions: clarifying identity development and self-acceptance, assessing the influence of self on society and developing coping skills, dealing with problems and uncontrollable factors, making good decisions, and connecting to a support group.

Clarifying Identity Development and Self-Acceptance

Information was gathered on Johnny's perceptions of who he is and how he feels about himself; earliest recollection of his gender identity and how he recognized it; and attitudes, values, and beliefs about his sexuality. The purpose of these leading questions was to determine if Johnny had a strong sense of identity or if his identify was fragile, uncertain, or confused. Identity is defined as a complex integration of cognitive, emotional, and social factors that make up a person's sense of self. These include gender (personal sense of being male or female), sex roles (social and cultural expectations of masculinity and femininity), personality (individual traits and disposition), and sexual orientation (Ryan & Futterman, 2001a). It is not uncommon for adolescents to experience confusion about their identity.

All of Johnny's responses were quite positive. He had a strong sense of who he is, and he was very much aware of when he first recognized that he was different. When he was about 3 years old, he remembered playing house, being the mommy and dressing up like mommies do. He stated that he has always felt like a girl, and he has never really tried to hide that. Johnny accepts his gender identity as female and has over a period of time integrated that identity with his personality and self-concept. He felt very comfortable and positive about his gender identity. For all practical purposes, Johnny accepted himself as female.

Following the session, I had to make an assessment of what I had just learned about Johnny and my own feelings and personal biases. I had flashbacks about my brother, who was in some ways similar to Johnny. My brother was very talented—a graduate of the Julliard School of Music in New York. He performed in many Broadway musicals and returned home to work at Vanderbilt and Fisk universities. He was shot in the back by one of his acquaintances. This reflection forced me to decide if I could effectively work with Johnny. On one hand, I knew that my principal and some teachers were not going to be happy with the outcome of our first counseling session. They wanted to see Johnny change his behaviors and be the boy he was born to be. On the other hand, my initial thoughts were that Johnny was comfortable with the way he was and that it was not our responsibility to force him to change his behaviors and his gender identity.

During that week I thought about Johnny a lot. Johnny was an individual who appeared to be cognitively rational with sound thinking.

I wasn't sure how I might help him, but I was willing to follow his lead to determine the agenda for future sessions. During the next session, Johnny and I agreed that our goals would be to look at interventions that would help him to maintain satisfaction with himself and to be safe.

Assessing the Influence of Self on Society and Developing Coping Skills

Johnny was able to recognize the reactions to himself from people in the school and community. Overall, society generally expects heterosexual behavior. This intervention focused on being able to deal with rejection by peers and family members, loss of friends, living with the stigma of being different, social isolation, his difficulties in academic involvement and participation in school and the community, and the wearing of female clothes and garments in school and in the neighborhood (Cooley, 1998).

At school, Johnny seemed to have many female friends. He chatted with them just as if he were one of them. Male students rejected him. He talked about his mother who was neutral about his coming out and his dad who at one time was physically abusive to him. His father disowned him because he felt Johnny was an embarrassment to him and the rest of the family. Johnny also had a brother who felt as his father did. His brother was unable to manage his feelings about Johnny dressing and prancing like a girl around the neighborhood. He rejected Johnny in order to save face with his friends.

We talked about the coping skills he had used previously and developed a list of new skills that he felt comfortable in using. Johnny admitted that his coming out was very self-affirming and that it made him feel really good about himself. However, he was also aware that he needed to develop skills to deal with a negative environment.

Dealing With Problems and Uncontrollable Factors

Remembering what had happened to my brother, I was concerned about Johnny's well-being. This intervention focused on problems/uncontrollable factors he might encounter, such as discrimination, violence, name-calling, and possibly being forced to leave home (Ryan & Futterman, 2001b). The accumulation of uncontrollable factors, particularly for an adolescent, can become unbearable.

I wanted Johnny to be well aware of the risks involved with coming out (Cooley, 1998). When a male discloses and demonstrates to the school and community that he wants to be or is a female, that's taking a big risk. We used role-playing to determine how Johnny might respond in a variety of situations to keep safe. Some of the scenarios included individuals who were angry at him because of the way he dressed or carried himself; being called names such as *freak, faggot, homo, transsexual*; strangers trying to physically take advantage of him; being tricked to get him in a situation where he is helpless; societal and institutional rules that might be discriminating in nature; and protecting himself from possible harm that might start with words but end with actions.

Adolescents whose behavior or style does not fit rigid definitions of appropriate maleness or femaleness often are labeled as *gay* or *lesbian*, whether they are or not. Those who do come out, as well as those who are labeled lesbian or gay, are often taunted, beaten, or driven from their homes, schools, religious groups, and communities.

Providing a safe learning environment in which Johnny felt comfortable role-playing the different scenarios and exploring his options was rewarding. It allowed discussion on society's value system and ways of thinking, and it challenged us to examine various perspectives and assumptions. Both verbal and nonverbal communication skills played a significant role because they could either escalate or deescalate a confrontation.

Making Good Decisions

Decision making is one of those preventive lessons that all students learn through classroom guidance sessions. However, with Johnny I wanted to know that he remembered the steps in the decision-making process. I wanted him to demonstrate that he could make conscious, quick decisions at the appropriate time for his own well-being and safety. I may have erred in the direction of being overly cautious, but I believed that Johnny's well-being and safety could be compromised if he was not able to think things through and possibly predict outcomes based on his own gut feelings.

It was important to remember that the senior school administrator had already very politely warned Johnny about his dress at school, and that some teachers had very blatantly expressed their displeasure with him. Johnny needed to be able to weigh his options and make the best decisions based on uncontrollable societal factors so that he was not contained in an area that limited his future options. In other words, Johnny might have to decide to do some things differently if he did not want to be harassed under the guise of school and district rules and regulations. Helping him to recognize his battles was extremely important.

Connecting to a Support Group

It is always comforting to know that there are others who feel as you do. Helping Johnny connect with the right community support group provided opportunities for him to socialize with others in a positive manner, access resources that specifically addressed his concerns, receive validation from sensitive and nonjudgmental counseling group work, and get the affirmations he needed for continued wholesome growth. Access to adult and peer support, accurate information, and resources helped enhance coping skills, self-esteem, and positive help-seeking behaviors (Muller & Hartman, 1998; Ryan & Futterman, 1998). Likewise, sharing information with Johnny's mother on parent support groups provided an option for her toward improving her relationship with Johnny and curtailing the dissonance between Johnny and his father and brother.

Outcomes

Johnny was successful in passing the eighth grade. He had poor attendance until the interventions. He stopped wearing girls' clothes to school. However, he did keep his long colorful fingernails, and he continued to wear wigs. These decisions he made on his own. Honestly, I was glad because work still needs to be done to accept the diversity that exists in our school. At home and on the weekends, Johnny wore female clothing. He met other students that he hung out with through his support group. He was excited about going to high school because the culture was much more accepting than our middle school culture. He would be allowed to wear what he wanted without repercussions.

As I think back about Johnny and his needs, I wonder if I did the right thing or if I could have done more. Surely, I have worked with other students who were somewhat confused about their identity. However, none was as certain as Johnny about his self-concept and gender identity. Johnny knew who he was and could express his feelings and wants with clarity.

I often think about my brother whose death had a great impact on my life. If society had been more knowledgeable and receptive to diversity during his time, he might still be here today. We cannot turn back the clock, but we can apply the multicultural competencies we learn in training in our daily lives to make this a better world for all people regardless of their differences.

Recommendations

There is much work to be done in schools, agencies, universities, businesses, and our global society before we can say that America is a nation that supports diversity. As such, the following recommendations are offered, especially for professional school counselors, and others who have an opportunity to apply them.

1. Work toward having system-wide polices written to support the acceptance of diversity in all school settings so as to foster a learning environment that is inclusive and equitable for all students.
2. Consider changes in school policies, curriculum, support services, and staff development. These are primary areas that must be addressed if schools are to become more sensitive to the needs of diverse student populations (Marinoble, 1998).
3. Train student leaders and facilitators to assist in and support a safe learning environment, as well as provide updated materials and resources for teachers. These can be powerful ways to make an impact.
4. Offer a school-wide program on issues pertaining to adolescent sexuality, homosexuality, lesbians, bisexuals. This is a statement in itself about the expectations of the school and the acceptance of its student/teacher population (Bauman & Sachs-Kapp, 1998).
5. Assist parents in better understanding the special needs of their adolescents by providing parenting classes on adolescent sexuality, organizing support groups, and connecting parents to available resources in the community.
6. Conduct a self-study of your own attitudes, beliefs, and knowledge about indigenous peoples, African Americans, Asian Americans, Hispanics, Latinos/Latinas, gays, lesbians, bisexuals, and transgendered people and other individuals who have mental/emotional, physical, and/or learning disabilities in your school (Haley-Banez, Brown, & Molina, 1999).
7. Participate in professional development and professional reading focused on multicultural/diversity education to enhance or improve your level of diversity acceptance.
8. Develop and promote a bill of rights with students that is inclusive of all youth in your school, i.e., ethnically, culturally, and linguistically diverse students; gay, lesbian, bisexual, and special needs students; and others not included in this list. Discuss and review the bill of rights through classroom guidance sessions.

9. Be an advocate for students by responding to negative, discriminatory, or oppressive comments made about students or teachers who are different. Seek to eliminate biases, prejudices, oppression, and discriminatory practices.
10. Develop broad-based support for diversity by establishing a school-community diversity committee with representatives from various ethnic groups inclusive of students, parents, teachers, religious leaders, mental health professionals, community agencies, and city council and board members.
11. Research federal and state laws related to discrimination and sexual harassment that might be applied to the school setting.
12. Actively engage in research involving diversity-related issues.

Conclusion

Professional school counselors are in a unique position in the schools as student advocates who can use a variety of approaches to promote diversity. Although administrators have the right of approval of school policies, as long as they support the system's policies, professional school counselors can exert their influence in an advisory capacity to develop school-wide policies that support and acknowledge diversity. Our children and youth must have a safe place to deal with the developmental, personal/social, career, academic, and diversity issues that confront them. Professional school counselors must be in the forefront of promoting these efforts.

References

American Psychiatric Association. (1994). *Diagnostic and statistical manual of mental disorders* (4th ed.). Washington, DC: Author.
American Psychiatric Association. (1998). *Position statement: Psychiatric treatment and sexual orientation.* Washington, DC: Author.
Bauman, S., & Sachs-Kapp, P. (1998). A school takes a stand: Promotion of sexual orientation workshops by counselors. *Professional School Counseling, 1*(3), 42–45.
Bullough, V. L., & Bullough, B. (1993). *Cross dressing, sex, and gender.* Philadelphia: University of Pennsylvania Press.
Cooley, J. J. (1998). Gay and lesbian adolescents: Presenting problems and the counselor's role. *Professional School Counseling, 1*(3), 30–34.
Goodrum, A. J. (2001). *Gender identity 101: A transgender primer.* Retrieved November 10, 2001, from http://www.users.qwest.net/

Haley-Banez, L., Brown, S., & Molina, B. (1999). Association for Specialists in Group Work principles for diversity-competent group workers. *Journal for Specialists in Group Work, 24*(1), 7-14.

Marinoble, R. M. (1998). Homosexuality: A blind spot in the school mirror. *Professional School Counseling, 1*(3), 4-7.

McIntosh, J. E. (1991). *The truth about transsexuals. So you wanna be a real girl?* Retrieved from http://www.diddigy.com/realgirl/truth.ht

Muller, L. E., & Hartman, J. (1998). Group counseling for sexual minority youth. *Professional School Counseling, 1*(3), 38-41.

Nangeroni, N. (2001). Gender identity. Retrieved November 11, 2001, from http//:www.gendertalk.com

Ryan, C., & Futterman, D. (1998). *Lesbian and gay youth: Care and counseling.* New York: Columbia University Press.

Ryan, C., & Futterman, D. (2001a). Experiences, vulnerabilities, and risks of lesbian and gay students. *The Prevention Researcher, 8*(1), 6-8.

Ryan, C., & Futterman, D. (2001b). Lesbian and gay adolescents: Identity development. *The Prevention Researcher, 8*(1), 1, 3-5.

Voltz, D. L. (1999). Empowering diverse learners at the middle level. *Middle School Journal, 30*(1), 29-36.

Chapter 16

Culturally Diverse Clients in Employment Counseling: What Do Multiculturally Competent Counselors Need to Know to Be Effective?

S. Craig Rooney and William M. Liu

This chapter discusses working with clients facing discrimination, managing racial and/or sexual identity, and dealing with dual-employment couple issues. These concerns are discussed within the framework of specific employability skills and interventions, as well as onsite services such as employee assistance programs.

R esearch and theory in multicultural competencies have revolved primarily around improving the client and counselor therapy relationship, and have recently discussed the need to extend services outside the direct therapy relationship (Toporek & Liu, 2001). A clear example of this dual competency is in the area of employment counseling. Counselors who help clients transition into new job settings and living environments need also be aware of potential problems that may affect the transition, work, and home life of their clients. To illustrate the necessity of understanding therapy and extratherapy issues, the work experiences and career lives of racial and ethnic minorities, as well as of lesbian women, gay men, and bisexual individuals (LGB), need to be highlighted. This chapter shows the dramatic increases of scholarship in these areas, and focuses as well on the lack of specific employment counseling information available when working with diverse clients. These deficits are addressed by suggesting similar and unique issues that may surface for employment counselors working with racial and ethnic minority, and LGB clientele. Specifically, this chapter discusses working with clients facing discrimination, managing racial and/or sexual identity, and dealing with dual-employment couple issues. These concerns are discussed within the framework of specific employability skills and interventions, as well as of onsite services such as employee assistance programs.

With the advent of the multicultural counseling competencies (Sue, Arredondo, & McDavis, 1992) and the metatheory for multicultural counseling (Sue, Ivey, & Pedersen, 1996), culture and context have been interwoven into many theoretical and applied counseling techniques. However, multicultural counseling competencies have not been fully explored in employment counseling. In employment counseling, importance is given to providing clients specific occupational interventions (Amundson, Westwood, & Prefontaine, 1995; Kellett, 1994) that, for many, need to be culturally sensitive interventions. Employment counselors deal with a wide range of issues such as providing adequate information for making good employment decisions, and facilitating a client's ability to be successful during employment transitions. Such transitions may include movement from educational settings to the world of work, or from an unemployed status to a working status. In essence, "employment counselors help job seekers make wise career decisions. . . . Personal traits, physical capacities and temperament are also considered. . . . They also offer clients job seeking skill development, resume writing, training information, and job development assistance" (Michigan Employment Counseling Association, 2001).

The purpose of this chapter is to assist employment counselors in conceptualizing work with diverse populations and cultural issues such as race, ethnicity, and sexual orientation. The chapter first looks at identity theories and then presents the case study of Mariana. The case is discussed in terms of several pertinent and important areas of skill development in employment counseling: resume writing, interviewing skills, and the individual's cultural presentation to potential employers. Successful intervention strategies are included in the discussion.

Identity Considerations

It is necessary to use theory to inform counseling practice. The theories presented here may be used to conceptualize the multiple issues, attitudes, and worldviews of clients in order to better integrate the information counselors receive into an overall counseling plan. The theories relevant for the case presented may seem to be different identity constructs (i.e., racial identity [RI] and lesbian, gay, bisexual [LGB] identity), but they are similar in important ways and are pertinent to career development (Byars & McCubbin, 2001; Croteau, Anderson, Distefano, & Kampa-Kokesch, 2000; Risdon, Cook, & Williams, 2000). Specifically, both sets of theories illuminate the process by which individuals in minority groups identify and confront dominant oppressive attitudes they have internalized as self-hatred (Sue & Sue, 1999) and move from dominant group identification (e.g., racism, homophobia, and hetero-sexism) toward self-acceptance and social action.

Although racial identity and sexual identity are conveniently catego-rized here as similar types of identity development (e.g., Cass, 1979), the different groups represented in racial and sexual identity theories have specific identity theories relevant for each community. For instance, among racial minorities, such as Asian, African, Latino, and American Indian, identity development paradigms exist that reflect unique charac-teristics and context of each community (e.g., Sue & Sue, 1999). Simi-larly, LGB identity represents at least three distinct communities. In lesbian identity development, women may experience feelings of differ-ence, connection with being lesbian, acceptance, making lesbian friends, and a lesbian relationship (Reynolds & Hanjorgiris, 2000). Among gay men, there may be the process of internal sexual identity development and group identity development occurring simultaneously (Fassinger & Miller, 1996). Among the three communities, it appears that bisexual individuals have received the least research attention (Chung & Katayama, 1996) and are relegated to invisibility in heterosexual, as well as lesbian and gay, worlds (Reynolds & Hanjorgiris, 2000). Counselors should consider how these different identities intersect in employment counseling.

Case Study

Because attention to issues of LGB people of color has been so scant in the professional literature (Fukuyama & Ferguson, 2000), we are present-ing the case of a LGB person of color. With the identity theories just described in mind and an eye toward application, consider the issues of resume writing, interviewing skills, and cultural presentation to poten-tial employers and how best to approach counseling Mariana.

Mariana is a 28-year-old third-generation Mexican American woman who identi-fies as bisexual. She has been in a 5-year relationship with a lesbian Latina. She has recently become unemployed as a result of downsizing in her company. Mariana had worked as a buyer for a major retail firm in the Midwest. She had been hired directly out of college when her employer visited her campus during a job fair. Mariana adapted easily into her position with the company, but faced frequent subtle insinuations that she was an affirmative action hire. Such communications from peers, and being one of a handful of people of color, made her cautious about expressing her cultural identity. She worked hard to mask her differences with White and heterosexual colleagues. During her 7-year tenure with the company, she often felt uncomfortable socializing at informal office parties and social events, and consequently was viewed somewhat as an outsider.

Mariana has sought out the services of an employment counselor. She presented with fears about finding a new job. Because she had held only one job, she was anxious about her resume and interviewing skills. Since her layoff, Mariana had found great relief and comfort by more openly identifying with the local Mexican American community. Having found support among several close Mexican American friends, a few family members, and also some lesbian friends, she and her partner have decided to have a commitment ceremony. They have also decided that it is important to be more open about their relationship and sexual minority statuses in all spheres of their lives.

Resume Writing

Although Mariana is comfortable with her identities as a Latina and bisexual, and is actively engaged in community activities, it is unclear if prospective employers will understand or embrace these aspects of her identities. Those unfamiliar with her cultures may not understand or appreciate her involvement with various groups and community organizations. This is not a small consideration. Employers typically may want to hire well-rounded individuals, and "other interests" on a resume are a way of displaying such broad interests and abilities. Employers may also feel uneasy about hiring an individual closely aligned with political, visible/vocal minority organizations.

An employment counselor working with Mariana should consider assessing her levels of RI and LGB identity development, and be prepared to talk with her about her own understanding of these identities. For example, given that Mariana had negative experiences being labeled as the affirmative action hire in her previous employment setting, it may be important to screen employment opportunities with regard to how they approach ethnic diversity within their organizational cultures. Also, because Mariana and her partner have decided they want to be out as sexual minorities in all spheres of their lives, she may wish to screen employers on the basis of their organization's stance on sexual minorities and partner benefits. If this is the case, an employment counselor can help Mariana tailor a resume that conveys her commitment to these communities.

Interviewing Skills

How can Mariana ask about her safety as a Latina bisexual without coming out as such (e.g., Risdon et al., 2000)? With a clear understanding of the meaning that Mariana attaches to being Latina, as well as of how she understands herself as bisexual, an employment counselor can tailor interviewing skills interventions to her specific situation. Obviously, many of the basic or generic skills of interviewing need to be applied to this case. More specific strategies, however, could now be discussed. For instance, a counselor could explore how explicitly she wants to raise concerns about her cultural identities during the interview process.

Employment counselors working with cultural minorities should be comfortable with helping clients learn how to ask direct, tactful questions about diversity in the workplace. Sometimes this may be difficult because direct confrontation may be counter to some cultural norms. But because Mariana is highly acculturated, she may choose to have questions for the interviewer(s) such as, "Does your organization have resources for ethnic minority employees? How does the organization feel about the need to have such resources?" Mariana may also wish to ask, "Has your organization ever had openly lesbian or bisexual staff? What was that experience like for the organization?" This type of direct questioning allows Mariana to receive direct responses from potential employers, as well as subtler, nonverbal responses to her questions (i.e., employer anxiety about answering certain questions). Although many cultural minority individuals may have well-developed skills for monitoring subtle reactions of others, employment counselors can assist them by supporting their recognition and interpretation of these messages.

Employment counselors might also consider forming a network for cultural minority applicants wherein they have access to employees from similar backgrounds who currently work in different occupational settings. This buddy system has the potential to allow clients like Mariana access to other Latina or lesbian/bisexual employees to gain information, strategies, and support.

Cultural Presentation

Unfortunately, within employment situations, discrimination and prejudice exist. For women, especially racial minority women, looking the part typically means reflecting the codes of normative femininity within the culture of the company or work site. In certain situations, normative femininity can be rather inflexible and traditionalist (e.g., women have long hair, wear skirts, wear makeup, and are deferential to men). Additionally, there are norms for race and ethnicity in employment situations. Sometimes the norm is to downplay cultural presentation or relegate it to sanctioned events (e.g., company picnic), to dissuade individuals from being too provocative in the workplace.

To address these issues, the counselor may work with Mariana on the Internet to examine prospective employers. An employment counselor working with her could help her process information about whether companies present a homogenous or a diverse view of people working in the organization. Through this process, Mariana could continue her own exploration about how comfortable she is presenting herself both as a Latina and as a bisexual. Such expression goes beyond identity development insomuch that persons at each stage of identity development may have different ranges of cultural expression. For example, some lesbian women may present in a manner that is stereotypical to employers unfamiliar with the lesbian community, whereas others may present in ways that do not elicit suspicions about their sexual orientation. Some individuals have a degree of control over this range of expression and presentation while others do not. Employment counselors sensitive to this reality could work with Mariana relative to her own degree of comfort in her cultural presentations and discuss potential hazards in work environments that want employees to present themselves within a narrow range of majority culture expressions.

Conclusion

All three of these areas—resume writing, interviewing skills, and cultural presentation—deal with overlapping issues for the employment counselor. Specifically, counselors should understand the importance of doing multicultural assessments of their clientele. This includes being familiar with identity development models and being able to assess clients' levels of minority identity development. They should be comfortable enough with their own identity development to be able to discuss these types of issues with their culturally diverse clientele. This inevitably will involve counseling situations in which the identities and cultural backgrounds differ between the counselor and client. Employment counselors should be prepared to address these differences with their clients, and seek to understand how their own backgrounds may have provided them with different experiences in the world of work than those faced by their clients. Further, in cases of minority individuals not indigenous to U.S. culture, employment counselors should be able to assess a client's level of acculturation and help evaluate the strengths and barriers to potential employment situations.

Additionally, it seems important that employment counselors discuss the potential ramifications of different choices of cultural presentation in the world of work. It is our view, however, that just providing this service is reactionary to the existing employment climates. Employment counselors should also explore avenues of change by creating new services (i.e., the network of persons of color and sexual minorities available to their clients), and exploring other avenues of changing existing workplaces.

References

Amundson, N., Westwood, M., & Prefontaine, R. (1995). Cultural bridging and employment counselling with clients with different cultural backgrounds. *Canadian Journal of Counselling, 29*, 206-213.

Byars, A. M., & McCubbin, L. D. (2001). Trends in career development research with racial/ethnic minorities: Prospects and challenges. In J. G. Ponterotto, J. M. Casas, L. A. Suzuki, & C. M. Alexander (Eds.), *Handbook of multicultural counseling* (2nd ed., pp. 633-654). Thousand Oaks, CA: Sage.

Cass, V. C. (1979). Homosexual identity formation: A theoretical model. *Journal of Homosexuality, 4*, 219-235.

Chung, Y. B., & Katayama, M. (1996). Assessment of sexual orientation in lesbian/gay/bisexual studies. *Journal of Homosexuality, 30*(4), 49-62.

Croteau, J. M., Anderson, M. Z., Distefano, T. M., & Kampa-Kokesch, S. (2000). Lesbian, gay, and bisexual vocational psychology: Reviewing foundations and planning construction. In R. M. Perez, K. A. DeBord, & K. J. Bieschke (Eds.), *Handbook of counseling and psychotherapy with lesbian, gay, and bisexual clients* (pp. 383-408). Washington, DC: American Psychological Association.

Fassinger, R. B., & Miller, B. A. (1996). Validation of an inclusive model of homosexual identity formation on a sample of gay men. *Journal of Homosexuality, 32*, 53-78.

Fukuyama, M. A., & Ferguson, A. D. (2000). Lesbian, gay, and bisexual people of color: Understanding cultural complexity and managing multiple oppressions. In R. M. Perez, K. A. DeBord, & K. J. Bieschke (Eds.), *Handbook of counseling and psychotherapy with lesbian, gay, and bisexual clients* (pp. 81-105). Washington, DC: American Psychological Association.

Kellett, R. (1994). The evaluation of career and employment counseling: A new direction. *Canadian Journal of Counselling, 28*, 346-352.

Michigan Employment Counseling Association. (2001). *What do we do?* Retrieved November 8, 2002 from http://www.geocities.com/Athens/Acropolis/6491/meca.html

Reynolds, A. L., & Hanjorgiris, W. F. (2000). Coming out: Lesbian, gay, and bisexual identity development. In R. M. Perez, K. A. DeBord, & K. J. Bieschke (Eds.),

Handbook of counseling and psychotherapy with lesbian, gay, and bisexual clients (pp. 35-55). Washington, DC: American Psychological Association.

Risdon, C., Cook, D., & Williams, D. (2000). Gay and lesbian physicians in training: A qualitative study. *Canadian Medical Association Journal, 162*(3), 331-334.

Sue, D. W., Arredondo, P., & McDavis, R. J. (1992). Multicultural counseling competencies and standards: A call to the profession. *Journal of Counseling & Development, 70,* 477-486.

Sue, D. W., Ivey, A. E., & Pedersen, P. B. (1996). *A theory of multicultural counseling and therapy.* Pacific Grove, CA: Brooks/Cole.

Sue, D. W., & Sue, D. (1999). Counseling the culturally different: Theory and practice (3rd ed.). New York: Wiley.

Toporek, R. L., & Liu, W. M. (2001). Advocacy in counseling: Addressing issues of race, class, and gender oppression. In D. B. Pope-Davis & H. L. K. Coleman (Eds.), *The intersection of race, class, and gender in counseling psychology* (pp. 385-416). Thousand Oaks, CA: Sage.

Chapter 17

Multiculturalism in Cyberspace: Hypertext Hyperbole or a Bridge Between People?

Michael D. Hawkins

This chapter focuses on the potential strengths and limitations of computer-mediated communication (CMC) in the delivery of counseling services. Various arguments surrounding cybercounseling are explored against the backdrop of our awareness that only through a clear understanding of an Internet-based client's cultural perspective can we hope to effectively engage in his or her virtual reality world. The Internet's growth as a major component in human communications and the growing use of CMC across cultures is discussed, as is online mental health seeking, clients' main concerns surrounding the activity, and how this applies to the practice of counseling. The ability to recreate one's self online and its implications for counselors and counselor educators are addressed. Also examined is the idea that online communities possess their own rich social constructs and the potential impacts this can have in online and face-to-face counseling settings and in online simulations for counselor training.

The use of computer-mediated communications in counseling is no longer a new practice. Over the last decade, the use of e-mail as a counseling media has spurred considerable research, writing, and teaching. Today, the American Counseling Association and the American Psychological Association recognize that counseling online takes place and have taken steps to provide ethical and practice-related guidelines for their members. The ACA's *Ethical Standards for Internet Online Counseling* were approved by its governing council in October 1999. The standards establish the types of electronic sites suitable for online counseling services, the counselor's responsibilities with regard to informing the client of the limitations of confidentiality over the Internet, and the appropriate steps to begin, maintain, and limit online counseling relationships. For psychologists and social workers an Online-Clinics Web site allows clients access to online practitioners. The goal of this site is to begin therapy online and provide for a transition to face-to-face sessions as the client and therapist make progress (Rabasca, 2000). Online resources for both practitioners' and clients' protections are now available to ensure, as much as possible, that privacies are protected, professional qualifications and identities are checked, and payment procedures for services rendered are understood (Hackerman & Greer, 2000).

Online counseling is a growing trend even as researchers across disciplines around the world are working to learn what impacts human communications in cyberspace will have on individuals and their social interactions (Kling, Crawford, Rosenbaum, Sawyer, & Weisband, 2000). Within this ongoing research there is information for the counselor or the counselor educator, much of which has direct applications for those devoted to cross-cultural counseling in both face-to-face (f2f) and text-to-text (t2t) settings.

There may be a correlation between increasing computer-mediated communication and an increasing multicultural environment. CMC is not merely related to the extended use of machines, but rather cyberspace communication can be an integral part of an individual's ongoing work to define self, worldview, and ultimately what it means to be human. In this context CMC becomes central to a discussion of cultural awareness and diversity.

The Shrinking Digital Divide

The term *digital divide* was coined to describe the gap between those people who had access to computers and the Internet and those who did not. Younger, better educated, more affluent, and technologically savvy people had access while older, less educated, and less affluent people with less technological sophistication did not. In 1995 this digital divide so concerned the U.S. Department of Commerce that it initiated a longitudinal study of the situation in the United States. The study was called *Falling Through the Net,* and the fourth report in this series was subtitled *Toward Digital Inclusion* (U.S. Department of Commerce, 2000). For this report data were collected through August 2000, and the report concluded that while a digital divide remained, both computer ownership and Internet access were increasing at a rapid rate. According to the findings, the gender gap on the Internet had nearly vanished. In 1998, 34.2% of men compared to 31.4% of women were using the

Internet in comparison to 44.6% of men versus 44.2% of women in 2000. Likewise the age gap was quickly narrowing. The rate of growth of Internet users age 50 was 53% from 1998 to 2000, more than that of any other age group and compared to a growth of 35% for people nationwide.

More recently researchers at the Pew Internet & American Life Project determined that during the second half of the year 2000, 43% of African Americans and 47% of Hispanics were online and their rates of use were increasing faster than either those of Euro-Americans or Asian Americans. In addition, 38% of households with under $30,000 annual income and 37% of those with a high school education or less were logging on (Rainie & Packel, 2000).

The availability of computers and the ease of access to the Internet, as well as lower prices, will continue to drive the market toward the time when almost everyone in the United States will be connected to the Internet. For counselors serving cross-cultural populations, there are implications. The number of people potentially seeking their services online will grow rapidly. Moreover, available data show that they are actively looking for those services.

Seeking Help on the Internet

Need for Health Information

According to Fox and Rainie (2000), 52 million American adults, 55% of all with Internet access, regularly search for health information on the Web. Of these health information seekers, 26% look for mental health information; 70% say the information helps influence their decision about how to treat the condition they research; and 28% say it helps them decide whether to seek help at all. The vast majority of mental health information seekers agree that what they like most about being able to look for information online are convenience, anonymity, and wealth of information (Fox & Rainie, 2000). This is especially true for women, minorities, and parents of children under 18. Those who stand to benefit also include individuals with physical or psychological barriers that make it difficult for them to travel, and others who might seek mental health services if it were not for a perceived stigma attached to the process. In addition, asking clients what online mental health sites they have visited and what information they found useful or influential can provide insight into how the client perceives the course of treatment or the expected outcome.

Consumer Concerns

American adults seeking mental health information on the Internet are particularly concerned about anonymity and accuracy of the information.

Anonymity.

The importance of anonymity online resonates strongly with what we know about the reluctance in many cultures different from the White U.S. culture to discuss personal matters with people outside the immediate or extended family. An online relationship might allow persons who have difficulties establishing f2f counseling relationships to pursue help.

The appeal of searching for information online may also speak to stereotypic labeling that women and racial and ethnic minority groups face when seeking mental health or other medical services. However, counselors should not assume that being online means abandoning gender, cultural, or ethnic beliefs and perceptions. To the contrary, there is evidence that in some parts of cyberspace groups have set up stringent defenses of their cultural and ethnic identities. In "Ain't Gotta Do Nothin But Be Brown and Die," Baird (1998) examined Native Americans' activities in online chat rooms. She found that they are extremely offended when non-Native Americans enter the room and pretend to be American Indians, and that there are designated room police who take immediate actions to identify the pretenders.

Accuracy of information.

Fox and Rainie (2000) cited two major concerns that emerged from their research. First, Internet users are wary of the accuracy of online information. Because of this, online users often check sources, such as the name of the organization or company sponsoring the site and providing data. Second, people are concerned about the privacy of their health information online, with African Americans women (75%) expressing the highest concerns, followed by Hispanics (69%). With this in mind, multicultural counselors should know of and refer f2f and t2t clients to appropriate online resources. Counselors who maintain their own online presence, whether to advertise services or provide information, should expect that their sites will be suspect until proven valid. Once proven accurate and useful, users are likely to bookmark the site and return to it. Any links a counselor provides to other sites should be carefully chosen because the content they present is likely to reflect directly on the counselor's site.

Conversely, counselors should make their clients aware of sites that offer mental health information that provide questionable information. There are, for instance, support group chat rooms that are not supervised by a mental health professional. If a client has experience with one of these sites, it might be a good idea for the counselor to visit it and decide what benefits it provides.

Given the enormous concerns about privacy, counselors who conduct business online should be certain to provide secure information transmission. A reputable third party should publicly verify the level of security. There are several online resources available that provide this service. One is available through www.metanoia.com (Hackerman & Greer, 2000) that provides consumers security and privacy ratings for sites of registered online mental health care providers. It also includes descriptions of the services offered, outlines their costs and payment procedures, and lets potential clients know whether or not the credentials of the provider have been checked and verified. The listings include counselors, psychologists, psychiatrists, and social workers with information about their expertise. Counselors with competencies to serve particular ethnic groups could include this information in their listings.

Counseling Challenges

Counselors who conduct business on the Internet are faced with new challenges. One is that their clients may be reinventing themselves, and another is that clients could experience online trauma.

Reinventing self in cyberspace.
Clients can redefine themselves, their cultural alliances, and the world in which they live through cyberspace interaction. When online, people are stripped of physical appearances. No longer identified by the sound of their voice, the way they walk, and the historical and environmental lenses that others see them through, people can be who they want to be. Self now includes the virtual reality persona (Ludlow, 1996), both as a tool for communicating and for projecting oneself to be as one wishes to be seen. This is a powerful statement about a person's ability to wrench free from the real-world's physical and social constraints that define the self and to become someone completely different in cyberspace, for better or for worse.

A person's cultural place online becomes a matter of individual preference and is subject to change. For some, particularly those who are socially or functionally disadvantaged (Miller, 1995), this can provide a sense of freedom. For others, it allows the creation of false, predatory identities.

For counselors online, a virtual reality persona creates profound questions about client identity and could confound attempts to use ethnic-specific counseling approaches or even to be multiculturally sensitive. Some might argue, however, that client anonymity or counselor uncertainty about a client's real-world identity might lead to a purer counseling approach in which counselors must focus on identifying and treating the problem, keeping in check any stereotypes. To certain clients anonymity and the opportunity to portray themselves as they wish may be more important aspects of the online therapeutic relationship, at least initially, than full disclosure. The counselor who understands and can work with this power of cyberspace to transform self will be better able to provide services online.

Clients who have created a strong online identity may have problems separating that construct from the real world. Ludlow (1996) said that if an individual has more and more satisfying social contacts in cyberspace, there is no reason that the virtual world can't have "greater claim" to that person's identity. Additionally, hyperpersonal communications (Walther, 1996) that are more powerful than those in the real world can create a loop that validates the false, but preferred, identity created online.

Online trauma.

Clients can suffer significant emotional trauma while participating in an online community. This is the "dark side" (Chenault, 1998) of the online world, in which threats of violence, sexual harassment, racism, and rape exist. In "A Rape in Cyberspace" (Dibbel, 1994), an event is described in which a computer-generated avatar, a cyberdoll representing a person in real-world space, broke into an online community and forced other characters to do things they did not want to. "They say he raped them that night.... They say that by manipulating the doll he forced them to have sex with him, and with each other, and to do horrible, brutal things to their own bodies" (p. 237). The violence described was a true reflection of the participants' feelings about what took place "right in the living room—right there amid the well-stocked bookcases and the sofas and the fireplace—of a house I've come to think of as my second home" (p. 237), a home that existed in cyberspace. One woman said that the trauma she experienced and the tears she shed were "real-life fact" and that they proved that the "emotional content" in cyberspace "was no mere playacting" (p. 242). Counselors who know that within a cybercommunity there is a genuine sense of social connectedness and reality that is separate from and potentially as powerful as a person's place in the real world will undoubtedly be better prepared to help those who experience either the pleasures or the perils of venturing into cyberspace.

Training Implications

The plasticity of identity and social or cultural milieu online can be transformed into a powerful tool for enhancing multicultural awareness in counselor education. McFadden (2000) proposed that simulations using avatars can offer students and counselors a safe environment in which to examine their social views and the consequences of those views. A simulated online community can allow students from around the world to work in an "identity workshop" (as cited in Silver, 2000). In the appropriate simulation, cross-cultural training could take on an entirely new dimension as we participate in another's worldview. When we place ourselves into the computer-generated constructs of other people, their characteristics become "an object to think with" (Seymour Papert as cited in Bruckman, 1993, p. 4). Our perspectives on and understandings of others can be enriched and enhanced by the experience.

Bruckman (1993) pointed out that in online virtual reality environments, gender is a matter of choice, and that in some of them it is possible to be gender neutral. This possibility of gender choice raises two important issues for counselor training. One is "the ways in which gender structures human interactions" and the other consists of "the ways in which [the online realities] help people to understand these phenomena by experiencing them" (p. 1).

Text-to-Text Versus Face-to-Face Communications

Because the biggest use of computer-mediated communication is e-mail (Rainie & Packel, 2000), the question before many is whether or not one can effectively counsel in a t2t environment. Can text even begin to provide clues and cues that will allow appropriate and effective interaction between counselor and client? Chenault (1998) argued that there is a slow but steady learning curve to interpreting in a t2t environment. She cited findings that persons who are experienced in CMC become highly adept at interpreting the feelings and underlying meanings of people in t2t communications. Emotion is also present in e-mail interactions, according to Chenault (1998). Some of these cues are as simple as which party talks more and whether the amount of communications between parties is equal.

Most experienced e-mail users will agree with this. We tend to look at text responses for signs that will help us interpret underlying meanings. If the font is different from that which the sender normally uses, we question it. Its color, size, whether it is regular, boldface, or italic, all play into our attempts to discern meaning. In the context of multiculturalism, e-mail text demands that we continually sharpen our knowledge of social, cultural, ethnic, and age-related communications styles.

Miller (1995) noted that in order to understand how we use t2t to present ourselves, we must first decide how it differs from f2f and then look to the resources available within t2t that allow us to make up the deficit. Most Internet users intuitively use time as a communications cue in e-mail. They are aware of the time lag between responses to important messages. They may wonder if the respondent is deep in thought about it, unhappy with it, unavailable to respond, or does not really care. Walther and Tidwell (1995) hypothesized that a slow t2t response is more intimate than a fast response to a social message, and that a social message sent at night conveys more intimacy than one sent during the day. Conversely, when responding to task messages, a prompt reply conveys more intimacy, and a task message sent during the day conveys more affection than one sent at night.

Disclosure is one form of communication that can generate "liking" in the t2t environment. Chenault (1998) pointed out that revealing leads to liking and liking leads to revealing. This feedback loop is already familiar to counselors in the f2f setting. Mental health practitioners who carefully practice disclosure online, using what we understand about the various cultural and ethnic attitudes toward sharing personal information, may find that it plays an even more prominent role in establishing trust in a t2t therapeutic relationship. Taking into account that it is presently not possible to be absolutely certain whether a cyberclient is being honest about his or her identity, and adding to that the likelihood that some online clients will purposely hide their real identities for reasons already discussed, the possibility arises that appropriate counselor self-disclosure can significantly strengthen an online relationship.

Conclusion

Within the online world there is an urgently growing sense of community (Silver, 2000), a new pluralism in which people are finding that they share values, attitudes, and beliefs with others they have never seen. This community is complex and multidimensional, and poses great promise for those who seek a deeper understanding of cross-cultural issues. But the world online requires enormous attention and thought; it changes on a daily basis. Members of the counseling profession must learn to navigate the Internet world wisely, to understand its effects on human behavior, to factor that understanding into their clinical methods, and to reach out to those on the Internet who find themselves in need of a counselor's services. The better informed we are of the opportunities and threats computer-mediated communication poses to people of all ethnic and cultural backgrounds, and the more we experience the Internet culture, the better we will be able to use this powerful new place to help bridge the gaps between peoples in both the virtual and the real worlds.

For those who want to know more about the practice of or research into cybercounseling, or who would like to explore mental health resources available on the Internet, a few of the hundreds of sites currently available are as follows:

- The International Society for Mental Health Online offers valuable information, including case studies and best practices from mental health professionals who are doing the work today, at ismho.org
- The American Counseling Association provides the organization's *Ethical Standards for Online Counseling* (1999) and a link to CyberCounseling, an online resource for information about cybercounseling and online counselor education, at www.counseling.org
- Behavior Online offers the *Journal of Online Behavior* at www.behavior.net
- Links to counseling and psychology resources online across a wide array of topics are available at http:/libnet.wright.edu/ libnet/subj/cou/cpmeta/mhc.html

References

American Counseling Association. (1999). *Ethical standards for Internet online counseling*. Retrieved October 29, 2002, from http://www.counseling.org/ resources/internet.htm

Baird, E. (1998, July). Ain't gotta do nothin but be brown and die. *CMC Magazine*. Retrieved May 29, 2002, from http://www.december.com/cmc/mag/ 1998/jul/baird.html

Bruckman, A. S. (1993). *Gender swapping on the Internet*. Paper presented at a meeting of the Internet Society, San Francisco, CA.

Chenault, B. G. (1998, May). Developing personal and emotional relationships via computer-mediated communication. *CMC Magazine*. Retrieved May 29, 2002, from http://www.december.com/cmc/mag/1998/may/chenault.html

Dibbel, J. (1994). A rape in cyberspace. In M. Dery (Ed.), *Flame wars* (pp. 237–261). Durham, NC: Duke University Press.

Fox, S., & Rainie, L. (2000). The online health care revolution: How the Web helps Americans take better care of themselves. Retrieved May 29, 2002, from http://www.pewinternet.org/reports/toc.asp?Report=26

Hackerman, A. E., & Greer, B. G. (2000). Counseling psychology and the Internet: A further inquiry. *Journal of Technology in Counseling, 1*(2). Retrieved May 29, 2002, from http://jtc.colstate.edu/vol1_2/cyberpsych.htm

Kling, R., Crawford, H., Rosenbaum, H., Sawyer, S., & Weisband, S. (2000). Learning from social informatics: Information and communication technologies in human contexts. Retrieved May 29, 2002, from http://www.slis.indiana.edu/SI/Arts/SI_report_Aug_14.doc

Ludlow, P. (1996). Self and community online. Retrieved May 29, 2002, from http://semlab2.sbs.sunysb.edu/Users/pludlow/intro5.html

McFadden, J. (2000). Computer-mediated technology and transcultural counselor education. *Journal of Technology in Counseling, 1*(2). Retrieved May 29, 2002, from http://jtc.colstate.edu/vol1_2/transcult.html

Miller, H. (1995). *The presentation of self in electronic life: Goffman on the Internet.* Retrieved May 29, 2002, from http://ess.ntu.ac.uk/miller/cyberpsych/goffman.htm

Rabasca, L. (2000, July/August). Therapy that starts online but aims to continue in the psychologists office [Electronic version]. *Monitor on Psychology, 31*(7). Retrieved May 29, 2002 from http://www.apa.org/monitor/julaug00/online.html

Rainie, L., & Packel, D. (2000). *More online, doing more.* Retrieved May 29, 2002, from http://www.pewinternet.org/reports/toc.asp?Report=30

Silver, D. (2000). Looking backwards, looking forward: Cyberculture studies 1990–2000. In D. Gantlett (Ed.), *Web studies: Rewiring media studies for the digital age.* Oxford, UK: Oxford University Press.

U.S. Department of Commerce. (2000). *Falling through the net: Toward digital inclusion.* Retrieved May 29, 2002, from http://www.ntia.doc.gov/ntiahome/fttn00/falling.htm

Walther, J. B. (1996). Computer-mediated communication: Impersonal, interpersonal, and hyperpersonal interaction. *Communication Research, 23,* 3–43.

Walther, J. B, & Tidwell, L. C. (1995). Nonverbal cues in computer-mediated communication, and the effects of chronemics on relational communication. *Journal of Organizational Computing, 5*(4), 355.

Part Four

Multicultural Organizational Development

Chapter 18

Against the Odds: Successfully Implementing Multicultural Counseling Competencies in a Counseling Center on a Predominantly White Campus

Mary A. Fukuyama and Edward A. Delgado-Romero

This chapter discusses the content and process of infusing multicultural counseling competencies in a university counseling center operating in a predominantly White campus. Systemic change at the agency level and at the larger system level is discussed. Concrete examples of organizational change, program development, and a critical incident involving racism are described. Recommendations are offered in the context that infusing multicultural competencies is an ever-evolving process.

University counseling centers are strategically situated to implement multicultural counseling competencies. Due to the multiple missions of providing clinical service, supervision and training, consultation, teaching and research, counseling center staff members have many opportunities to put theory into practice and to test the efficacy of current models of MCC. This chapter is written from the perspectives of two counseling psychologists employed on large predominantly White university campuses. Cumulatively, we have over 30 years of experience spanning the past three decades, and we offer both historic and recent perceptions of the infusion of multiculturalism in counseling and student affairs, specifically in the context of our work at the University of Florida, which is a *predominantly White institution*. This term is more than a static descriptor of racial and ethnic demographic categories. It refers to the historical and current dominance by those of Euro-American (Caucasian) background. This dominance can be seen in demographics (predominantly White alumni, students, faculty, and staff) and in the curriculum as well as in the power structure of a university. For example, at the University of Florida this cultural dominance is evident in the official mission of the university, which is stated as "Linking the experiences of Western Europe with the traditions and histories of all cultures." Consequently, it can be quite challenging to implement MCC in a predominantly White institution.

Multicultural counseling competencies were developed by the Association of Multicultural Counseling and Development in a series of landmark articles (Sue, Arredondo, & McDavis, 1992; Arredondo et al., 1996) that have produced both competencies as well as behavioral, outcome-based explanatory statements. Arredondo and Arciniega (2001) stated the following as the philosophy underlying MCC:

> All counseling is multicultural in nature; sociopolitical and historical forces influence the culture of counseling beliefs, values and practices and the world-view of clients and counselors; and ethnicity, culture, race, language, and other dimensions of diversity need to be factored into counselor preparation and practice. (p. 266)

In keeping with the application orientation of this book and the behavioral and outcome-based statements of current MCC writings (e.g., Arredondo et al., 1996), this chapter discusses, in four sections, infusing MCC in the University of Florida (UF) Counseling Center, innovative MCC programming, MCC work within the larger system (institution), and current trends and recommendations.

Infusing Multicultural Counseling Competencies in the UF Counseling Center

The University of Florida was founded in the mid-19th century as an institution of higher education for White males. It opened its enrollment to women in 1947 and was racially integrated in 1958. It is a publicly funded, comprehensive, land-grant, research institution. Of the approximate enrollment of 44,000 students, the ratio of women to men is now 51:49; ethnic minority enrollment is at 22% (African American 6.5%, Hispanic 9.4%, and Asian American or Pacific Islander 6.0%); and there are about 2,000 international students (University of Florida, 2001b). In terms of faculty and staff, the percentages of racial and ethnic minorities are much lower (African American 4%, Hispanic 3%).

The UF Counseling Center has been in operation for almost 70 years and has maintained a strong commitment to service and training from a humanistic and developmental perspective. The primary mission of the

UF Counseling Center has been to provide psychological services (counseling, psychoeducational programming, and consultation services) to the campus community. Concerns for social justice and social change have been predominant themes over the years, especially since the social revolutions around issues of gender roles (women's liberation), and racism (civil rights) of the 1960s. Initial efforts by the UF Counseling Center to be responsive to the needs of ethnic minority students and women were initiated in the late 1970s through walk-in clinics oriented to make counseling more easily accessible to these minority populations (Bingham, Fukuyama, Suchman, & Parker, 1984). Various clinical services were subsequently extended to culturally diverse students through therapy and support groups (e.g., Gay, Lesbian, Bisexual Support Group; Women of Color Group; Men's Group), outreach workshops (e.g., Biracial Identity), and other psychoeducational interventions (e.g., programs, brochures, Web site).

As a general rule, however, individuals rather that systemic infrastructure carried out social activism until awareness about multicultural counseling competencies reached new levels through the efforts by the leadership of AMCD and of American Psychological Association (APA) Divisions 17 (Counseling Psychology), 44 (Society for the Psychological Study of Lesbian, Gay, and Bisexual Issues), and 45 (Society for the Psychological Study of Ethnic Minority Issues) through their MCC programming at APA conventions and articles in their peer-reviewed journals. The Counseling Center was aided immensely by guidelines for working with ethnic, linguistic, and culturally diverse populations established by the APA Office of Ethnic Minority Affairs (1991) and, more recently, guidelines for working with gay, lesbian, and bisexual clients developed by Division 44 of APA (APA, 2001).

An important first step in implementing multicultural counseling competencies is developing a mission statement. The UF Counseling Center's multicultural mission statement, which follows in its entirety, hopefully provides a model for extending this work to other university counseling centers.

The promotion of human welfare is the primary principle guiding the professional activity of the counseling psychologist and the counseling psychological service unit. Consistent with this principle, we believe that each person has worth and should be treated with dignity and respect. We value acceptance and appreciation for all differences among people, including those of race, gender, sexual orientation, ethnicity, functional ability, socioeconomic status, age, and religious affiliation. We believe that valuing cultural diversity facilitates human growth and development and enhances the quality of life in our community and on our campus. Therefore, we deplore acts of bigotry, discrimination, and social injustice. Because of these beliefs, we are committed to enhancing our awareness and understanding of cultural diversity on our campus at all levels. Our mission is to actively incorporate this philosophy into our professional activities. These activities include clinical services, training, outreach and consultation, written materials, staff selection and development, policies and procedures, administrative support services, paraprofessional services, research, teaching and scholarly activity. (University of Florida, 2001a, p. 2)

In order to support MCC efforts, a Multicultural Services Committee was formed in the early 1990s to provide a resource base and support system for carrying out these initiatives. Although there is some debate in the literature between focusing multicultural counseling competencies in one organizational structure (e.g., one committee, one academic course) versus infusing it into the whole system (Copeland, 1983), we have found that both are necessary.

The UF Counseling Center has a long tradition of training counselors and psychologists as a practicum site for both counselor education and counseling psychology programs, and as an APA-accredited predoctoral internship site. Multicultural counseling competencies were first introduced into training through a multicultural seminar with predoctoral interns, and multicultural issues increasingly have been infused into all training and trainee evaluations. In implementing MCC training, we were guided by the operationalization of multicultural competencies (Arredondo et al., 1996), available research (e.g., Pope-Davis, Reynolds, Dings, & Ottavi, 1994), and feedback from accreditation site visitors. A byproduct of increased MCC awareness was an increased emphasis on the selection of multiculturally competent trainees.

Increased competence on the part of trainees challenged the staff to evaluate themselves and update their own MCC skills. Training and working with culturally diverse and MCC-savvy graduate students, many of whom had just emerged from state-of-the-art multicultural training programs, was a welcome challenge but also has been what Pope-Davis, Liu, Toporek, and Brittan-Powell (2001) termed a *difficult multicultural transformation*.

Another example of the interface of multicultural counseling competencies in providing training and service can be found in our intern consultation projects. Predoctoral interns negotiate consultation services with various units on campus depending upon their professional interests. In recent years, the majority of the consultation projects have reflected multicultural priorities, for example, diversity training at the

Jewish Student Center, programs directed toward international students and their spouses, and interventions with the McNair Student Scholars Program and minority student support services. Through these consultation projects, interns learn the organizational development skills (Sue, 1995) necessary to implement multicultural counseling competencies in settings outside the center.

Ongoing staff development is a priority at the center, and having a tradition of active staff development helped the staff consider the need for systemic (versus individual) changes and training in multicultural counseling competencies. Staff noted that it was easier to focus on the MCC of trainees than to focus on the MCC of the training staff. As a remedy, programs on race and gender in supervision, for example, were presented as part of ongoing staff development. Summer work groups also were formed to dedicate time to study and implement MCC in UF Counseling Center operations, with such tasks as developing a mission statement and philosophy of training, assessing the UF Counseling Center's operations with a checklist (see Ponterotto, Alexander, & Grieger, 1995), and reviewing all aspects of clinical service from a MCC perspective. However, it became evident that in order to continue MCC development in our agency, the center needed both to hire staff who were trained in MCC and to open our efforts to obtaining feedback from a skilled MCC consultant.

The staff set out to diversify its composition. Through the efforts of the UF Counseling Center director and the vice president of student affairs, three ethnic minority counselors were hired, one on an existing line and two on new lines targeted to minorities. These counselors brought personal, clinical, and research experience in working with African American and Latino/a populations and increased the overall level of multicultural counseling competencies. In addition, the staff decided to provide MCC training for support staff and made racial, ethnic, and linguistic diversity a priority for hiring support staff as well.

The process of infusing multicultural counseling competencies with the staff moved to a deeper level by bringing in an outside MCC expert consultant to help facilitate staff communications around MCC issues. This was an important step in continuing to develop trust among the staff on this topic. Annual all-day staff retreats have enabled the staff to discuss further their concerns and to see how to continue to infuse MCC into the operations of the UF Counseling Center. Based on one of the consultant's recommendations, we make time each semester to focus on MCC issues during our normally scheduled staff meetings.

We have found that it is important to proactively address MCC issues rather than wait for conflicts or issues to arise and that scheduling this time into the hectic pace of the semester is the only way to make sure it happens.

The physical change of the UF Counseling Center to reflect a multicultural environment in which diverse students would feel welcome was a relatively easy step to take. The decorations were changed to reflect diverse cultures, the selection of magazines in the waiting room was expanded, and major cultural holidays and important dates were recognized (e.g., a Kwanzaa display). A multicultural library that included both books and videotapes was also created for use by staff and trainees.

In terms of academic and research activities, the staff from the UF Counseling Center has affiliate faculty status with the counseling psychology and/or the counselor education academic programs, and several staff members teach in these programs. UF Counseling Center staff have infused multicultural counseling competencies into existing courses and developed specific multicultural counseling courses. In addition, the staff have contributed scholarly works examining MCC practices (Fukuyama, 1994; Funderburk & Fukuyama, 2001; Murphy, Wright, & Bellamy, 1995), as well as contributed to innovative MCC efforts, such as the special issue of the *Journal of Counseling & Development* that featured personal narratives about racism (Delgado-Romero, 1999; Fukuyama, 1999).

This section so far has focused on the content of our MCC infusion. However, the process of incorporating multicultural counseling competencies has taken years and continues to be an ongoing discussion. It should be noted that the importance of administrative support cannot be minimized, and in our case, the support of the UF Counseling Center director as well as the vice-president of student affairs has been critical. Through active support from the administration, it has been possible to hire new staff, bring in consultants, transform our physical environment, and have the resources to attend national MCC conferences. There is no substitute for active MCC leadership from the top.

A number of other process issues have occurred while infusing multicultural counseling competencies. For example, territorial issues arose when selecting staff for seminars, courses, or committee assignments. The Multicultural Services Committee and coordinator time allotments were raised to be equal to other administrative committees, such as training and clinical services. Staff cooperation was enlisted in order to complete the self-study process. Feelings of exclusiveness or inclusiveness were addressed. We made special efforts to avoid tokenism or slotting people of color as the experts, or presuming Whites were not committed to multiculturalism. We continue to discuss how to integrate core competencies for counseling with emerging multicultural competencies.

Innovative MCC Programs

Within the UF Counseling Center there have been two high profile innovative MCC programs. The first is a Brown Bag Diversity Lunch Series for which UF Counseling Center staff presented creative programs dealing with diversity. The series drew capacity participation partly due to an innovative sponsorship by a local eatery. The audience was made up of undergraduates and university staff, and at present there have been 40 programs over 4 years with over 800 participants. Topics varied and included conversations about gender-bending and sex roles, SES (class), spirituality, racism, interracial dating, and transgender identity.

The second was a response to the ending of affirmative action programs in higher education admission in the State of Florida. Research indicated that the end of affirmative action would disproportionately affect the number of African Americans among students on campus. Therefore, the vice president for student affairs sponsored a grant initiative to departments within Student Affairs that wanted to proactively address this issue. In response, the UF Counseling Center director and members of the staff created ASPIRE (African American Student Program for Improvement and Retention in Education). This program funded three postdoctoral counselors to dedicate 8 hours a week each on projects related to African American student retention and enrichment. ASPIRE counselors consulted with and provided programming for the Institute of Black Culture, university programs (such as Achievement In Mainstreaming [AIM], the McNair Student Scholars Program, the Dean of Students Office, the Association of Black Faculty, the Counsel of Negro Women, and college-specific mentoring programs) as well as for community support systems such as churches. Without the grant, funding such an effort would not have been possible.

In addition to these two in-house programmatic efforts, the UF Counseling Center provides a range of outreach workshops to the campus community, including workshops in residence halls and classroom presentations. We consistently provide staff for programs for an annual event known as People Awareness Week—a week dedicated to celebrating campus cultural diversity. A recent activity included offering a cultural art/collage project in which students were invited to create images of their cultural identities from magazine pictures and art supplies and place them on a bulletin board strategically located near the Student Union.

Multicultural Competency Work
Within the Larger System

Working within the larger institutional system has presented its own challenges. Many of our student affairs colleagues are aware of the need for multicultural competence, and we have had division-wide programming on the need for multicultural competence in Student Affairs. However, we have also experienced some conflict. For example, one administrator believed that specific training in multicultural competence was not necessary, that the right person could learn on the job. This hiring philosophy ran counter to the notion of multicultural competence and led to a great deal of staff turnover and dissatisfaction. The UF Counseling Center staff repeatedly pointed out the need for (and availability) of multiculturally competent personnel, but their pleas were ignored. This interaction was a reminder that once we step outside the UF Counseling Center, we have to interact and deal with people who may not share our dedication to multicultural competence.

One critical incident captures the complexity, both within the UF Counseling Center and across the campus, of implementing multicultural competencies. On the day of a popular and competitive student government election in which a Latino was a candidate for president (and therefore would have control of a $9 million budget), the Institute of Hispanic/Latino Cultures was spray-painted with the words, "No Spick [sic] for president."

The reaction across campus was swift as the slur made front-page news. A segment of campus felt the slur was politically motivated and another segment felt unsafe and traumatized. Many Latino/a students reported it was the first time that they had experienced being a target of racism. Tension was high across campus, and anger seemed the prevalent mood. Immediately the UF Counseling Center staff was called upon to help deal with the issue. The fact that relationships had already been established between the Latino community and some UF Counseling Center staff was critical in our staff being seen as credible.

The staff had to deal with their own reactions as they tried to help students both in therapy sessions and in outreach. Thankfully, the MCC training and dedicated staff time (retreats, training) in talking about difficult multicultural issues paid off. The staff was able to rally together to make a proactive statement to the campus. We decided to write a letter to the editor of the campus newspaper emphasizing the need for unity and reminding students that the UF Counseling Center was a place where they could share their feelings. The newspaper refused to run the letter (and letters from campus ministry and other supportive groups), instead choosing to print inflammatory letters or to ignore the issue altogether. Subsequently, we paid for an ad that read, "When one of us is hurt, all of us are hurt. Hate speech hurts. Resist racism."

Some of the staff worked directly with the targeted student candidate and other members of the community as they tried to express their feelings of anger, outrage, and fear. In conjunction with other student affairs staff, the UF Counseling Center staff coordinated two events, a speak-out for students and a question-and-answer session with administrators. Both events were successful and demonstrated a great deal of multicultural sensitivity. However, one student angrily decried the meetings, saying it was a counseling session designed to pacify the students into inaction. Despite our best efforts to be helpful, this was a reminder that we represent the administration and that students may not make distinctions when employing us-vs.-them thinking.

Current Trends and Recommendations

The process of infusing multicultural counseling competencies has been somewhat like an accordion, expanding and contracting. Similar to therapy, progress may seem more like two steps forward and one step backwards. Change is difficult for most people, and resistance is to be expected. At worst, one may encounter backlash, hostility, and invalidation of multicultural counseling competency efforts. Staff members who are dedicated front-liners for MCC initiatives may burn out. Minority staff members, in particular, run the risk of role overload and stress. To counteract these hazards, it is important to have recognition by the full staff that infusing MCC is everyone's responsibility, and that self-care and balance in lifestyle are important. Rotating job responsibilities, providing professional development leaves, and providing ongoing support are essential for the well-being of active MCC staff.

We cannot overemphasize the importance of hiring culturally diverse staff, of following the spirit (if not the law) of affirmative action, and reaching a critical mass in personnel (about one third of faculty and interns). We have found it invaluable to have a consultant take an objective look at the relationships and dynamics in our UF Counseling Center. Often dealing with multicultural issues can be a personal and intense process, and having an outside consultant helps to diffuse defensiveness and territoriality. In addition, by using objective data such as the results of the multicultural competency checklist (Ponterotto et al., 1995) or research on training (e.g., Constantine & Gloria, 1999; Manese, Wu, & Nepomuceno, 2001), we are able to see the efforts of our UF Counseling Center in a national context. Similarly, we have found that national conferences and professional Internet listservs serve the function of providing context, support, and inspiration for multicultural counseling competency work.

It has been pointed out that what is missing from multicultural competency research is the client perspective of multicultural counseling competencies (Fuertes, Bartolomeo, & Nichols, 2001; Pope-Davis et al., 2001). We suggest that counseling center staff members are ideally situated to be leaders in this research. In addition, counselors can marshal their clinical strengths to contribute to the MCC literature through clinical case studies (e.g., Hansen, Pepitone-Arreola-Rockwell, & Greene, 2000) that illustrate MCC issues. However counselors have to be willing (and get institutional support) to navigate the highly politicized waters of multicultural research.

The process of infusing and energizing multicultural counseling competencies on a predominantly White campus is ongoing and ever-evolving. Just as it is challenging to keep up with new developments in the counseling profession itself, it is equally challenging to keep abreast of changes in consciousness regarding MCC (e.g., Holcomb-McCoy & Myers, 1999). Ongoing professional development and peer supervision (Pope-Davis & Coleman, 1997) and staying current with MCC research are essential features of all vital MCC counseling centers. Some recommendations for consideration include developing a bilingual (Spanish/English) counseling training program, continuing to hire MCC competent staff members that reflect underserved populations, and updating current organizational structures to reflect multicultural counseling competencies (e.g., intake forms, supervisory evaluations, outreach efforts).

Conclusion

Infusing MCC has been and continues to be a challenging and exciting part of being at the UF Counseling Center. The rewards far outweigh the frustrations as we become more adept at mastering and infusing multicultural counseling competencies into the life of the Counseling Center and the institution.

References

American Psychological Association. (2001). *Guidelines for psychotherapy with lesbian, gay, and bisexual clients.* Retrieved July 2, 2001, from http://www. apa.org/pi/lgbc/guidelines.html.

American Psychological Association, Office of Ethnic Minority Affairs. (1991). *Guidelines for providers of psychological services to ethnic, linguistic, and culturally diverse populations.* Washington DC: Author.

Arredondo, P., & Arciniega, G. M. (2001). Strategies and techniques for counselor training based on the multicultural counseling competencies. *Journal of Multicultural Counseling and Development, 29,* 263-273.

Arredondo, P., Toporek, R., Brown, S. P., Jones, J., Locke, D. C., Sanchez, J., & Stadler, H. (1996). Operationalization of the multicultural counseling competencies. *Journal of Multicultural Counseling and Development, 24,* 42-78.

Bingham, R. P., Fukuyama, M. A., Suchman, D., & Parker, W. (1984). Ethnic student walk-in: Expanding the scope. *Journal of College Student Personnel, 25,* 168-170.

Constantine, M. G., & Gloria, A. M. (1999). Multicultural issues in predoctoral internship programs: A national survey. *Journal of Multicultural Counseling and Development, 27,* 42-53.

Copeland, E. J. (1983). Cross-cultural counseling and psychotherapy: A historical perspective, implications for research and training. *Personnel and Guidance Journal, 62,* 10-15.

Delgado-Romero, E. A. (1999). The face of racism. *Journal of Counseling & Development, 77,* 23-25.

Fuertes, J. N., Bartolomeo, M., & Nichols, C. M. (2001). Future research directions in the study of counselor multicultural competency. *Journal of Multicultural Counseling and Development, 29,* 3-12.

Fukuyama, M. A. (1994). Critical incidents in multicultural counseling supervision: A phenomenological approach to supervision research. *Counselor Education and Supervision, 34,* 142-151.

Fukuyama, M. A. (1999). Personal narrative: Growing up biracial. *Journal of Counseling & Development, 77,* 12-14.

Funderburk, J., & Fukuyama, M. (2001). Feminism, multiculturalism, and spirituality: Convergent and divergent forces in psychotherapy. *Women and Therapy, 24,* 1-18.

Hansen, N. D., Pepitone-Arreola-Rockwell, F., & Greene, A. F. (2000). Multicultural competence: Criteria and case examples. *Professional Psychology: Research and Practice, 31,* 652-660.

Holcomb-McCoy, C. C., & Myers, J. E. (1999). Multicultural competence and counselor training: A national survey. *Journal of Counseling & Development, 77,* 294-302.

Manese, J. E., Wu, J. T., & Nepomuceno, C. A. (2001). The effect of training on multicultural counseling competencies: An exploratory study over a 10-year period. *Journal of Multicultural Counseling and Development, 29,* 31-40.

Murphy, M. C., Wright, B. V., & Bellamy, D. E. (1995). Multicultural training in university counseling center predoctoral psychology internship programs: A survey. *Journal of Multicultural Counseling and Development, 23*, 170–180.

Ponterotto, J. G., Alexander, C. M., & Grieger, I. (1995). A multicultural competency checklist for counseling training programs. *Journal of Multicultural Counseling and Development, 23*, 11–20.

Pope-Davis, D. B., & Coleman, H. L. K. (Eds.). (1997). *Multicultural counseling competencies: Assessment, education and training, and supervision*. Thousand Oaks, CA: Sage.

Pope-Davis, D. B., Liu, W. M., Toporek, R. L., & Brittan-Powell, C. S. (2001). What's missing from multicultural competency research: Review, introspection, and recommendations. *Cultural Diversity and Ethnic Minority Psychology, 7*, 115–138.

Pope-Davis, D. B., Reynolds, A. L., Dings, J. G., & Ottavi, T. M. (1994). Multicultural competencies of doctoral interns at university counseling centers: An exploratory investigation. *Professional Psychology: Research and Practice, 25*, 466–470.

Sue, D. W. (1995). Multicultural organizational development: Implications for the counseling profession. In J. G. Ponterotto, J. M. Casas, L. A. Suzuki, & C. M. Alexander (Eds.), *Handbook of multicultural counseling* (pp. 474–492). Thousand Oaks, CA: Sage.

Sue, D. W., Arredondo, P., & McDavis, R. J. (1992). Multicultural counseling competencies and standards: A call to the profession. *Journal of Counseling & Development, 70*, 477–486.

University of Florida. (2001a). *Counseling center policies and procedures manual*. Gainesville, FL: Author.

University of Florida. (2001b). *UF facts and rankings*. Retrieved July 2, 2001, from http://www.ufl.edu/facts.html

Chapter 19

Transforming College Campuses: Implications of the Multicultural Competencies Guidelines

Kwong-Liem Karl Kwan and Deborah J. Taub

Using a self-report approach, the authors discuss how existing guidelines of multicultural competencies can be integrated into the existing roles of college counseling and student personnel, including counseling (e.g., prevention, support interventions), administration (e.g., top-down involvement, multicultural mission), teaching (e.g., curriculum development), program development (e.g., student orientation, faculty training), and consultation (e.g., staff development). Strategies that are found to be effective as well as challenges that are yet to be overcome are shared. Throughout the chapter, the authors argue that a multilevel approach to fostering a culture of multicultural competencies ought to be reinforced if the multicultural mission of college campuses is to be realized. In particular, the authors emphasize that multicultural competencies ought to be developed at both organizational and individual levels, and that commitment to the multicultural mission must come from senior administration and faculty. Thus the authors call for college counseling and student personnel to serve as catalysts and change agents to transform college campuses through multicultural competencies.

The U.S. college student population has never been more diverse. In 1976 non-White students made up 16% of the college student population; in 1997, they comprised 27% of the student body (National Center for Education Statistics [NCES], 2001). Aided by the rise of the public sector in American higher education and by a number of mostly federal financial aid programs, access to higher education in the United States has expanded from a narrow focus on educating the elite, such as White males, sons of landowners (Gardner, 1999). With students of diverse backgrounds reaching a critical mass on campuses, institu-

217

tions of higher education have undergone a process of change, from tolerance, with an expectation of assimilation, to recognition of the special needs of this group of students (Trow, 1973).

Despite such changes, a number of studies have indicated that college student professionals may be less than equipped to address the academic and adjustment needs of the increasing students from various racial and ethnic groups. For instance, Black students who attended predominantly Black liberal arts institutions reported significantly more benefits from their overall college involvement than those who attended predominantly White liberal arts institutions. Black and Latino students were found to express a preference to disclose to faculty of their own ethnicity than to White faculty. Only about one third of African American and Hispanic students who began a bachelor's degree attained their degree 4 years later (Smith, 1997).

Biographical documents (e.g., Suskind, 1998) reporting various adjustment challenges of non-White students in predominantly White universities have been supported by empirical studies. Latino students reported that overt discrimination and subtle indications of ethnic tension inhibited their transition to college (Hurtado, Carter, & Spuler, 1996), and that physical, social, institutional, and climate factors in the academic environment affected retention and graduation (Hernandez, 2000). Patterson-Stewart, Ritchie, and Sanders (1997) found that African American students attributed feelings of not belonging in academia to invisibility that emerged when they encountered White students and faculty. African American roommate pairs reported significantly greater roommate satisfaction than did African American–White roommate dyads, who reported significantly less roommate satisfaction than did White–White dyads (Phelps et al., 1998). Other empirical studies also have documented the effects of racial and cultural climate on the adjustment difficulties and academic performance of non-White college students (Anaya & Cole, 2001; Berger & Milem, 2000; Brown, 2000; Flowers & Pascarella, 1999; Sedlacek, 1999).

Usefulness of Multicultural Counseling Competencies

Guidelines on multicultural competencies (American Psychological Association, 2002; Arredondo et al., 1996; Sue, Arredondo, & McDavis, 1992) enable college student professionals to identify, explain, and act upon these ongoing and difficult racial and cultural issues on the increasingly multicultural college campus. Culling from our knowledge and experiences, we discuss here how existing guidelines of multicultural competencies can be integrated into counseling and mentoring, training and teaching, and consultation and program development.

We urge all college student professionals not to designate the multicultural missions as their duties but as our obligations, i.e., as obligations of everyone on campus. Although recognizing that changes may need to progress in small steps, we emphasize that multicultural competencies ought to be developed at both organizational and individual levels (Sue et al., 1998), and that commitment to the multicultural mission must "come from the top" (Sue & Sue, 1999, p. 212).

We need to identify causes that contribute to the adjustment difficulties of non-White students so that culturally sensitive preventive and intervention programs can be designed and implemented. First-generation college students who grew up primarily with their own ethnic peers often raise the questions of "Where do I fit in?" and "Do I belong here?" These self-doubts are likely related to a number of factors. First, given the lack of academic role models within the family (and perhaps among their ethnic peers), adjusting to being a college student can be a novel and unfamiliar experience. Second, students who grew up in ethnic enclaves and are of lower socioeconomic status may lack personal experience in interacting with White and middle-class people, such as the majority of students and faculty they meet on campus. Third, the lack of peers from similar ethnic and cultural backgrounds for personal and social support often expose them to struggles between wanting or not wanting to be "White," and to worrying about how changing their identification might be perceived as a sellout by their own ethnic peers and parents.

Using the multicultural counseling competency framework, college student professionals therefore realize that they need to (a) have knowledge of precollege demographic backgrounds and related ethnocultural experiences; (b) develop an empathic understanding of their impact on non-White students' subsequent feelings of being different, whether real or perceived, and the corresponding sense of self- and social alienation; and (c) possess skills to gather and integrate such knowledge in the helping, advising, and counseling process.

Counseling–Mentoring

We believe that a combined counseling–mentoring approach needs to be provided to educate and psychologically equip these students for the college experience. Such counseling–mentoring needs to be offered both early in and throughout these students' college years. It is our experience that personal, preentrance contacts are effective ways to understand and prepare for these students' academic and day-to-day personal needs, and to cultivate a sense of support and community necessary for their subsequent adjustment. Informal meetings with these students throughout the academic years also enable the faculty to monitor students' progress and address unexpected academic and adjustment issues that might arise.

Along with personal mentoring, mentors can also help sponsor and mobilize support groups for non-White students. Such groups provide reality-checking grounds for students who encounter incidents of racism inside and outside the classroom. Often victims of racism may feel confused, harbor repressed anger, and resort to denial to cope. Prolonged racism perpetuates powerlessness and hopelessness, which might lead to poor academic performance and attrition (McEwen, Roper, Bryant, & Langa, 1996). Thus these support groups allow students a much-needed outlet to voice their concern and for the faculty mentors to help students confront these issues. With a critical mass and collective voice, these groups can help propose changes to the multicultural mission of the curriculum, and the recruitment and retention of non-White students on campus. An example of such a group is the Ethnic Minority Affairs Committee (EMAC) of the Department of Educational Psychology at the University of Nebraska-Lincoln (see Ethnic Minority Affairs Committee, 2002).

We need to identify, network with, and encourage faculty members and current students on campus who have understanding and experiences working with these non-White students to serve as counselor–mentors. Initially, we may enlist support by providing consultation services to faculty members, presidents of multicultural student associations, and directors of diversity offices on campus.

Such counseling–mentoring, however, is not exclusively the duty of non-White faculty and student mentors, nor does it always require racial and ethnic match between mentors and mentees. Although we believe that it is important to expose these students to faculty and student role models of the same racial and ethnic group, we echo Sue and Zane's (1987) position that the treatment effectiveness of racial and ethnic match remains an empirical question. Models of racial and cultural identity development (Atkinson, Morten, & Sue, 1998; Helms, 1995) have informed us that both White people and visible racial and ethnic people can be differentiated along their psychological identification with the White group or their own group as the identity reference group. The first author once assumed that a visible American Indian college student professional would accept an invitation to guest lecture on a multicultural counseling topic; instead, a less salient American Indian college student professional later invited himself to deliver the lecture. Such incidents illustrate that skin color alone cannot indicate identification and psychological affiliation with racial and ethnic group. Thus we are constantly reminded of the biasing effects of racial salience when identifying and selecting counselor–mentors committed to the cause of multiculturalism on campuses.

Teaching Students and Training the Trainers

Systematic transformation to a multicultural environment calls for professionals responsible for the training mission of the university to be equipped with multicultural competencies. What do we know about the status of multicultural competencies among college student professionals? Talbot (1996) found that students in the eight largest graduate training programs in student affairs reported having (a) limited experience with diverse populations prior to graduate school, (b) limited knowledge about diversity and the needs of diverse populations, and (c) limited behaviors seeking experiences with diverse populations. Thus the need to redevelop and strengthen the multicultural mission of the curriculum is evident. Yet the next generation of college student professionals is not the only group that needs training. In fact, these findings were not surprising when interpreted in light of data reported by Talbot and Kocarek (1997), which found that faculty in graduate training programs in student affairs had limited experience, knowledge, and behaviors related to diversity. The lack of knowledge (beyond the recognition level) about diverse populations among the graduate faculty is a cause for concern.

We need to identify who needs to be trained. Discussions about the revisions of curricula have focused primarily on students in training when we may also need to train the trainers. If existing graduate faculty members are to be responsible for the training of multiculturally competent student affairs professionals, they themselves must possess the necessary attitudes and beliefs, knowledge, and skills articulated by guidelines of multicultural competencies. Faculty members need to know the role played by student affairs in serving diverse students. Current faculty can seek education through conferences, workshops, coursework at their own or a neighboring institution (in such departments as psychology, sociology, multicultural studies), online courses, consultation, and directed reading.

We need to be able to suggest to college student professionals what needs to be learned. We want to reinforce that the tripartite, awareness-

221

knowledge-skill model provides an effective framework for training multicultural competencies. Along with knowledge acquired through textbooks (e.g., Atkinson et al., 1998; Sue & Sue, 1999), empathic and experiential learning can be facilitated by incorporating other reading and media materials. We have found Janet Helms' book, *A Race Is a Nice Thing to Have* (1992), helpful in facilitating an understanding of racial identity. The article by Peggy McIntosh (1988/2001) on White privilege and male privilege has enabled many to understand the "invisible package of unearned assets that [White people] can count on cashing in each day" (p. 95). Both Helms and McIntosh offer useful and challenging exercises for understanding the implications and impact of race and culture on identity and interpersonal experiences.

To help trainees develop an empathic understanding of non-White people's experiences and conflicts in White environments, we have found *A Hope in the Unseen* (Suskind, 1998), *Best Intentions* (Anson, 1987), and *Bury My Heart at Wounded Knee* (Brown, 2001) useful. The Suskind and Anson books are particularly effective given their focus on the college experiences of their protagonists. Instructional videos such as *Skin Deep* (Reid, 1995), *Black Is . . . Black Ain't* (Riggs, 1995), and *Racism 101* (Lennon & Bagwell, 1988) as well as commercial films such as *My Family* (Thomas & Nava, 1995) and *Losing Isaiah* (Koch, Foner, & Gyllenhaal, 1995) can provide experiential information and serve as stimuli for class discussion, particularly for students without much previous knowledge. *Skin Deep*, which features a diverse group of students discussing their experiences with race and racism, offers a useful companion discussion guide. The authors of this chapter have found these materials useful for enhancing student learning in multicultural classes.

We support Midgette and Meggert's (1991) argument that the model of only a single course is insufficient to train multiculturally competent professionals. When students' multicultural training is left up to a single class, students are likely to view multicultural issues in isolation rather than integrate them into their practice and conceptualizations. Multicultural competencies call for faculty to make a concerted effort to integrate multicultural knowledge into the training curriculum (e.g., college student development theory, counseling theories and techniques, career development), and to structure practica and internships so as to expose trainees to multicultural client populations. Thus, it is important for faculty to network so as to connect student trainees with practicum and internship supervisors at training sites that provide services to non-White students.

Along with the multicultural guidelines (e.g., Arredondo et al., 1996), we need to have knowledge of criteria of various accreditation bodies (e.g., Council for the Accreditation of Counseling and Related Programs, Council for the Advancement of Standards in Higher Education) to guide our development and evaluation of the multicultural competencies of counseling and college student affairs training programs. By evaluating the extent of adoption of national and accreditation standards in the curriculum, we could assess faculty multicultural awareness of and responsiveness to the multicultural mission of the profession.

Beyond meeting national and accreditation standards, the commitment to multicultural competence on the part of the training program must be clear and explicit. The College Student Personnel Program in the Counseling and Personnel Services Department at the University of Maryland at College Park, for example, has adopted a set of multicultural principles that articulate the program's commitment to multiculturalism (College Student Personnel, 1999). Among these principles is an emphasis on self-knowledge, a commitment for action against oppression, and a responsibility to become an agent of change.

Consultation and Program Development

A vice president of student affairs (a White male) of a university in the Midwest once invited two college student professionals to deliver a workshop to increase multicultural awareness and sensitivity of a staff of college administrators and faculty members. Before the workshop started, several faculty members articulated to the vice president that "we are not going to lower our admission standards just to increase minority enrollment."

Efforts to enhance organizational multicultural competencies can be incredibly frustrating. In this scenario, faculty and administrators operated from (a) the deficient model—that Black and Latino students, in particular, are intellectually inferior, (b) fears that non-White students might lower the university's academic standards, and (c) assumptions that standardized tests (e.g., SAT) are culturally valid and reliable and the sole indicators and predictors of success in college.

We may consider applying certain cognitive strategies and counseling skills when confronted with these challenges. First, we could expect and develop skills to recognize resistance, which often is subtler than the preceding scenario. We realize that resistance often reflects struggles of the larger system rather than targets the individual consultant. Second, we could apply empathy skills to listen and understand reasons for resistance. We could use the counseling techniques of empathic listening and reflection to enable consultees to recognize and confront their own biases. Third, we could take small, incremental steps toward enhancing organizational multicultural competencies. As such, we need to continue to establish rapport and create opportunities for resisting parties to listen to multicultural messages while strengthening the relationships and collective voice of supportive faculty and administrative units. On a more proactive level, we believe that organizational multicultural competencies can be best promoted through programming and hiring practices.

Hiring Practices

As Komives and Kuh (1988) articulated, the quality of a unit can be no better than the quality of the staffing. The limited number of non-White trainees in graduate programs leads inevitably to a limited number of non-White candidates in the hiring pool. Thus, as noted by Sagaria and Johnsrud (1991), "by increasing the minority presence in student affairs, student services divisions can cultivate a more racially and culturally diverse campus environment, which can in turn enhance the achievement of minority students" (p. 105). As cited by Patitu and Terrell (1998), a minority staff person was hired to assist financial needs of minority students—particularly Native American Indians—at the University of Montana. Since that hiring, the number of students who have received aid has increased dramatically.

Therefore, "it is imperative that every staff position be filled with an individual who, in addition to having the knowledge, skills, and ability to do the job, appreciates diversity and is willing to empower diversity" (Kearney, 1993, p. 275). We cannot understate that criteria for multicultural competencies ought to be explicitly listed as a central component, rather than as a miscellaneous item, in the selection and evaluation of candidates, especially the higher level administrators. We need to work with various campus units (e.g., serve as a search committee member) to adopt, develop, incorporate, and employ standards of multicultural competencies in the recruitment and selection of faculty and staff members.

Programming

Outreach activities and programs represent another powerful, proactive way to enhance organizational multicultural competencies. Programs can be focused on small, specific units, or be campus-wide. Residence halls represent an individual campus unit that presents both a challenge and an opportunity for students to develop multicultural relations: for many students this may be their first experience to live in proximity to the racially and culturally different. Such contacts might lead to race-related tension and conflict, or understanding, appreciation, and the development of community. Films and videos, such as *Frosh: Nine Months in a Freshman Dorm* (Goldfine & Geller, 1993) and *Skin Deep* (Reid, 1995), can be used to stimulate discussion and dialogue. Hughes (1994) has provided a framework and suggestions for multicultural programming in residence halls.

Campus-wide efforts frequently take the form of major speakers invited to campus or of celebration weeks or months (e.g., African American History Month). Another popular approach is a freshman book program in which every incoming first-year student is assigned to read the same book, which is then discussed in a variety of formats including first-year classes. DePaul University, for example, used Suskind's book for this purpose in fall 2000; the Web site supporting this endeavor and providing guiding questions can be found at www.depaul.edu/~firstyr/hope.html.

Needs assessments and program evaluations must be constructed and conducted carefully to ensure that the perspectives of underrepresented students are identified. It is important, therefore, to collect information about race and ethnicity in the process and to examine results by these variables. Sampling methods also need to be examined for unintentional biases.

Conclusion

The needs of our increasingly multicultural campus cannot be served exclusively through a designated person or multicultural centers. Throughout the chapter, we have reiterated the tenet that each college student professional and student service unit within the institution has the responsibility to transform our campuses using guidelines of multicultural competencies. Beyond knowing these guidelines, let us walk the talk and make it happen.

References

American Psychological Association. (2002). *Guidelines on multicultural training, research, practice, and organizational change for psychologists.* Retrieved November 1, 2002, from http://www.apa.org/pi/multiculturalguidelines.pdf

Anaya, G., & Cole, D. G. (2001). Latina/o student achievement: Exploring the influence of student–faculty interactions on college grades. *Journal of College Student Development, 42*, 3–14.

Anson, R. A. (1987). *Best intentions: The education and killing of Edmund Perry.* New York: Vintage Books.

Arredondo, P.,Toporek, R., Brown, S. P.,Jones,J., Locke, D., Sanchez,J., & Stadler, H. (1996). Operationalization of the multicultural counseling competencies. *Journal of Multicultural Counseling and Development, 24,* 42–78.

Atkinson, D. R., Morten, G., & Sue, D.W. (1998). *Counseling American minorities* (5th ed.). San Francisco: McGraw Hill.

Berger, J. B., & Milem, J. F. (2000). Exploring the impact of historically Black colleges in promoting the development of undergraduates' self-concept. *Journal of College Student Development, 41,* 381–394.

Brown, D.A. (2001). *Bury my heart at wounded knee: An Indian history of the American West.* New York: Holt.

Brown, T. L. (2000). Gender differences in African American students' satisfaction with college. *Journal of College Student Development, 41,* 479–487.

College Student Personnel Program. (1999). *Multicultural principles.* College Park: University of Maryland.

Ethnic Minority Affairs Committee, University of Nebraska at Lincoln. (2002). Retrieved May 29, 2002, from http://tc.unl.edu/edpsych/EMAC.html

Flowers, L., & Pascarella, E. T. (1999). Cognitive effects of college racial composition on African American students after 3 years of college. *Journal of College Student Development, 40,* 669–677.

Gardner, J. N. (1999, September). *The freshman seminar: History, benefits, effectiveness, findings from national research.* Paper presented to the Purdue University Lilly Endowment Retention Initiatives, West Lafayette, IN.

Goldfine, D., & Geller, D. (Directors/Producers). (1993). *Frosh: Nine months in a freshman dorm.* Palo Alto, CA: Horizon Unlimited.

Helms, J. E. (1992). *A race is a nice thing to have: A guide to being a White person or understanding the White persons in your life.* Topeka, KS: Content Communications.

Helms, J. E. (1995). An update of Helms' White and people of color racial identity models. In J. Ponterotto, M. Casas, L. Suzuki, & C. Alexander (Eds.), *Handbook of multicultural counseling* (pp. 181–198). Newbury Park, CA: Sage.

Hernandez, J. C. (2000). Understanding the retention of Latino college students. *Journal of College Student Development, 41,* 575–588.

Hughes, M. (1994). Helping students understand and appreciate diversity. In C. C. Schroeder & P. Mable (Eds.), *Realizing the educational potential of residence halls* (pp. 190–217). San Francisco: Jossey-Bass.

Hurtado, S., Carter, D. F., & Spuler, A. (1996). Latino student transition to college: Assessing difficulties and factors in successful college adjustment. *Research in Higher Education, 37,* 135–157.

Kearney, P. A. (1993). Professional staffing. In R. B. Winston, Jr., & S. Anchors (Eds.), *Student housing and residential life* (pp. 269–291). San Francisco: Jossey-Bass.

Koch, H. W., Jr., Foner, N. (Producers), & Gyllenhaal, S. (Director). (1995). *Losing Isaiah* [Motion picture]. United States: Paramount Pictures.

Komives, S. R., & Kuh, G. (1988). "The right stuff": Some thoughts on attracting good people to student affairs work. In R. B. Young & L. V. Moore (Eds.), *The state of the art of professional education and practice* (pp. 1-20). Washington, DC: Commission on Professional Education in Student Personnel.

Lennon, T., & Bagwell, O. Producers. (1988). *Racism 101* [Television broadcast]. Washington, DC: Public Broadcasting System.

McEwen, M. K., Roper, L. D., Bryant, D. R., & Langa, M. J. (1996). Incorporating the development of African American students into psychosocial theories of student development. In F. K. Stage, G. L. Anaya, J. P. Bean, D. Hossler, & G. D. Kuh (Eds.), *College students: The evolving nature of research* (pp. 217-226). Needham Heights, MA: Simon & Schuster.

McIntosh, P. (1988/2001). White privilege and male privilege: A personal account of coming to see correspondences through work in women's studies. In M. L. Andersen & P. H. Collins (Eds.), *Race, class, and gender* (4th ed., pp. 95-105). Belmont, CA: Wadsworth/Thomson.

Midgette, T. E., & Meggert, S. S. (1991). Multicultural counseling instruction: A challenge for faculties in the 21st century. *Journal of Counseling & Development, 70,* 136-141.

National Center for Education Statistics. (2001). *Digest of educational studies 2000* (NCES 2001-034). Washington, DC: Government Printing Office.

Patitu, C. L., & Terrell, M. C. (1998). Benefits of affirmative action in student affairs. In D. D. Gehring (Ed.), *Responding to the new affirmative action climate* (pp. 41-56). San Francisco: Jossey-Bass.

Patterson-Stewart, K. E., Ritchie, M. H., & Sanders, E. T. W. (1997). Interpersonal dynamics of African American persistence in doctoral programs at predominantly White universities. *Journal of College Student Development, 38*(5), 489-498.

Phelps, R. E., Altshul, D. B., Wisenbaker, J. M., Day, J. F., Cooper, D., & Potter, C. G. (1998). Roommate satisfaction and ethnic identity in mixed-race and White university roommate dyads. *Journal of College Student Development, 39*(2), 194-203.

Reid, F. (Producer/Director). (1995). *Skin deep: Building diverse campus communities* [Motion picture]. Berkeley, CA: Iris Films. (Available from California Newsreel, 149 Ninth Street, San Francisco 94103)

Riggs, M. T. (Producer/Director). (1995). *Black is ... Black ain't* [Motion picture]. United States: Independent Television Service. (Available from California Newsreel, 149 Ninth Street, San Francisco 94103)

Sagaria, M. A., & Johnsrud, L. K. (1991). Recruiting, advancing, and retaining minorities in student affairs: Moving from rhetoric to results. *NASPA Journal, 28,* 105-120.

Sedlacek, W. E. (1999). Black students on White campuses: 20 years of research. *Journal of College Student Development, 40,* 538-550.

Smith, T. M. (1997). Issues in focus: Minorities in higher education. In *The condition of education 1996* (NCES 96-304). Retrieved May 2002, from http://nces.ed.gov/pubsoid/CE96/C96006.html

Sue, D. W., Arredondo, P., & McDavis, R. J. (1992). Multicultural counseling competencies and standards. A call to the profession. *Journal of Counseling & Development, 70,* 477-486.

Sue, D.W., Carter, R.T., Casas, J. M., Fouad, N.A., Ivey, A. E., Jensen, M., LaFromboise, T., Manese, J. E., Ponterotto, J. G., & Vazquez-Nutall, E. (1998). *Multicultural counseling competencies: Individual and organizational development.* Thousand Oaks, CA: Sage.

Sue, D. W., & Sue, D. (1999). *Counseling the culturally different: Theory and practice* (3rd ed.). New York: Wiley.

Sue, S., & Zane, N. (1987). The role of culture and cultural techniques in psychotherapy. A critique and reformulation. *American Psychologist, 42,* 37–45.

Suskind, R. (1998). *A hope in the unseen: An American odyssey from the inner city to the Ivy League.* New York: Broadway Books.

Talbot, D. M. (1996). Master's students' perspectives on their graduate education regarding issues of diversity. *NASPA Journal, 33,* 163–178.

Talbot, D. M., & Kocarek, C. (1997). Student affairs graduate faculty members' knowledge, comfort, and behaviors regarding issues of diversity. *Journal of College Student Development, 38,* 278–287.

Thomas, A. (Producer), & Nava, G. (Director). (1995). My family [Motion Pictures]. United States: New Line Productions.

Trow, M. (1973). *Problems in the transition from elite to mass higher education.* San Francisco: Carnegie Commission.

228

Chapter 20

Applying Multicultural Competencies in Predominantly White Institutions of Higher Education

Patricia Arredondo

Applied research in White institutions of higher education (WIHE) has yielded valuable data to guide diversity initiatives. This chapter highlights the Blueprint for Diversity Management, currently being applied in WIHE, and outlines multicultural competencies that lead to institutional best practices. Topics discussed include learning organizations, the role of consultants, and multiculturalism and diversity as catalysts for organizational change.

Three case examples set the multicultural stage for this chapter. They are disguised versions of real scenarios that are playing out across college and university campuses today. Such situations arise for colleges and universities of all sizes, colleges within large universities, and smaller units, e.g., academic departments or counseling centers. Owing to their experiences as change agents of individual, group, and organizational behaviors and as practitioners of multicultural counseling competencies, counselors have the best preparation to become involved as consultants to White institutions of higher education (WIHE).

- *Case 1:* The dean of a college of education requested a retreat to discuss concerns about retaining faculty of color. His request was for all faculty members to participate.
- *Case 2:* The provost of a network of community colleges indicated that the tenured faculty were not interested in the system-wide cultural diversity initiative. The faculty reported that they were carrying an overload of teaching and advising assignments and were unable to take additional work. Al-

though the community colleges were located in very multicultural, multilingual areas, they were not retaining students or junior faculty of color.

- *Case 3:* A counseling and career center at a Midwest university sought to develop multicultural competency for its staff. Students they were serving were increasingly older, international, gay and lesbian, and ethnic and racial minorities. The clinicians reported feeling unprepared for multicultural counseling experiences. Additionally, clients expressed frustration with the receptionist who spoke quickly, creating stressful communications.

Specific themes and desirable objectives have generally emerged from requests to me from White institutions of higher education (WIHE) for organizational diversity consultation. WIHE organizations in general

1. place their highest emphasis on the attraction, enrollment, hiring, and retention of students, faculty, and staff of color;
2. are interested in promoting a sense of campus community and inclusiveness for all constituencies;
3. express an interest in addressing diversity, broadly speaking, e.g., gender, physical disability, and sexual orientation; and
4. are well intentioned but not necessarily experienced in managing change processes that focus on change through diversity and multicultural competency.

The focus on multiculturalism and diversity in White institutions of higher education continues to increase (American Council on Education [ACE] and American Association of University Professors [AAUP], 2000; Grieger & Tolliver, 2001). The motivating factors are demographic changes pointing to an increase in school-aged ethnic minority populations and a decrease in White Americans (U.S. Census, 2000); the inability of predominantly WIHE to successfully attract and retain students of color at both the undergraduate and graduate levels (Grieger & Tolliver, 2001); projections about skills, educational content, and technology competency needs in the workforce (Judy & D'Amico, 1997), which WIHE must respond to; and the current economic viability of institutions of higher education in their historic form for the traditional student they were designed to educate in a socially segregated society (ACE & AAUP, 2000).

A recent court case, *Gratz v. Bollinger*, was supported in belief that the attainment of diversity in the university's composition was in the state's best interest, and that the admissions process justified this (Robbenolt & Walker, 2001). Through Internet access it is possible to read about diversity-related initiatives taking place at institutions such as Cornell, University of Maryland, and Fisher College of Business at the Ohio State University, among others (diversityatwork.online.com, 2001). Herein reported are practices to promote organizational culture change. These include attention to mission statements, more pluralistic curriculum, faculty multicultural development, and diversity or multicultural training. A recent study on diversity in college classrooms (ACE & AAUP, 2000) indicated that through deliberate and systematic attention to multicultural curriculum and multiracial and multiethnic classrooms, enhanced educational outcomes are possible. Another major study on the diversity debate in higher education found that diversity in its many forms does bring benefits to individuals, institutions, and society at large (Chang, Witt, Jones, & Hakuta, 2000).

Personal Framework

Since 1985, I have practiced as a consultant, interfacing with a wide range and size of more than 400 organizations, including many WIHE. Specific consultation to college and universities has been in response to different types of requests. The three examples given at the beginning of the chapter mirror some of the requests and contexts. Because the requests and contexts vary, my philosophy is to customize my approach, still holding to my guiding principles, models, and methodologies, which are described later in this chapter, but making adaptations to meet the client's diversity change objectives.

My focus has been on addressing change through a focus on diversity and multiculturalism. Thus my background as a helping professional and educator, with a particular expertise in cross-cultural education and training and multicultural competencies, has brought great value to my diversity-related consulting. It has allowed me to take a combined counseling, developmental, and psychoeducational approach, grounded in multicultural competencies. My work is guided by mutual respect, collaboration, and ethical behavior. I see myself as a collaborator and facilitator of organizational change processes, not an expert with the answers.

My consultation approaches and tools have been enhanced over the years as a result of collaboration with other consultants who offer their particular technical expertise, and through learning from organizations where I have provided services. For example, based on a multiyear evaluation of more than 50 diversity initiatives in nonprofit organizations in the 1990s, I developed a Blueprint (see Figure 20.1) that guides my diversity management consultation (Arredondo, 1996).

Multicultural Counseling Competencies

AMCD's multicultural counseling competencies (Arredondo et al., 1996; Sue, Arredondo, & McDavis, 1992) provide an excellent frame of reference in consulting to White institutions of higher education. Multicultural counseling competencies are based on the rationale that culture is embedded in many institutional forms and all aspects of counseling practices; sociopolitical and historical forces influence contemporary orientations in counseling; and cultural competency and ethical practice are interrelated (Sue et al., 1992).

Multicultural counseling competencies have three domains: Counselor Awareness of Own Cultural Values and Biases, Counselor Awareness of Client's Worldview, and Culturally Appropriate Intervention Strategies. In a WIHE context, these counselor competencies can be adapted to WIHE Awareness of Own Cultural Values and Biases, WIHE Awareness of Constituencies' (faculty, staff, students, and community) Worldviews, and Culturally Appropriate Intervention Strategies.

Subsumed within these domains are the content areas of attitudes and beliefs, knowledge, and skills. The 31 original competencies (Sue et al., 1992) specify aspirational statements for culturally skilled counselors and are centered on concerns for ethnic and racial minority populations receiving counseling services in predominantly White agencies. In another AMCD-initiated document, "Operationalization of Multicultural Counseling Competencies" (Arredondo et al., 1996), 119 behavioral statements were added, offering direction for how to apply the 31 competencies. The specificity of the behavioral statements provides direction for education and training, assessment and research, and clinical practice. According to Sue (2001), there are multidimensional facets to multicultural competence allowing for applications for different purposes and in different contexts, e.g., societal and institutional.

AMCD's multicultural competency publications represent the first professionally supported document that addresses multiculturalism in counseling and psychology. As a result, educators and researchers are creating opportunities to apply them in different settings (e.g., school, marriage and family counseling, group work), for infusion in counselor education and training (Arredondo & Arciniega, 2001), and as tools to address institutional racism and oppression (Arredondo, 1999). Although most of the literature on MCC focuses on education and training and counseling practice, more attention is now being given to multicul-

Figure 20.1
Blueprint for Organizational Diversity

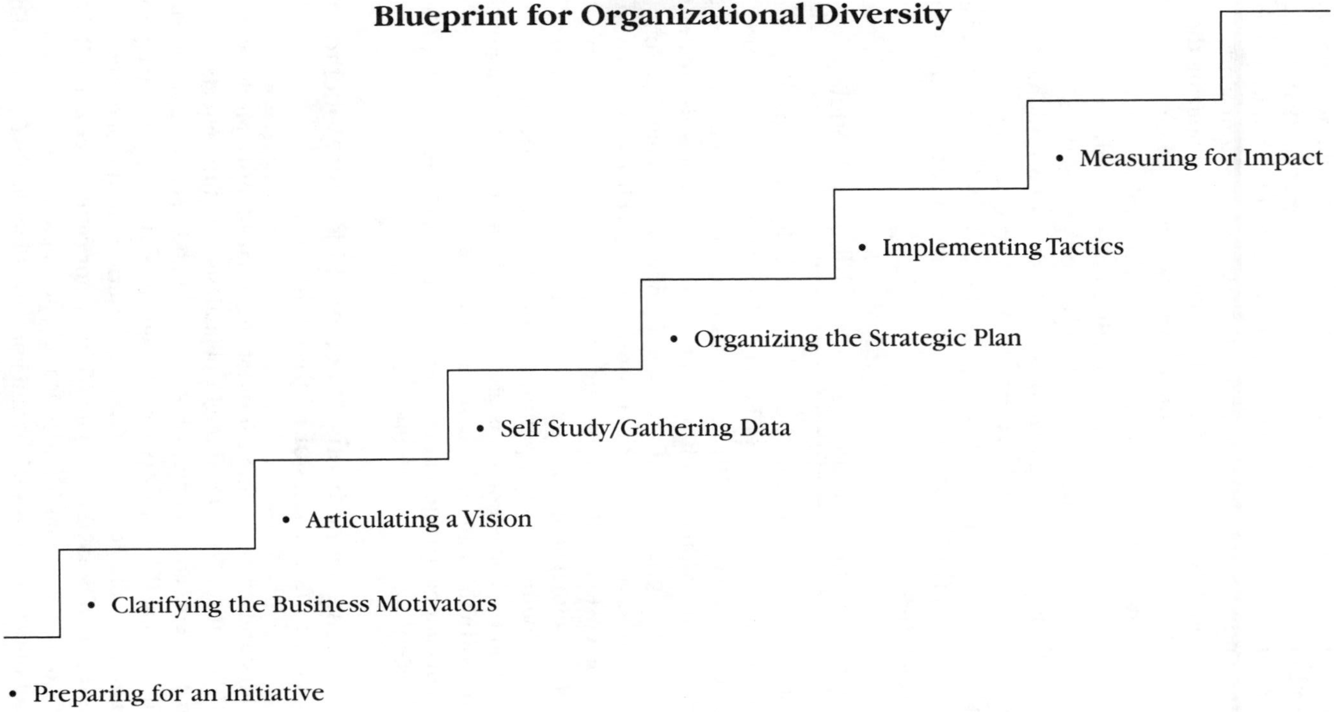

- Measuring for Impact
- Implementing Tactics
- Organizing the Strategic Plan
- Self Study/Gathering Data
- Articulating a Vision
- Clarifying the Business Motivators
- Preparing for an Initiative

© Empowerment Workshops, Inc., 1997.

233

tural competence in organizational development (American Psychological Association [APA], 2002; Arredondo, 1996; Sue et al., 1998; Sue, 2001).

A Midwest counseling center staff (Case 3) admitted they were not sufficiently knowledgeable about the experiences and worldview of clients from different cultural backgrounds. Again, by utilizing the multicultural competence model, the center staff began to engage in professional development seminars based on the multicultural counseling competencies, allowing them to gain knowledge about their clients as more complex individuals, not as a stereotype based on limited sociocultural information (e.g., age or sexual orientation). Additionally, they came to recognize that the receptionist was serving as a gatekeeper, perhaps unintentionally perpetuating institutional racism and other forms of exclusion (Ridley, 1995). She too became engaged in the center's change processes.

Dimensions of Personal Identity Model

An added new feature in the 1996 multicultural counseling competencies is the Dimensions of Personal Identity Model (see Figure 20.2) (Arredondo & Glauner, 1992), a tripartite, interdependent conceptualization of an individual's multiple identities. The model adds greater flexibility to the application of the MCC framework in White institutions of higher education for several reasons: (1) individuals are portrayed as multidimensional, affected by immutable identities, including racial and ethnic (A dimension); (2) individuals are influenced by different contexts, including the sociopolitical, economic, and historical (C dimension); and (3) consideration is given to areas in one's life that are based on opportunities and access, or lack thereof, such as work experience and educational background (B dimension). It is posited that the A and C dimensions have a direct influence on B dimensions.

Applying Dimensions of Personal Identity Model to White Institutions of Higher Education

Understanding the Dimensions of Personal Identity Model within a WIHE context allows for thoughtful analysis about the effects of institutional systems and practices, both positive and negative, intentional and unintentional (Ridley, 1995), on individuals and groups. Referring to the community college faculty (Case 2) described in the beginning of the chapter, we observed that some White senior faculty (see A and B dimensions of the Personal Identity Model) perhaps had little awareness of sociopolitical barriers such as anti-immigrant legislation (A and C dimen-

Figure 20.2

Dimensions of Personal Identity

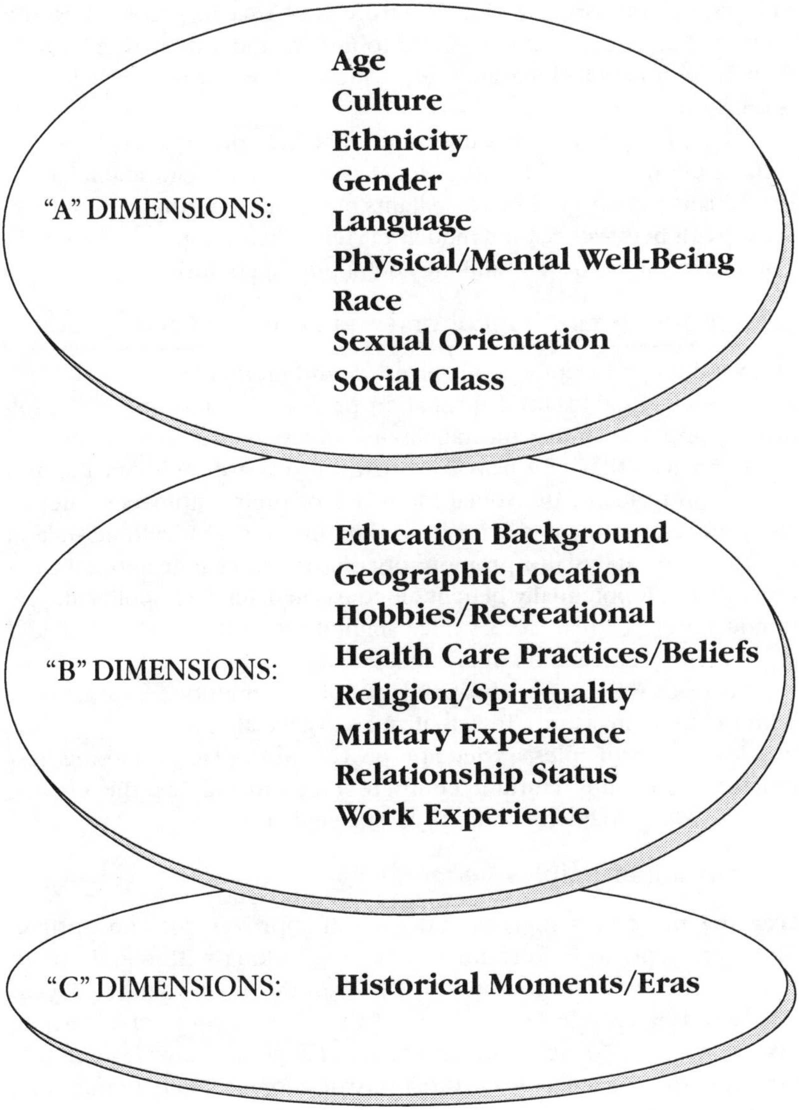
"A" DIMENSIONS:
Age
Culture
Ethnicity
Gender
Language
Physical/Mental Well-Being
Race
Sexual Orientation
Social Class
"B" DIMENSIONS:
Education Background
Geographic Location
Hobbies/Recreational
Health Care Practices/Beliefs
Religion/Spirituality
Military Experience
Relationship Status
Work Experience
"C" DIMENSIONS:
Historical Moments/Eras

© Arredondo & Glauner, 1992
Empowerment Workshops, Inc.

sions). We hypothesized how such personal characteristics of the White faculty may affect the enrollment and retention (B dimensions) of ethnic and linguistic minority students and faculty. I have posited that each White institution of higher education has its own profile of identity dimensions and organizational culture, and that in recognizing the dominant dimensions, it is possible to understand why particular individuals or groups feel marginalized within a WIHE or do not believe it is accessible.

Prior to applying multicultural counseling competencies and the Dimensions of Personal Identity Model as part of an organizational diversity initiative, counselors or consultants may want to further equip themselves with perspectives and models currently being applied with WIHE. This can help to broaden thinking and minimize confusion.

Premises About Multicultural and Diversity Consultation

My personal philosophy about diversity and multiculturalism in WIHE and in society guides my consultation practices. I subscribe to the following premises: Multiculturalism and diversity are facts of life, not trends or fads that will pass. All organizations are multicultural and diverse, in terms of the social identities of their employees, clients, and vendors; and there is diversity within diversity. Multiculturalism and diversity are catalysts to promote organizational change and development that will potentially benefit all constituencies. Sociopolitical, economic, and historical factors have shaped the culture of a WIHE and affect the implementation of its mission.

A serious WIHE diversity agenda requires a multidimensional plan with outcome measures. To actualize an organizational diversity initiative, learning principles, a tried and proven work plan promoting best practices, and multicultural competencies must guide the change process (APA, 2002; Arredondo, 1996; Sue et al., 1998).

Learning Principles

Learning principles suggest that for self-improvement and optimal functioning, organizations must be willing to look within and out, to become learners, and to apply this learning to their change process (Morgan, 1997; Senge, 1990). Some of the best practices of a learning organization are to "scan and anticipate change in the wider environment and to detect significant variations; develop an ability to question, challenge, and change operating norms and assumptions; and to allow a strategic direction and pattern of organization to emerge" (Morgan, 1997, p. 90).

For instance, the learning condition for White institutions of higher education is that there are new and potential constituencies reflecting national demographic changes and shortcomings within the existing WIHE systems and services to serve these constituencies. The resulting learning for WIHE leadership must consist of asserting and leading institutional change. According to multicultural counseling spokespersons (D'Andrea et al., 2001), the positive aspects of the multicultural movement far outweigh the negative aspects related to the diversification of the United States.

The Blueprint for Diversity Initiatives

The Blueprint (Arredondo, 1996) is a multiphase methodology for planning, implementing, and evaluating a WIHE diversity initiative (see Figure 1). The Blueprint design includes tasks applied in clinical work (e.g., data gathering, diagnosis, and treatment planning), making it a user-friendly tool for counselors who are consultants. It uses a developmental model (Arredondo, 1996; Arredondo et al., 1996) that includes the following developmental tasks:

- preparation for an initiative
- clarification of organizational motivators
- organizational self-study
- strategic planning based on measurable objectives
- implementation of strategies and techniques
- evaluation of objectives and particular strategies

When following the Blueprint, multicultural counseling competencies are applied to assess a WIHE's cultural competencies. A few examples from my work with the three WIHE cases previously discussed are included here. The MCC statements are modified to refer to WIHE rather than the "culturally skilled counselor" (Sue et al., 1992).

Preparation.
During the preparation phase when consulting with the college of education, I collaborated with a diversity committee composed entirely of faculty. Their concern was the retention of faculty of color. Tenure-track faculty were leaving prior to completing the typical tenure review process, and several senior faculty of color, few in number, were being recruited successfully by other WIHE.

The first MCC domain refers to "awareness about attitudes and beliefs" and how these manifest in relationship to culturally different individuals and groups (Sue et al., 1992). In other words, this competency allows for discussion of worldviews and how these may vary cross-culturally for individuals within the same department. Prevailing beliefs of the college were articulated as individualism, self-reliance, publish versus perish work ethics, excellence in teaching, and professional service. Though the values applied to all faculty members, discussions revealed differences in expectations for faculty of color. For example, the junior faculty were typically not mentored. They arrived with little to no previous experience in academia and stepped into a multi-tasked role. As also occurs, faculty members of color are sought out to serve on various committees to ensure diversity representation, and by students of color, who seek role models and mentors. In WIHE, the latter tasks are generally not given the same weight in a formal faculty evaluation process as publications and teaching. Junior faculty of color who overinvest in student advisement and service are at risk, but without guidance and mentoring, they will not know this.

In this setting, senior faculty of color had proved themselves by achieving tenure but, as they often stated, at a cost. Some of these costs included having their research agendas challenged, receiving lower evaluations by students, lacking peer collegiality, and having to be better in all tasks than their White colleagues.

This preparation phase allowed me to gather quantifiable data with respect to engagement and retention of faculty and students of color, the prevailing cultural norms of the college and the university in which it was housed regarding cultural and linguistic pluralism, and other background data about the WIHE. In so doing, the following competency statements emerged and are recommended for application in this first phase. Multiculturally competent White institutions of higher education

- understand their prevailing worldview, how it is operationalized through standards, policies, and practices, and its differential effects for individuals of differing cultural backgrounds;
- recognize the strengths and limitations of past institutional experiences with groups not historically part of their mainstream White culture; and
- recognize the sociopolitical factors within the institution that distribute privilege and power differentially based on cultural heritage and gender.

Clarifying Motivators.
This task provided another opportunity for the college diversity committee to understand contextual reinforcements. The concern about

retaining and hiring faculty of color was not just one of racial and ethnic representation. The departure of previous faculty created an image and public relations problem. Students were upset; agencies and public schools that had collaborated with these faculty members wondered about future relationships with the college; and faculty of other departments across the university quietly questioned the dean's commitment to diversity. As the college prepared for new hiring plans, concerns were raised about how to attract potential faculty of color. What might be the social impact based on the recent track record?

Again, guiding competency statements emerged. Multiculturally competent White institutions of higher education

- recognize the social impact of their institutional image and practices on different constituencies;
- recognize the perceptions of their institution held by different cultural groups; and
- recognize that their motivators for promoting institutional diversity must include putting values expressed through mission statements to practice.

Organizational Self-Study.

All three White institutions of higher education engaged in an organizational climate self-study, utilizing various tools, to determine how systems, policies, and practices affected their constituencies. These included a survey, cultural audit, MCC inventory (unpublished documents), and focus groups.

At the Midwest counseling center, the MCC inventory revealed desirable areas for enhancing multicultural competence including more information about specific ethnic identity development theories, acculturative stress, and the use of non-English languages in therapy. Through the cultural audit, baseline data were gathered about institutional practices to promote (or not promote) diversity through public relations materials, hiring practices, the center's physical ambiance, and visible statements about the value of diversity and multiculturalism.

One of the MCC Explanatory Statements (Arredondo et al., 1996) reads, "can recognize and discuss examples in which racism or bias may actually be embedded in an institutional system or in society" (p. 71). To try to explore this competency guideline with the community colleges, faculty and staff completed the organizational climate survey. Findings indicated that women, regardless of status, were experiencing sexism; staff were feeling like second-class citizens, disrespected primarily by faculty; and both faculty and staff of color reported more mistrust, exclusion from program decision making, and primary responsibility for representing diversity issues on campus committees.

Self-studies are a key phase in the Blueprint methodology. Findings provide White institutions of higher education with necessary data to develop strategic plans with measurable objectives and various systemic interventions. The latter may include multicultural competency, diversity, and sexual harassment training, revisions to hiring and performance management plans, and other tangible practices that can promote a diversity initiative and, simultaneously, multicultural competence.

Additional Competencies to Guide
WIHE Multicultural Competence

Beyond the recommended MCC, there are additional methods that can be drawn from the existing documents (APA, 2002; Arredondo et al., 1996; Sue et al., 1992). A few have been adapted to guide organizational multicultural competency development.

Multiculturally competent White institutions of higher education

- are able to exercise institutional intervention skills on behalf of all members of their campus community (employees, students, and clients). They can help individuals determine whether a problem stems from racism or bias in others so that victims of racism do not inappropriately personalize problems (Arredondo et al., 1996, p. 71);
- develop community-based relationships with organizations that can serve as partners and resources in promoting a diversity initiative;
- are familiar with sociopolitical influences that impinge on the life of racial and ethnic minorities, including racial profiling, anti-immigration and bilingual education legislation, and other forms of institutional racism within a WIHE (Ridley, 1995); and
- recognize that sexism, classism, homophobia, and disability insensitivity undermine respect and inclusion of all members of the campus community.

Conclusion

Consultation with different colleges and universities continues to indicate the necessity of a systemic approach to plan and implement organizational change driven by diversity and multicultural considerations. I believe there are many opportunities for counselors to play a central role in change efforts and hope that this chapter sparks interest and activity to do so.

References

American Council on Education and American Association of University Professors. (2000). *Does diversity make a difference? Three research studies on diversity in college classrooms.* Washington, DC: Author.

American Psychological Association. (2002). *Guidelines on multicultural education, training, research, practice, and organizational change for psychologists.* Washington, DC: Author.

Arredondo, P. (1996). *Successful diversity management initiatives.* Thousand Oaks, CA: Sage.

Arredondo, P. (1999). Multicultural counseling competencies as tools to address oppression and racism. *Journal of Multicultural Counseling and Development, 77,* 102-108.

Arredondo, P., & Arciniega, M. (2001). Strategies and techniques for counselor training based on the multicultural counseling competencies. *Journal of Multicultural Counseling and Development, 29,* 264-272.

Arredondo, P., & Glauner, T. (1992). *Personal dimensions of identity model.* Boston: Empowerment Workshops.

Arredondo, P., Toporek, R., Brown, S. B., Jones, J., Locke, D. C., Sanchez, J., & Stadler, H. (1996). Operationalization of the multicultural counseling competencies. *Journal of Multicultural Counseling and Development, 24,* 42-78.

Chang, M., Witt, D., Jones, J., & Hakuta, K. (Eds.). (2000). *Compelling interest. Examining the evidence on racial dynamics in higher education.* Report of the American Educational Research Association (AERA) Panel on Racial Dynamics in Colleges and Universities. Palo Alto, CA: Stanford University.

D'Andrea, M., Daniels, J., Arredondo, P., Ivey, M. B., Ivey, A. E., Locke, D. C., O'Bryant, B., Parham, T. A., & Sue, D. W. (2001). Fostering organizational changes to realize the revolutionary potential of the multicultural movement. In J. G. Ponterotto, J. M. Casas, L. A. Suzuki, & C. M. Alexander (Eds.), *Handbook of multicultural counseling* (2nd ed., pp. 222-253). Thousand Oaks, CA: Sage.

Grieger, I., & Toliver, S. (2001). Multiculturalism on predominantly White campuses. In J. G. Ponterotto, J. M. Casas, L. A. Suzuki, & C. M. Alexander (Eds.), *Handbook of multicultural counseling* (2nd ed., pp. 825-845). Thousand Oaks, CA: Sage.

Judy, R. W., & D'Amico, C. (1997). *Workforce 2020.* Indianapolis, IN: Hudson Institute.

Morgan, G. (1997). *Images of organization.* Thousand Oaks, CA: Sage.

Ridley, C. R. (1995). *Overcoming unintentional racism in counseling and therapy.* Thousand Oaks, CA: Sage.

Robbenolt, J. K., & Walker, J. C. (2001). Challenges to affirmative action in university admissions: The role of social science. *Monitor on Psychology, 32,* 20.

Senge, P. M. (1990). *The fifth discipline*. New York: Doubleday.

Sue, D.W. (2001). Multidimensional facets of cultural competence. *The Counseling Psychologist, 29*, 790–821.

Sue, D. W., Arredondo, P., & McDavis, R. (1992). Multicultural counseling competencies: A call to the profession. *Journal of Counseling & Development, 70*, 477–483.

Sue, D. W., Carter, R. T., Casas, J. M., Fouad, N. A., Ivey, A. E., Jensen, M., LaFromboise, T., Manese, J. E., Ponterotto, J. G., & Vazquez-Nutall, E. (1998). *Multicultural counseling competencies: Individual and organizational development.* Thousand Oaks, CA: Sage.

U. S. Census Bureau. (2000). *2000 Census.* Washington, DC: U.S. Department of Commerce.

Chapter 21

Multicultural Practices in Historically Black Institutions: The Case of Lincoln University

Queen Dunlap Fowler

Lincoln University in Missouri, as a historically Black institution, illustrates the characteristics of an institution devoted to cultural diversity. Its services, activities, resources, curriculum, library, and student organizations demonstrate multifaceted programs creating a multicultural environment. This multifaceted approach provides students repeated exposure to cultural diversity in many environments and from many sources. Thus multiculturalism is not simply one course, an isolated assignment, a discussion, or a lecture within a course, but a university's mission or policy-driven commitment that makes it possible for various service programs, administrative units, and academic departments to create a multicultural environment on campus that includes the recruitment and retention of a diverse faculty and student body.

Creating a multicultural environment in schools, college campuses, and other educational institutions, including those that are predominantly Black, is a high priority for public and private education in the United States. The increasing cultural diversity in the current student body points to the need for institutional commitment to a multicultural environment. The incentive for addressing multiculturalism includes many factors, such as economic development, state and governmental funding and regulations, and societal changes including in values and cross-cultural affiliations. Identifying practices at historically Black colleges and universities (HBCUs) illustrates the characteristics that HBCUs have adopted to fulfill their multicultural commitment. Lincoln University, an HBCU in Jefferson City, Missouri, is profiled as an example of one such institution.

Lincoln University's mission statement has served as the catalyst for achieving racial diversity. Lincoln is the only 4-year state institution in Missouri to have achieved significant diversity in its student enrollment, and serves as a multicultural institutional model. This success, however, has created a paradox and has implications for the future of Lincoln University and HBCUs across the nation. Lincoln is 1 out of 4 of over 100 HBCUs where a majority of students are White. Because White students now constitute the majority, the university is at a crossroad with regard to its mission. Can Lincoln University maintain its traditional HBCU designation if the majority of its students are White? This phenomenon requires further study and open discussion by political and education leaders.

Lincoln University is a historically Black institution that began as Lincoln Institute in 1866. During the Civil War, Black soldiers were taught to read and write by White officers, such as Lt. Richard Baxter Foster. After the war, the soldiers of the 62nd and 65th "colored" infantries discussed ways of continuing their education. Most of these Black soldiers came from Missouri, and the goal established was to create a school in Missouri for "the special benefit of freed African Americans" (Lincoln University, 2000–2001, p. 11). Through contributions from these soldiers and other philanthropists, money was raised to establish Lincoln Institute (Savage, 1939).

The initial years were financially difficult. In 1879, Lincoln officially became a state-supported institution when the school's property was deeded to the State of Missouri. Thus Lincoln became the first land grant institution in the nation in 1890. Lincoln Institute became Lincoln University in 1921 through a bill introduced by Walthall Moore, the first African American to serve in the Missouri legislature.

During its 135-year history, Lincoln has supported a number of educational opportunities for students, including for many years the Laboratory High School and Elementary School. During the 1940s, the only school of law in Missouri accepting African American students was at Lincoln. Lincoln also provided a school of journalism (Marshall, 1966).

In 1954, the United States Supreme Court handed down the ruling in *Brown v. Board of Education*, and Lincoln University responded by opening its doors to all applicants who met its entrance criteria. During this period, Missouri artist Thomas Hart Benton painted a mural depicting the history of Lincoln, which hangs in Page Library (Holland, 1991).

Today, Lincoln University maintains its open enrollment policy, providing an education to the widest range of people possible. Lincoln University has undergraduate programs as well as graduate programs. As a

244

continuation of its land grant status, Lincoln conducts research in agriculture and provides cooperative extension services. It has both residential and nonresidential students and international students.

Multicultural Environment at Lincoln University

From its inception, Lincoln Institute was diverse, with its first principal, Lt. Richard Baxter Foster, being White and the men of the 62nd and 65th colored infantries being Black and newly freed slaves. Their diverse composition prevented them from using both the local White church and the local colored church (Savage, 1939). Later the faculty and administrators of Lincoln represented additional diversity through the hiring of both Whites and Blacks. In 1868, Superintendent T. W. Parker recommended that Lincoln be designated as a school to train colored teachers for the State of Missouri (Savage, 1939). In 1870, W. H. Payne became the first Black principal hired to lead Lincoln Institute. The American Missionary Society previously paid his salary and continued to do this after he was hired at Lincoln.

After the *Brown v. Board of Education* decision in 1954, 18 White students were admitted. Later that number doubled, and 3 years later, White students outnumbered Black students. White students came in large numbers to attend the school that was close to home and very reasonably priced. The cost to attend Lincoln was only $750, compared to $1,300 at the University of Missouri ("The School That," 1958). Students were also attracted to the school's other features: small classes, intimate instruction, and a wide range of educational programs, including day and evening courses and education at the graduate, undergraduate, high school, elementary, and nursery school levels. White students mixed freely with Black students in the cafeteria, library, band, football team, choirs, and theatric productions. It was reported in *Ebony* that one White student said, "I know several of my friends who were prejudiced and a little hesitant about going to Lincoln. Some of them went and learned two lessons, one from books and one from people" ("The School That," 1958, p. 20). Elaine Abers, a wife and mother of four children, was one of the first Whites to graduate from Lincoln. She did so in a record time of 3 years, and with a grade point average that made her the class valedictorian of 1957. Also noted in *Ebony* was that "the only Negro in a classroom at Lincoln was [the] professor...." (p. 18).

According to the 2000–2001 annual report, 1,079 Black and 2,012 White students attended Lincoln. There were 29 Hispanic/Latino, 14 Native American, 20 Asian or Pacific Island, and 167 nonresident international students, as well as 26 students of other origins. Thus the student body was made up of 3,347 racially diverse students (Lincoln University, 2000-2001).

Multicultural Learning Opportunities

Today, Lincoln University makes multicultural learning a priority. As stated in its latest bulletin, Lincoln University's vision is to be "a premier, historically Black, land-grant open admissions university . . . where social and cultural diversity are an integral part of student-centered learning" (Lincoln University, 2000-2001, p. 13). This vision is implemented through required classes in the general education program as well as through elective classes for more focused study. In compliance with state regulations, the university requires all students to take a general cultural diversity class. To further enhance this goal, there is an institutional requirement that all students take a course focusing on international cultural diversity. Students applying for the bachelor of arts degree are required to complete 12 hours of foreign language. Focused study is also available in African American culture. Students may choose to minor in Black studies. This minor immerses students in African American culture through study of its history, literature, art, and music (Lincoln University, 2000-2001). Furthermore, it exposes students to a broader understanding of the global Black experience through the study of the cultures in Africa, the Caribbean, and other countries with Black societies.

The Lincoln University Cooperative Extension (LUCE) Program addresses the needs of diverse constituencies, with an emphasis on critically underserved populations, by helping to improve their physical, social, economic, and environmental conditions. Extension specialists share the benefits of scientific research through education programs that they have designed and implemented for their target clientele (Lincoln University, 2000-2001).

Campus Programs

The university provides programs to assist students with their learning. One of these is the Student Success Program that is designed especially to embrace the open admission policy of the university. This uniquely designed program allows for students who are admitted under an academic probationary contract. According to the Office of Student Retention (2001), the program is structured in a manner to help less-prepared students to adjust to the rigors of college and to become connected with their new university family. Prospective students seeking admission to the university who have a low ACT score and less than a 2.00 cumulative high school grade point average are given an opportunity to be admitted to Lincoln University, upon a favorable recommendation from a high school counselor. These students sign a probationary contract before admission to the university is granted.

Student Support Services (SSS), another program, is a federally funded program designed to serve low-income students, first-generation college students, and students with disabilities. The program helps students to remain in college until they earn their bachelor degrees. SSS at Lincoln University has made a strong, positive impact upon the lives of many students. After almost 12 years of service, it has helped approximately 274 participants graduate from the university. Services such as tutoring, secondary school academic advisement, peer counseling, the College Survival Lecture series, and career and cultural explorations successfully retain students each year.

The Third Annual Summer Enrichment Academy was held on campus June 11–July 8, 2000. Twenty-five high school students from St. Louis, Kansas City, Jefferson City, and the Bootheel resided on campus for 4 weeks of intensive, integrated learning experiences that focused on academic and out-of-classroom activities. Four of the 25 participants enrolled as full-time students in the university in fall 2000 (Lincoln University, 2000–2001).

Cultural Education Resources

The university offers a number of resources that support multicultural learning. The Lincoln University Library, in the Ethnic Studies Center/Archives, is host and home to a number of multicultural exhibits and events. Exhibit pieces are displayed throughout the center from various cultures, including Native American, Korean, African, Egyptian, German, and Jewish. One collection of note is the Challie King Collection of African artifacts, which is often used as the display in the primary exhibit case of the library. Exhibits of Native American pottery and African jewelry and artifacts are on display outside the center. The Ethnic Studies Reading Room, a conference room, is decorated with an African carving, African mud cloth, a lithograph series on U.S. civil rights leaders, busts of Frederick Douglass and George Washington Carver, and many paintings depicting the history of Lincoln University.

Paintings by African American artists depicting African American themes are on display throughout the library. In addition, on the first floor, a mural painted by the Missouri artist Thomas Hart Benton tells the story of Lincoln University's beginnings. The library staff utilizes these paintings when groups come to tour the library. People of all ages, as well as Lincoln students, learn here the university's history and are exposed to a multicultural climate. The librarians dressed in cultural costumes for a recent open house to inform the faculty about the resources in the library.

The library staff also works in the community to promote multicultural themes. On one occasion, displays were prepared and staffed by the library personnel at the Juneteenth Celebration and at a Jefferson City multicultural festival. Members of the library staff narrate ethnic stories to children who visit the library or attend multicultural festivals in the community.

The library prioritizes funds to purchase multicultural books. These are cataloged under headings with various ethnic descriptions and placed in a special area of the stacks next to the Ethnic Studies Center. Special emphasis is placed on books by and about African Americans. These are labeled as Black bibliography books and also housed in the stacks outside the Ethnic Studies Center.

The Agriculture and Extension Information Center houses videos on topics related to the university's land grant status as well as videos on cultural diversity (Lincoln University, 2000–2001). The Office of Retention facilitates organizations and activities to encourage international students to remain at the university. This includes the International Students Association, which meets weekly to discuss issues of interest to international students. Activities are organized for the National Week of International Awareness, including a panel discussion on stereotypes, myths, and misperceptions; multicultural music and food at the student cafeteria; all sports appreciation day; and a day of international fashion.

The university is involved in providing culturally diverse programs to the central Missouri community, such as the "Share in the Arts" series of nine programs during the year. Prominent artists, musicians, and speakers are featured in the Richardson Fine Arts Center. The President's Concert is held in the spring with nationally known musicians presenting classical, spiritual, and gospel renditions. Lincoln University's music department is also involved in concerts throughout the year. The diversity in their music selections is one of the most attractive aspects of their programming. The work of American and international musicians is featured, as are jazz and classical music, Negro spirituals, and traditional American fare.

The Lincoln University Dance Troupe is a vital part of the Department of Health and Physical Education. The troupe is a modern jazz company with a repertoire that includes ballet, ethnic, street, and lyrical dance forms. Musical selections for the group vary from spiritual and classical to contemporary and popular. Membership is open to all enrolled students who meet audition requirements established by the artistic director. The Dance Troupe provides cultural entertainment to the Lincoln University community, gives opportunities for creative expression, shares in the training of dance specialists, and assists the university's recruitment program for the university by performing at high schools both in and out of state (Lincoln University, 2000–2001).

Financial Resources

The Department of Student Financial Aid has as a fundamental purpose offering a diverse financial aid program that affords equal opportunity to qualified students who want to attend Lincoln University. Lincoln University's student default rate for tuition payment is 12%, well below the national average of 23% at many HBCUs (Burd, 2001). Lincoln University provides a program of one-on-one counseling to assist students in budgeting, saving, and spending their financial aid packages in the most economically feasible manner possible. Students are also taught how to use their finances in their University Seminar General Education 101 class. Every student has to do a budget in this class. Financial care enables students to succeed and is one of the most nurturing aspects of Lincoln University.

Student Organizations

Lincoln University supports student organizations that promote cultural diversity on campus. Barrier Breakers is one such organization specifically devoted to heightening awareness of multicultural issues. Membership in Barrier Breakers is open to faculty, staff, students, parents, and interested community members. The organization puts on monthly programs relating to diversity on campus and in the community. These may involve invited speakers, panel discussions, and round tables. For example, one invited speaker spoke on his experiences as a survivor of the Japanese concentration camps and of racism, which listeners could relate to current forms of societal racism. The topics of other invited speakers have included interracial relationships and biracial persons, the language of Mark Twain's novels, the experience of international students on campus, and homophobia. An annual coffeehouse is held by Barrier Breakers, at which campus members display artwork and put on other presentations. Discussion is facilitated and encouraged (Pat Pollock, personal communication, November 16, 2001).

There are eight Greek organizations on campus. Alpha Kappa Alpha and Delta Sigma Theta sororities were established in 1930, and Alpha Phi Alpha and Omega Psi Phi fraternities were established in 1936. A Sigma Gamma Rho sorority chapter was established in 1936. Phi Beta Sigma was the last sorority to be established on campus, in the fall of 1949; Zeta Phi Beta was the last fraternity to be established, in 1950. These are all historically Black fraternities and sororities, although they have been integrated on some campuses. In Lincoln University, these sororities remain culturally and socially diverse in their projects on campus and in the community. They are nationally recognized; membership can transfer when students leave Lincoln University; and there are also graduate chapters. Each fraternity and sorority has special initiation activities, music, and "steps" that are held at various times throughout the year, thus contributing to the diversity of Lincoln University and its culture.

As already indicated, Lincoln University of Missouri is one of the most ethnically diverse institutions of higher education in the United States. Data reveal that over the past 15 years Lincoln University's Statement of Mission and concentrated efforts to create a heterogeneous student body have succeeded. At the state level, data reveal that by 1998 Lincoln University stood out as the only institution in Missouri to have achieved a measure of racial diversity in student head count. White students comprise the overwhelming majority of students in 11 of 13 public institutions in Missouri. Black students comprise 6% of the total students enrolled in 4-year public institutions of higher education. One historically Black college in St. Louis (Harris Stowe State College) has a 79% Black student population. Thus with the exception of Lincoln University, Missouri institutions remain essentially either White or Black.

Perspectives on Other Historically Black Colleges and Universities

The techniques profiled here that Lincoln University utilizes have been used by other HBCUs. Ohio Dominican College in Columbus, Ohio, has been working on improving its multicultural education program since 1980 (Carroll & Matesich, 1993). Its methods include celebrating minority contributions to science and culture by recognizing significant minority scholarly achievement each year and by promoting the interaction of its own faculty with faculty from other universities with expertise in multiculturalism and in HBCUs. Walker, Bandele, and Mellion (1998) of Southern University and A&M College in Baton Rouge, Louisiana, have recommended that the agricultural programs at HBCUs

250

be used for multicultural opportunities. These include providing books and curriculum materials that discuss African American achievements in agriculture, promoting a series of Black history videos, and providing multimedia presentations. In a paper presented at an annual meeting of the American Educational Research Association, Charles Carter (1998) emphasized the need to recognize multicultural education as an "additive process" that occurs throughout the student's experiences at the university (p. 3).

Berg-Cross, Craig, and Wessel (2001) have proposed four guidelines that might be applied to HBCUs and predominantly White institutions (PWIs): having a comprehensive review of courses in which diversity issues are addressed; curriculum changes being grounded in the larger mission or diversity statements of the university; utilizing coalitions and student involvement; and setting forth explicit diversity goals in classes. However, professional programs, such as the business school at an HBCU, Howard University, and those in a PWI school, Stanford, might assume that multicultural issues are less apparent in their work. In these programs there is a lack of courses with a multicultural emphasis, and multicultural issues are not integrated into the curriculum (Berg-Cross et al., 2001). Nevertheless, at both these universities, multiculturalism is a significant part of the graduate programs in history, English, and the social sciences (Berg-Cross et al., 2001).

Howard University has 1,245 full- and part-time faculty, 36% of whom are females. Out of 1,036 full-time faculty, 61% are Black; 16% are White; 1% each are Asian, Hispanic, and Native American; and 12% are recorded as unclassifiable. Howard has the largest number of Black scholars and perhaps the most diverse community of scholars in the world. Faculty members of color have found working in Howard's environment rewarding (Berg-Cross et al., 2001). National statistics indicate that 12% of full-time faculty members are minorities, of whom 9.2% are people of color, and faculty members of color report that they "experience exclusion, isolation, alienation, and racism" (Berg-Cross et al., 2001, p. 858).

Many African Americans with PhDs decide to teach at PWIs due to better compensation and working conditions. Because HBCUs are perceived as exclusively African American, it is hard to get funds from other ethnic groups and from those wanting to promote multiculturalism. Donors who want to give money to promote multiculturalism often give it to PWIs, perhaps assuming that it is best spent there as multiculturalism is more of a concern in PWIs. Howard University, however, has an advantage because it has a large number of international alumni and faculty, and thus receives funding from international sources (Berg-Cross et al., 2001).

In many institutions, mental health treatment is stigmatized, which often keeps students from seeking mental health services. This is especially true with African Americans. Howard University's counseling center has made a number of efforts to decrease the stigma associated with seeking out mental health services. Acknowledging that African Americans are often group-centered, and that efforts should be made to include the group modality when working with them, the counseling center at Howard has developed a number of group services and outreach, both supportive and therapeutic. Because a number of diversity themes can be played out in the group setting (Berg-Cross et al., 2001), HBCUs are in a unique position to offer training opportunities in multicultural counseling.

Conclusion

Due to the unique mission of HBCUs, they have the opportunity to be centers in which multicultural issues can be brought to the forefront. HBCUs have the opportunity to become premier institutions in terms of bringing a large group of diverse students together in a place where their needs are recognized, and of providing an education that pays attention to diverse backgrounds and contributions of culture. Regardless of the variation of approaches and distinctions of cultural pluralism, the end product should be to make ethnic diversity and cultural pluralism better understood as integral parts of the educational process. Additionally, identifying practices in similar (e.g., other HBCUs) and different institutional (PWIs) settings may determine whether results are positive or at least workable in a predominantly Black institution.

References

Berg-Cross, L., Craig, K., & Wessel, T. (2001). Multiculturalism at historically Black colleges and universities. A case study of Howard University. In J. G. Ponterotto, J. M. Casas, L. A. Suzuki, & C. M. Alexander (Eds.), *Handbook of multicultural counseling* (2nd ed., pp. 849–868). Thousand Oaks. CA: Sage.

Burd, S. (2001, October–December). Rift emerges over independence of federal financial aid office. *Chronicle of Higher Education, 48*(7), p. A271.

Carroll, W. J., & Matesich, M. A. (1993). *Diversity and the urban campus: The Ohio Dominican response.* (ERIC Document Reproduction Service No. ED 358 215)

Carter, C. (1998). *The moccasin on the other foot dilemma: Multicultural strategies at a historically Black college.* (ERIC Document Reproduction Service No. ED 421 057)

Holland, A. F., with Roberts, T. R., & White, D. (1991). *The soldiers' dream continued: A pictorial history of Lincoln University of Missouri.* Jefferson City, MO: Lincoln University.

Lincoln University. (2000-2001). *2001-2003 Undergraduate bulletin.* Jefferson City, MO: Author.

Marshall, A. P. (1966). *Soldiers' dream: A centennial history of Lincoln University of Missouri.* Jefferson City, MO: Lincoln University.

Office of Student Retention of Lincoln University. (2001). *Student success program* [Brochure]. Jefferson City, MO: Author.

Savage, W. S. (1939). *History of Lincoln University.* Jefferson City, MO: Lincoln University.

The school that was too good to die. (1958). *Ebony, 13,* 17-24.

Walker, C., Bandele, O., & Mellion, D. (1998). *Multicultural education: Ways to utilize the historically Black land grant agricultural programs.* (ERIC Document Reproduction Service No. ED 427 097)

Note. A special thanks is extended to Elizabeth Wilson, director of Iman E. Page Library, Lincoln University, for her collaboration, editing, and staff assistance with this effort; to Mary Heady, archivist; Sharon Proctor, information technologist/assistant to the librarian; and to E. F. Braun, library assistant, for their assistance with the research and other supportive resources for the completion of this chapter.

Chapter 22

Multiculturalism in the Military

Jim Henderson

Multiculturalism in the military can be characterized as an ongoing process that is constantly under improvement. This chapter outlines through a historical perspective how one segment of society has achieved some success in diversifying its population. It is obvious that this achievement has not come easily, nor did it happen overnight, nor is it complete. In fact, it has taken over 225 years to get to this point in the American military experience.

The military might be considered America's foremost example of diversity and multiculturalism. About 40% of the military are minorities and women. Military members embrace a value system based on integrity, honor, and performance. They also have a strong work ethic, an attitude of winning, and a can-do orientation.

The military is held in such high esteem because the military places a premium on unit cohesion and morale. Physical and moral courage, discipline, and a professional code of conduct are strongly valued, whereas these professional attributes are foreign to most civilian communities. In addition, the military has a separate justice system with unique requirements that do not exist in civilian life.

There have, of course, been many attempts to "civilianize" the military over the years. As far back as post World War II, a review board under General Jimmy Doolittle set out to change military life. Training was made less demanding and rigorous, military norms were softened and made more relative to civilian norms. However, as T.R. Fehrenbach (1998) wrote in his classic study of the Korean conflict, *This Kind of War*, "By the very nature of its missions, the military must maintain a hard and illiberal view of life and the world. Society's purpose is to live; the military's is to stand ready, if need be, to die" (p. 2). Therefore the military must be counted on to be prepared for this eventuality, so that the society it protects will survive (Mackubin, 1999).

African Americans in the Military

Early in 1945, the military had the foresight to see that in order to become a unified organization, to become one entity, the races must not be separated. Therefore, the then secretary of war, Robert P. Patterson, appointed a board of three general officers to investigate the Army's policy with respect to African Americans and to prepare a new policy providing for the efficient use of African Americans in the Army. This board, together with the President's Committee on Civil Rights, met during the years from 1945 to 1950 to determine how best to integrate the military services.

In January 1948, President Truman ended segregation in the armed forces and the civil service through administrative action (i.e., executive order) rather than through legislation. The Army, Marine Corps, and Navy refused to abide by the order immediately. However, by January 22, 1949, the Air Force completed plans for full integration of its units, and by June 7, 1949, the Navy accepted an integration plan for its units. By January 14, 1950, the Army approved an integration plan, and by October 1953, the Army announced that 95% of African American soldiers were serving in integrated units (Geselbracht, 1969). Thus integration continued from the end of 1940s through the early 1950s in the military.

In civilian society, Blacks nevertheless continued to experience discrimination. As Ulysses Hollimon, a baseball player with the Birmingham Black Barons in the Negro League, said,

> The military was integrating during the early 50s, and when I came back from Europe and the guys would go off base to get something to eat or go to the clubs, we all rode the same bus into town. When we got off of the bus the Blacks would go one way and the Whites would go another. When we headed back to the base we got back on the same bus together and went back to the base, and then out of sight of the general public, we were once again integrated. Segregation was still strong in the community while integration was a way of life in the military. (Hollimon, 2000, p. 1)

Women in the Military

President Clinton, on June 25, 1995, at the groundbreaking of the Women in Service of America Memorial, said

> Women have been in our service ... since George Washington's troops fought for independence, clothing and feeding our troops and binding their wounds. They were in the struggle to preserve the Union as cooks and tailors, couriers and scouts, even as spies and saboteurs. Some were so determined to fight for what they believed that they masqueraded as men and took up arms.

256

Women were also there during World Wars I and II, and our military establishment brought women into the ranks to serve, for example, in the Army as WACS (Women's Army Corps), in the Navy as WAVES (Women Accepted for Voluntary Emergency Service), in the Coast Guard as SPARS (Semper Paratus Always Ready–Women's Reserve), in the Air Force as WASPS (Women Air Force Service Pilots), and in the Marines (Women Marines). They worked in shipyards and factories, and they endured bombs, torpedoes, disease, and deprivation to support our fighting forces from the beaches of Normandy to the Pacific Islands.

Despite this history of bravery and accomplishment, women were too long treated as second class soldiers. They could give their lives for liberty, but they could not give orders to men. They could heal the wounded and hold the dying, but they could not hold the highest ranks. They could take on tough assignments, but they could not take up arms. Still they volunteered, fighting for freedom, fighting for the right to serve to the fullest of their potential. From conflict to conflict, from Korea to Vietnam to the Persian Gulf, women have overcome slowly the barriers to their full service to America (Defense Equal Opportunity Management Institute [DEOMI], 2001b).

Particularly since the 1970s, the role of women in the military has steadily increased. The most recent changes occurred between 1992 and 1994, when both legislative and policy changes expanded opportunities for women by opening more occupations and organizations to women. Congress has taken a keen interest in this process, and the congressional report for the Defense Authorization Act for fiscal year 1997 included as a special interest item a directive to the Secretary of Defense to evaluate the performance of the military services in integrating women into occupations previously closed to them. The report also asked for an assessment of the effects of this integration on readiness and morale.

Table 22.1 gives the percentage of positions that were open to women before and after 1993 (Harrell & Miller, 1997):

Table 22.1

Percentages of Positions Open to Women Before and After 1993

Service	Before April 1993 (%)	After Law and Policy Changes (%)
Army	61.0	67.2
Navy	61.0	91.2
Air Force	97.0	99.4
Marine Corps	33.0	72.0
Total	**67.4**	**80.2**

Careers for women in the military today tend to be concentrated in administration and supply areas. Women are underrepresented in tactical operations, in the areas that yield our general and flag officers. However, although women's representation in aviation remains low, it has risen recently. Aviation is a greatly valued career path, bringing rewards and career opportunities in the military as well as in the private sector. Achieving increased representation of women will largely depend on increasing their numbers in career-enhancing occupations. Overall, many women in the military feel that they have been treated fairly and that the equal opportunity climate is better in the military than in the private sector.

Asian Americans in the Military

Like other minority groups, Asian Americans have experienced exclusion. During World War II, most Asian Americans were not treated as American citizens. Japanese Americans, for example, were put in internment camps. Nevertheless, many Asian Americans fought for the United States during World War II, and Japanese American soldiers, who made up the 100th Battalion/44 Regimental Combat Team, played a major role in the war (Ryan, 2000).

Native Americans in the Military

Many Native American Indians served honorably during the United States' wars but fared no better than other minority group. The term *Native American* means citizens of the United States who are of American Indian, Alaska Native, or Native Hawaiian ancestry. Some Native Americans are members of federally recognized Indian tribes, others are not. Congress has enacted statutes that benefit Native Americans generally and other statutes that benefit specific groups of Native Americans—members of federally recognized Indian tribes or Alaska Natives.

Homosexuality in the Military

In 1993, amidst allegations that homosexual military servicemen and -women were being singled out for investigation and harassment, Defense Secretary William Cohen announced a 3-month review of military policy toward homosexuals. Since 1993, the Pentagon has had a "don't ask, don't tell" policy, meaning the Defense Department says it will not ask about members' sexual preference, and homosexual members are told not to discuss their sexuality. However, since the policy went into effect, the number of discharges for homosexuality in all the services has gone up over 80%. In 1998, 1,149 cases were reported, compared to 597 in 1994. The policy was a compromise between President Clinton, who had advocated allowing homosexuals to serve openly, and Congress, which had passed a law saying it is illegal for gays in the military to discuss their sexuality (MacNeil-Lehrer, 2000).

Defense Equal Opportunity Management Institute (DEOMI)

Propelled by the Civil Rights Movement of the 1960s and to counteract a national policy of segregation and inequality, a virtual Magna Carta for race relations training was issued in 1971 in the military. The violent and nonviolent disorders of the late 1960s were the catalyst that convinced military leaders that race relations education must be provided to every member of the Armed Forces.

An interservice task force examined the causes and possible cures of poor race relations within the military. The task force, chaired by Air Force Major General Lucius Theus, brought out Department of Defense Directive 1322.11. This directive established the Race Relations Education Board and, in 1971, created the Defense Race Relations Institute (DRRI), whose mission was "to enhance leadership and readiness by fostering Equal Opportunity (EO) and Equal Employment Opportunity (EEO) programs and positive human relations through world class education, training, and research" (DEOMI, 2001a).

Since then the Institute has expanded to meet the needs of field commanders and agency heads. As a result, the Institute now addresses a wide array of issues that include sexual harassment, sexism, extremism, religious accommodations, and anti-Semitism. To reflect this new growth, the Institute's name was changed in 1979 to the Defense Equal Opportunity Management Institute (DEOMI 2001a).

Conclusion

Multiculturalism in the military can be characterized as a continuing project in action. Black Americans might experience covert racial prejudice, such as in promotions to the higher ranks. Women have progressed significantly in promotions and have been accepted into career areas previously denied to them. As in the civilian population, Asian Americans and Native American Indians tend to assimilate well in military life.

Homosexuals, regardless of their race, can simply retain their sexual orientation as a private matter.

The military is an example of how organizations might develop multiculturally.

References

Defense Equal Opportunity Management Institute (DEOMI). (2001a). *DEOMI history*. Retrieved November 7, 2001, from http://www.patrick.deomi/deomi.htm

Defense Equal Opportunity Management Institute (DEOMI). (2001b). *Women's History Month 2001*. Retrieved November 7, 2001, from http://www.patrick.deomi/deomi.htm

Fehrenbach, T. R. (1998). *This kind of war: The classic Korean War history*. Dulles, VA: Brasseys, Inc.

Geselbracht, R. (1969). *The Truman administration, and the desegregation of the Armed Forces*. Retrieved June 6, 2001, from http://wwwtrumanlibrary.org/deseg1.htm

Harrell, M. C., & Miller, R. (1997). *New opportunities for military women, effects upon readiness, cohesion, and morale*. Retrieved November 7, 2001, from http://www.ran.org/publications/MR/MR896

Hollimon, U. (2000). *True baseball*. Retrieved June 6, 2001, from http://www.truebaseball.com/hd.htm

Mackubin, T. O. (1999). *The military: What is it good for?* Retrieved February 27, 2001, from http://www.IntellectualCapitol.com

MacNeil-Lehrer. (2001). *Gays in the military*. Retrieved November 7, 2001, from http://www.pbs.org/ne...forum/january00/gays_military.html

Ryan, F. (2000) *Japanese-Americans in the military*. Retrieved November 7, 2001, from http://www.fatherryan.org/hcompsci/ms.htm

Afterword

The Competent Practice of Multicultural Counseling: Making It Happen

Judy Lewis

A s this book, *MCC Guidebook*, so aptly demonstrates, the effective practice of multicultural counseling can be infused into every one of the settings and specialties of our profession, from school setting, to private mental health counseling, to employment counseling, to college counseling centers, to organizational consultation, to graduate training programs, to community outreach, to family counseling, to group counseling, to Internet services, to social justice work, and so on. The diverse authors who have come together in this publication possess the knowledge, awareness, and skills that underlie multicultural competence. Their descriptions of successful interventions provide conclusive proof that the multicultural perspective is not only theoretically sound but also practical, not only right but also necessary. Undoubtedly, multiculturalism is at the heart of everything we do as counselors and as counselor educators.

Common Themes

The strategies and settings described in each of the chapters are distinctive. Yet we can find commonalities that help to shed new light on the practice of multicultural counseling. I noticed several common themes running through the previous chapters. Among these themes are

- the importance of creating safe places for multicultural exploration,
- the need for authentic commitment to multiculturalism among people in leadership and policy-making positions,
- the value of interactions and personal connections across difference,
- the usefulness of strategies built on active outreach,

- the acceptance of a collectivistic orientation, and
- the connection between multiculturalism and social/political advocacy.

Safe Places

Pedersen, in his chapter on the use of simulations for developing multicultural competence, says that he tries to create a "safe space to ask dangerous questions." Many other authors also describe the use of safe places when asking dangerous questions, such as exploring one's White racial attitudes, as in the training activities of Sandhu and Looby; analyzing whether to be outed or not, as Rooney and Liu address in employment counseling; or discussing multiculturalism with an all-White administration and faculty, as in the case of Arredondo. Creating safety and trust while having difficult dialogs is central to multiculturalism, as is creating an environment in which clients from oppressed groups feel secure enough to engage in the counseling process.

Fukuyama and Delgado-Romero, for instance, describe their university counseling center's Brown Bag Diversity Lunch Series, in which undergraduates and staff have conversations about such topics as gender-bending and sex roles, class, spirituality, racism, multiple cultural identities, and transgender identity. McLean, in his chapter on Black gay shame, talks about providing a safe space that is affirming and nonjudgmental, allowing clients to address shame issues and to move toward healing. Hogan, in her chapter on multicultural school counseling, emphasizes the importance of making the school a safe place for diversity of all kinds. Frey, a White mental health counselor, creates a safe place for a sexually abused adolescent in foster care and who disidentifies with his Native American culture. The creation of the safe space may well be a necessary component underlying all multicultural practice, whether in counseling, education, training, or consultation.

Authentic Commitment

Authentic commitment to multiculturalism is another key component at the core of effective practice. Consider, for instance, the higher education settings described by Fukuyama and Delgado-Romero and by Kwan and Taub. Fukuyama and Delgado-Romero emphasize the fact that conscious efforts at multicultural development are as important for trainers as they are for trainees and write about the inclusion of such programs as "race and gender in supervision" as part of ongoing staff development. They also stress the importance of paying attention to multicultural competence and membership in underrepresented groups when hiring new counseling center staff. Kwan and Taub say that "the commitment to multicultural competence on the part of a training program must be clear and explicit." They too emphasize hiring practices, stating that multicultural competencies should be explicitly listed as a central component in the selection and evaluation of candidates, especially at high administrative levels. Arredondo's description of her extensive consultation on multicultural organizational development reveals her commitment to and energetic advocacy in changing White institutions of higher learning.

Interactions and Connections

Roysircar, with the assistance of Webster, Germer, Palensky, Lynne, Campbell, Yang, Liu, and Blodgett-McDeavitt, points out in the first chapter of this book that experience contributes to multicultural competence and that "it is ideal to get out of the classroom and into multicultural interactions in order to experience the issues of race, ethnicity, culture, class, power, and privilege as part of everyday reality." Similarly, Santiago-Rivera and Moody write in their chapter on mentoring toward the development of multicultural competence that "while one can become exposed to information and specific strategies through a mentor, ultimately real learning takes place by doing (i.e., interacting with people from culturally diverse backgrounds)." Counselors who make these kinds of connections as part of their everyday lives are the ones who are most likely to be able to follow McLean's suggestion that we choose those treatment modalities that are most sensitive to the needs of the clients we serve (in his example, the use of cognitive-behavior techniques to help deconstruct shame experienced by Black gay men). Roysircar and her colleagues, in their analysis of counselor trainee process, describe the psychological attributes of the personal connection/alliance counselors make in their multicultural community outreach.

Outreach

It is, of course, important for counselors to develop the kinds of connections that can help them develop and maintain multicultural competence. Reaching out into the environment is also important for another purpose: providing a welcoming atmosphere that encourages clients to make use of counseling services. Whether because of distrust or cultural conventions, individuals who are part of oppressed groups are often hesitant to seek counseling on their own. Virtually all of the authors in this book describe methods they have used to make counseling services accessible and inviting. Fukuyama and Delgado-Romero, for instance, describe the walk-in clinics, support groups, and outreach workshops that they devised to respond to the needs and interests of culturally diverse students. Kwan and Taub sponsor and mobilize support groups that provide an outlet for non-White students to explore their reaction to prolonged experiences of racism. McLean writes about the importance of counselors being active and visible in the communities they serve.

Collectivist Orientation

Sensitivity to the values of the communities within which they work requires that counselors try to become comfortable with a collectivist orientation that may seem at odds with their own individualistic values. Inman and Tewari, in describing their work with South Asian families, point out that the collectivist orientation underlying many families' values must be understood and become a part of family-based interventions in individual counseling. Inman and Tewari, Madison-Colemore and Moore, and Frey describe the use of the cultural family genogram in their respective chapters. Frey, to ease the transition of her client from foster care and the process of cultural identity development in adolescence, involves older siblings in counseling as well as in guardianship and supervision roles with her client. Portman, in describing her approach to group work, also emphasizes the merit in incorporating collectivistic methods that are responsive to the worldviews of so many nonmajority cultural groups. Collectivism is inherent in the work of Santiago-Rivera and Moody as well. They suggest that counselor educators create learning environments that promote collectivism, including, for example, encouraging research teams as a means of promoting collaboration. Roysircar's seven co-authors were graduate students in her research team, who collaborated in the evaluation of training and participated in her experiential training as well. Thus her student coauthors were mentored in the participant–observer qualitative methodology considered suitable for multicultural enquiries.

Social/Political Advocacy

A final theme running through many of the chapters of this book regards the close connection between multicultural competency and social and political advocacy. As McLean writes, "competent multicultural counselors can be change agents for social justice in the community," attempting to eliminate the biases and discrimination that affect our clients. Santiago-Rivera and Moody also suggest that counselors and educators take advocacy roles in their communities, working on such issues as inequality in access to health care, exposure of low-income and minority communities to environmental contamination, and other effects of White privilege. They suggest, in fact, that a social justice perspective should be infused in all of our work. Specific examples of advocacy in action are provided by Fukuyama and Delgado-Romero, who describe their proactive approaches to working with the larger systems in their institution.

As Roysircar and her colleagues point out in the first chapter of this book, it is difficult and challenging to teach multicultural counseling and to practice it. Yet the models are there for us in the *MCC Guidebook* to see, choose, modify, and implement. Throughout this book, we have read about successes in counselor education: Faubert and Locke's delineation of the pedagogy of liberation; and Sandhu and Looby's process-oriented activities to increase counselor trainees' White racial identity development. We have read about successes in the practice of counseling across many settings: Frey's mental health counseling with a Native American adolescent referred to her by social service; and Avilés's step-by-step sociocultural assessment, which includes treatment as well as feedback from his Puerto Rican college client who reported academic difficulties and depression. The question we must face as a profession is how to infuse multiculturalism so thoroughly into every aspect of the counseling profession that proficient practice becomes commonplace, rather than exceptional. In reaching this goal, our professional associations have a major role to play.

Association Role

In order to be proficient in the practice of counseling in any specialty area, an individual must possess and apply a multicultural perspective. The idea that multiculturalism is central to effective practice must, therefore, be infused throughout every aspect of the counseling profession. Our professional associations can help to ensure that multiculturalism is recognized as central, not tangential, to everything we do as counselors only if they first move toward bringing multiculturalism to the center of the associations themselves.

In recent years, the American Counseling Association, with the help and guidance of the Association for Multicultural Counseling and Development, has taken steps toward infusing multiculturalism into its programs and activities. It is interesting to note that some of the same themes running through the chapters of this book are just as relevant to association work as they are to multicultural counseling. We can identify examples of attempts to create safe places for multicultural exploration, engender authentic commitment among members of leadership, generate interactions across difference, use outreach strategies, and become involved in social/political advocacy.

In 2001, the then-AMCD President Victor Bibbins led an experiential exercise on multiculturalism for the members of a council made up of ACA division presidents and region chairs. This exercise allowed participants to generate their own questions concerning multiculturalism and diversity and to discuss them in very small groups. Each small group then reported to the group as a whole. This type of workshop is notable for the provision of a structure that gives people the option to share what they wish of themselves and to explore questions that might be seen as risky in less secure environments. This experience provides just one example of the many training sessions in which the skills of AMCD leaders have been used to encourage and enhance multicultural exploration among members of the counseling profession.

The fact that this workshop was provided for the leaders of ACA's divisions and regions also points to a movement toward commitment to multiculturalism among association leaders. Multicultural and diversity training is mandated by ACA policy to take place at meetings of the association's Governing Council, and the talents of AMCD leaders are put to good use there also. Former AMCD presidents Bernal Baca and Thomas Parham provided Governing Council training in 2000 and 2001, respectively. A growing commitment to multiculturalism is also demonstrated by policies that require conference programs and other professional development offerings to address multicultural and diversity issues.

Leadership commitment also makes it more likely that interactions and personal connections across difference will take place in the organizational context. For example, the committee appointments made by each year's incoming ACA president are subject to review to ensure that all committees are diverse in their makeup. For the year 2001–2002, ACA President Jane Goodman selected as her theme *Unity Through Diversity*, indicating her desire to enhance interaction across differences of all kinds. In the previous year, *Celebrando el espiritu latino*, a series of programs celebrating Latino cultures, took place at the annual conference and included a Latino Town Meeting led by leaders of AMCD's Latino Interest Network.

These kinds of activities make it more likely that cross-cultural interactions will take place within the association context, but outreach to encourage participation by people of diverse cultures is needed as well. In 2001 and 2002, ACA reached out by implementing leadership training that was designed to increase the participation of people from groups currently underrepresented in leadership positions in ACA and its divisions.

The more participation we have from people of diverse cultures the more likely it is that we will become more open to a collectivist orientation. This phenomenon also makes it more likely that we will continue to advocate strongly for issues of social justice. In 2001, ACA's Governing Council passed a resolution stating that the association would work toward the elimination of stereotypical Native American images in schools and universities. The association's strategic plan calls for the inclusion of human rights issues as part of the public policy and legislation agenda each year.

All of these examples demonstrate that movement toward infusion of a multicultural perspective in our associations and in our practice of counseling is taking place. Although some people may believe that we have already accomplished this goal, we are, in reality, only beginning the journey. It takes collaboration and a proactive stance to make multiculturalism commonplace in our associations and in our professional practice. This book itself is a first-rate example of what collaboration and action can do to move our profession along the road to true commitment.

Judy Lewis, PhD
President, 2000–2001
American Counseling Association

Index

Accreditation and multicultural
counseling competencies,
222-223
Acculturation
bidimensional model, 135-137
employment counseling and,
190-191
guidance for, 6
Accuracy of information in
cybercounseling, 196-197
Adams, E. M., 164
Adolescents and sexual identity,
173-183. *See also* School
counseling of adolescents for
sexual identity
Advocacy
counselor's advocating on behalf
of Black gay clients, 117
social/political advocacy, 264-265
teaching skills to client, 6
Affirmation Model for therapy, 71
African American gay men, 109-118
characteristics of successful
counselors for, 111, 113-114
cognitive restructuring model for
therapy, 116, 263
community resources for support
of, 116
counseling implications, 115-117
creation of multicultural
relationship, 113-114
deconstructing shame of, 114-115

flexible counseling approach,
115
framework for counseling of,
111-115
racism and, 110-111
safe places created for
multicultural exploration, 262
shame and, 110-111
theoretical grounding for
counseling of, 112-113
African American women
culture-centered existentialism in
therapy for, 153-160
privacy issues of health
information online, 196
substance abuse, 67-80
barriers to treatment, 71
case study, 69-71
cultural history/herstory, 72-73,
75
drinking patterns, cultural
comparisons, 68
empowerment techniques, 73,
75-76
History, Employment, Rapport,
and Spirituality (H.E.R.S.)
therapeutic model, 68,
72-76, 77
previous research on, 68
rapport with client, 73, 76
research needs, 77
spirituality and, 73, 76

African American women (*continued*)
   substance abuse (*continued*)
      therapy models designed for,
         71-72
African Americans
   college enrollment and graduation,
      218
   ethnic and sexual identity of Black
      gay males, 109-118. *See also*
      African American gay men
   existential interventions for, 153
   Internet access by, 195
   in military service, 256
   women. *See* African American
      women
Africentrism and Black gay males, 112
Age differences and Internet use, 195
Alcohol abuse. *See* Substance abuse
Almeida, R., 42
AMCD. *See* Association for
   Multicultural Counseling and
   Development
American Counseling Association
   AMCD. *See* Association for
      Multicultural Counseling and
      Development
   publications of. *See specific
      publication by title*
   role in multicultural counseling,
      265-267
American Indians. *See* Native
   Americans
American Psychological Association's
   Healthy Lesbian, Gay, and
   Bisexual Students Project, 117
Anger of students in multicultural
   education, 46
Anonymity in cybercounseling, 196
Anson, R.A., 222
Anxiety
   existential therapy for, 150, 151, 158
   result of experiential training of
      multicultural counselors, 10-11
Aponte, J. F., 84
Arciniega, M., 20

Arranged marriages, 100
Arredondo, P., 20, 41, 129, 131, 132,
   137
ASERVIC. *See* Association for Spiritual,
   Ethical, and Religious Values in
   Counseling
ASGW (Association for Specialists in
   Group Work), 142-143
Asian Americans
   family counseling, 97-107. *See also*
      South Asian family counseling
   Internet access by, 195
   in military, 258
   substance abuse of, 68
Aspy, C. B., 73
Assessment procedures
   case study with Latina woman,
      88-93
   client's barriers, 84
   counselor's barriers, 82-83
   decision making for treatment,
      87-88, 92, 94
   environmental factors, 84
   establishing rapport and data
      gathering, 85, 88-89
   identifying cultural data, 86, 89-90
   incorporating other clinically
      relevant data, 87, 91-92
   interpreting cultural data, 86-87,
      91
   Latina women, 81-95
   Multicultural Assessment
      Procedure (MAP), 85-88
   multicultural variables and, 81-85,
      93
   person-based factors, 82-84
   postassessment feedback, 88, 93
   process factors, 84-85
   recommendations for practice,
      93-94
Assimilation and acculturation, 136
Association for Multicultural
   Counseling and Development
   (AMCD), 20, 163, 265-267
   MCC publications of, 232

Index

Association for Specialists in Group Work (ASGW), 142–143
Association for Spiritual, Ethical, and Religious Values in Counseling (ASERVIC), 162, 163
Authentic commitment to multiculturalism, 261, 262–263

Baca, B., 266
Baden, A., 18
Baird, E., 196
Bandele, O., 250
Bangladesh. *See* South Asian family counseling
Barriers
  African American women in substance abuse treatment, 71
  client's barriers in assessment procedures, 84
  counselor's barriers in assessment procedures, 82–83
  result of experiential training of multicultural counselors, 10
Behrens, J. T., 18
Berg-Cross, L., 251
Bergin, A. E., 162
Bernier, J. E., 41
Berry, J. W., 130, 135, 137
Bhutan. *See* South Asian family counseling
Bibb, A., 42
Bibbins, V., 266
Bibliography, usefulness of, 102, 103, 222
Biopsychological Model for therapy, 71
Bixsexuals
  employment counseling case study of Latina bisexual woman, 187–190
Black colleges and universities, 243–252. *See also* Historically Black colleges and universities (HBCUs); Lincoln University

Black culture. *See headings starting with "African American"*
Black identity development (nigrescence), 25
Blueprint for Organizational Diversity, 232, 233, 237–240
  clarifying motivators, 238–239
  organizational self-study, 239–240
  preparation phase, 237–238
Boatright, K. J., 18
Bollywood films, 100
Brazilian education, 54–55
Brittan-Powell, C. S., 208
Brown, S. P., 20, 21, 232
Brown v. Board of Education, 244, 245
Buber, M., 152

Canfield, A. A., 51
Carter, C., 251
Carter, R. T., 41, 111
Casas, J. M., 41, 111
Center for Substance Abuse Prevention, 67
Chatham, L. R., 68
Chenault, B. G., 199, 200
Chickering, A. W., 45
Child abuse perceived in Native American culture, 123
Classroom learning of multicultural counselors, 55–59
  assignments, 59–60
  book reports, 60
  listening skill development, 55–56
  meta-discussions on classroom discussions, 57, 59
  research papers, 59–60
  role playing, 57–58
  seating arrangement of room, 56–57
  teachable moments, 57
Clinton, B., 256
CMC. *See* Computer-mediated communications

Cognitive development of counselors
  complexity and multidimensional
    thinking, 83, 93
  of multicultural counselor
    students, 45
Cognitive therapy
  effectiveness of, 116, 263
  sexual aggression, 126
Cohen, N. H., 39
Cohen, W., 258
Collectivism, 264
  group work and collectivistic
    nature, 141–146
  mentoring and learning
    environment to promote,
    43–44, 46
  Native American culture of,
    141–142, 144
Colleges and universities. See also
    specific institution by name
  ACA resolution to eliminate
    stereotypical images of Native
    Americans in, 267
  counseling. See University
    counseling and multicultural
    counseling competencies
    (MCC)
  historically Black colleges and
    universities, 243–252. See also
    Historically Black colleges and
    universities (HBCUs)
  predominantly White institutions
    of higher education, 229–242.
    See also White institutions of
    higher education (WIHE)
The Color of Water: A Black Man's
    Tribute to His White Mother
    (McBride), 25
Common themes in practice of
    multicultural counseling,
    261–265
Community relations and resources.
    See also Outreach activities;
    Support groups

  for support of African American
    gay men, 116
  White institutions of higher
    education and community-
    based partnerships and
    resources, 240
Computer-mediated communications
    (CMC), 193–202. See also
    Cybercounseling
  digital divide disappearing, 194–195
  text-to-text versus face-to-face
    communications, 199–200
Conformity Model for therapy, 71
Contact methods, 115. See also E-mail
Coping skills and sexual identity
    counseling, 178
Corey, A. T., 120
Cose, E., 24–25
Counselors for Social Justice (CSJ), 43
Cox, C. I., 164
Craig, K., 251
Credibility of counselor, 83
Creswell, J. W., 7
Critical Incidents (simulation in
    multicultural training), 34–35
Cross, W. E., Jr., 25
Cultural genogram
  African American women, 72–73,
    75, 264
  kinship network mapping,
    123–124, 264
  South Asian family, 101–102, 103,
    264
Cybercounseling, 193–202
  accuracy of information, 196–197
  anonymity online, 196
  challenges of, 197–199
  consumer concerns, 196–197
  digital divide disappearing,
    194–195
  ethics of, 193–194
  health information on the Internet,
    195
  online trauma, 198–199

privacy issues, 196-197
reinventing self in cyberspace, 197-198
seeking help on the Internet, 195-200
sites offering resources, 201
text-to-text vs. face-to-face communications, 199-200
training implications, 199

D'Andrea, M., 83
Day, L. E., 68
de Monteflores, C., 109
Decision making
by counselor, 83
in sexual identity counseling, 179-180
Defense Equal Opportunity Management Institute (DEOMI), 259
Defenses of counselors, culturally related, 82
Deficit Model for therapy of minority clients, 71, 223
DePaul University and freshman reading program, 225
Depression
existential interventions for, 153
Native Americans and, 86-87
Diagnostic and Statistical Manual of Mental Disorders (DSM-IV), 87, 94, 175-176
Dimensions of Personal Identity Model, 234-236
Direction, need for, and existential therapy, 154, 157
Disability insensitivity at White institutions of higher education, 240
Diversity Conference (State University of New York at Albany, Department of Educational and Counseling Psychology), 44

Domains of multicultural competency development, 20-26, 41-42, 232
"Don't ask, don't tell" policy, 258-259
Doolittle, J., 255
Drawings to facilitate client communication, 123
Drug abuse. *See* Substance abuse
Duran, B., 127
Duran, E., 127
Durran, A., 41

Educational issues
colleges and universities. *See* Colleges and universities; *specific institution by name*
school counseling of adolescents, 173-183. *See also* School counseling of adolescents for sexual identity
for South Asians, 101, 105
training of counselors. *See* Training of multicultural counselors
E-mail as counseling media, 193, 199-200
Emotional reactions of students in multicultural education, 46
Empathic connection through mutual self-disclosure, 9
Employment counseling, 185-192
cultural presentation, 189-190
identity considerations, 186-187
interviewing skills, 189
Latina bisexual woman (case study), 187-190
resume writing, 188-189
support groups, 189
Empowerment techniques
African American women and substance abuse, 73, 75-76
existentialism and culture-centered counseling, 151
Environmental factors in assessment, 84

Epp, L. R., 149
Ethical Standards for Internet Online Counseling (ACA), 193, 201
Exchange of cultural information, 9-10
Existentialism and culture-centered counseling, 149-160
  African American client (case study), 154-160
  application to practice, 150-154
  constant change and evolution of people, 150-151
  content versus context, 153-154
  definition of existentialism, 149-150
  freedom of choice, 151, 152, 158
  goals and strategies, 151-153
  hope, 151
  initial assessment and counseling sessions, 157-159
  literature review of interventions and inventories, 152-153, 154
  self-awareness of counselor and, 150
  therapist's sharing of own values and beliefs, 152
Experiential training of multicultural counselors, 3-15, 263
  benefits from application of cultural knowledge, 6
  components of course, 5
  culturally consistent tasks for trainees, 6
  evaluation of, 5
  framework of, 5-6
  goal of, 5
  informed consent of minority client, 6
  learning from client's stories, 4, 5
  method, 6-8
  mixed method design, 7
  negative multicultural thoughts, 11
  participants and procedures, 6-7
  positive multicultural thoughts, 13
  process notes, 7-8
  qualitative results, 8-11
  quantitative results, 11-13
  relating with individual in local community, 5-6
  self-reported multicultural competencies, 7
  understanding the client, 4, 5
  weekly journaling of trainees, 7

Faith. *See* Religious beliefs; Spirituality
Falling Through the Net (U.S. Department of Commerce report), 194-195
Family counseling. *See also* Family relationships
  South Asians, 97-107. *See also* South Asian family counseling
Family Institute of New Jersey, 42
Family relationships. *See also* Cultural genogram
  African American client (case study), 155-156
  Black gay males and family system theory, 112-113
  Native American sexually reactive youth, assessment and treatment, 124-125
Faubert, M., 54
Feedback
  postassessment feedback, 88, 93
  training of multicultural counselors, 48, 208
Fehrenbach, T. R., 255
Feinberg, L., 41
Foreign language native speakers in counseling classes, 52-53, 58
Fouad, N. A., 41, 111
Fowler, J. W., 165-168, 169
Fox, S., 195, 196
Freedom of choice in existentialism, 151, 152, 158
Freire, P., 54-55
Fukuyama, M. A., 163-164

Galbraith, M. W., 39
Gard, G., 18
Garica Preto, N., 42
Gay Black males, 109–118. *See also*
    African American gay men
Gender identity disorder, 176
Gender roles and differences
    employment counseling, 189–190
    Internet access, 194–195
    Polish family, 134
    South Asians, 98–99, 104
    White institutions of higher
        education and, 240
Generative words, 54–55
Genogram, cultural. *See* Cultural
    genogram
Goodman, J., 266
Gratz v. Bollinger, 230
Grief counseling and existential
    therapy, 150, 154
Group work, 141–146
    incorporating Native American
        perspectives in, 145–146
    literature review, 142–144
    skills for group workers, 143
Guilt of students in multicultural
    education, 46
Gutkin, T. B., 41

Hanley, C. P., 164
Harmony and balance in group work,
    146
HBCUs. *See* Historically Black colleges
    and universities
Health information on the Internet,
    195
Helms, J. E., 19, 222
Herd, D., 68
Here-and-now orientation, 145, 151
H.E.R.S. *See* History, Employment,
    Rapport, and Spirituality
Higher education. *See* Colleges and
    universities
Highlen, P. S., 164

Hill, C. E., 7
Hill, C. L., 81, 82, 85, 86, 87
Hispanics
    ACA programs and Latino cultures,
        266
    college enrollment and graduation,
        218
    existential interventions for, 153
    Internet access, 195
    privacy issues of health
        information online, 196
    women. *See* Latina women
Historically Black colleges and
    universities (HBCUs),
    243–252
    agricultural programs, 250–251
    guidelines to encourage diversity,
        251
    Lincoln University, 243–250. *See
        also* Lincoln University
    mental health treatment, 252
    other colleges and universities,
        250–252
History, Employment, Rapport, and
    Spirituality (H.E.R.S.)
    application to case study, 73–76
    development and components,
        72–73
    research needs, 77
    therapeutic model for substance
        abuse, 68
History, Identity, and Spirituality
    (H.I.S.) therapeutic model, 72
Hofstede, G., 32, 34
Holistic mapping in assessment and
    treatment of Native American
    sexually reactive youth,
    123–124
Hollimon, U., 256
Homophobia
    African American gay men and,
        110–111
    transgendered persons and, 176
    White institutions of higher
        education and, 240

Homosexuality. *See also* Homophobia
  Black men. *See* African American
    gay men
  in military, 258-259
  not mental disorder, 176
Hoopes, D. S., 46
Hope and existentialism, 151
Howard University, 251, 252
Hubbell, R., 18
Hudak, H., 42
Hughes, M., 225
Hughes, T. L., 68
Humanism and Black gay males, 113

Identity considerations
  cybercounseling, 197-198
  Dimensions of Personal Identity
    Model, 234-236
  employment counseling, 186-187
  racial salience and, 220-221
  sexual identity counseling,
    177-178. *See also* Sexual
    identity
Imitation of Life (film by Hunter &
  Sirk), 25
Immediacy of time, 145
Immigrants
  Polish. *See* Polish immigrants
  South Asians. *See* South Asian
    family counseling
Indians, American. *See* Native
  Americans
Individualism vs. collectivism,
  43-44
Informal settings for counseling,
  115
Information Processing Strategy (IPS)
  and development of White
  racial identity, 19-20
Informed consent of minority client
  for participating in experiential
  training, 6
Institutions of higher education. *See*
  Colleges and universities

Integration
  acculturation and, 136
  in military, 256
Interactions and connections to
  multiculturalism, 261, 263. *See
  also* Experiential training of
  multicultural counselors
International Society for Mental
  Health Online, 201
Internet. *See* Cybercounseling
Interviewing
  Polish immigrant client (case
    study), 129-135
  skills and employment counseling,
    189
Intimacy in South Asian families,
  100-101, 104, 105
Isensee, R., 114
Ivey, A. E., 32, 41, 83, 111
Ivey, M. B., 83

Jackson, J. D., 18
Japanese American soldiers, 258
Jensen, M., 41, 111
Johnson, J.A., 149
Johnson, L. R., 84
Johnsrud, L. K., 224
Jones, J., 20, 21, 232
*Journal for Specialists in Group
  Work*, 142
Journal of Online Behavior, 201

Kahn, H. I., 164
Kinship network mapping,
  123-124
Kiselica, M., 40
Kocarek, C., 221
Kohlberg, L., 165
Komives, S. R., 224
Kuh, G., 224
Kuo, P.Y., 82
Kuo-Jackson, P.Y., 42, 120, 131, 135
Kwan, K. L., 136

Lafferty, L. C., 51
LaFromboise,T., 41, 111
Latina women. *See also* Hispanics
    assessment procedures case study,
        88-93
    drinking patterns, cultural
        comparisons, 68
    employment counseling case study
        of Latina bisexual woman,
        187-190
Learning from stories of the client
    experiential training of
        multicultural counselors, 4, 5
    Native American metaphors and
        story telling, 122-123, 126,
        127
    Polish immigrant, interviews of,
        130-131, 133-135
    South Asian family counseling, 102,
        103-104
    validation of client's belief system
        and, 83
Li, L. C., 81, 82, 85, 86, 87
Life skills coaching, 6
Lincoln University, 243-250
    background of, 244-245
    campus programs, 246-247
    cultural education resources,
        247-249
    financial resources, 249
    multicultural environment,
        245-250
    multicultural learning
        opportunities, 246
    student organizations, 249-250
Linguistic competency, 83
Liu,W. M., 208
Locke, D. C., 20, 21, 54, 232
Loiacano, D. K., 110
Loss, sense of
    African American client (case
        study), 154-160
    existential therapy for, 151, 154
Loya, G. J., 42, 131, 135
Ludlow, P., 198

Manese, J. E., 41, 111
MAP (Multicultural Assessment
    Procedure), 85-88
Marcantonio, R. J., 68
Marginalization and acculturation, 136
Marriage issues and South Asians,
    100-101, 104
McBride, J., 25
McDavis, R. J., 20, 41, 129, 131, 132,
    137
McFadden, J., 199
McGoldrick, M., 42
MCI (Multicultural Counseling
    Inventory), 7
McIntosh, P., 222
Meaninglessness, existential therapy
    for, 151, 158
Medical Model for therapy, 71
Meggert, S. S., 222
Mellion, D., 250
Mentoring. *See also* Mentoring of
    counselor trainees
    counseling-mentoring approach on
        college campuses, 219-221
Mentoring of counselor trainees, 6,
    39-50, 264
    definition of mentoring, 39-40
    developmental level of students, 45
    learning environment to promote
        collectivism, 43-44
    multicultural competencies and
        considerations in course
        teaching, 45-47
    development strategies, 43-44
    progress of students when
        developing, 46-47
    research on development of,
        41-43
    strategies to facilitate learning,
        47-48
    multiple sources for, 40
    opportunities to enhance
        professional and multicultural
        competency development, 44,
        263

Mentoring of counselor trainees
(*continued*)
philosophical framework for
course construction, 45-46
Mexican Americans. *See* Hispanics;
Latina women
Midgette, T. E., 222
Military, 255-260
African Americans in, 256
Asian Americans in, 258
Defense Equal Opportunity
Management Institute (DEOMI),
259
homosexuality in, 258-259
Native Americans in, 258
women in, 256-258
Miller, H., 200
Mills, G. E., 59
Minority clients. *See specific minority
(e.g., African American, Asian
American, Latina)*
Moore Hines, P., 42
Multicultural Assessment Procedure
(MAP), 85-88
Multicultural counseling
competencies (MCC)
development of racial identity of
White counselor trainees and,
20-21
development strategies, 43-44
domains. *See* Domains of
multicultural competency
development
mentoring and, 41-48
research on development of, 41-43
school counseling of adolescents
for sexual identity, 173-174
university counseling using. *See*
University counseling and
multicultural counseling
competencies (MCC)
White institutions of higher
education using, 232-234, 240
Multicultural Counseling Inventory
(MCI), 7

Myers, L. J., 164
Mystical awakening model of spiritual
identity, 164

Narratives of client. *See* Learning from
stories of the client
National Institute on Drug Abuse, 68
Native Americans
ACA resolution to eliminate
stereotypical images of, 267
assessment and treatment of
sexually reactive youth,
119-128
case study, 120-121
cognitive interventions, 126
counselor's cultural growth,
119-120
family involvement, 124-125
guiding orientation, 121-122
holistic mapping of
experiences, 124
holistic mapping of
relationships, 123-124
interventions, 122-125
juvenile court proceedings, 125
metaphors and story telling,
122-123, 126, 127
reentry into family, 125-126
safe places created for
multicultural exploration,
262
theoretical foundations, 120
depression and suicide rate,
86-87
group work and collectivistic
culture of, 141-142, 144-146
harmony and balance concepts,
146
implications of, 146
noninterference or mutual
respect, 145-146
value of immediacy of time, 145
in military, 258
in online chat rooms, 196

Nepal. *See* South Asian family
  counseling
Nguzo Saba and African communal
  living, 116–117
Nigrescence, 25
Nonaction as form of action, 152
Noninterference in group work,
  145–146

Ohio Dominican College, 250
Online counseling. *See*
  Cybercounseling
Optimal Theory Applied to Identity
  Development (OTAID) model,
  164–165
Organizational development, 203–267
Other-awareness
  cultural awareness of counselor,
    111
  development of, 93
  interviewing immigrant in course
    project, 133–134
  racial identity development of
    White counselor trainees, 24–25
  result of experiential training of
    multicultural counselors, 8
Outreach activities, 261, 263–264. *See
  also* Community relations and
  resources
  universities, 211–212, 224–225

Pain
  in African American culture, 153
  existential therapy for, 150, 151,
    153
Pannu, R., 136
Parenting classes on adolescent
  sexuality, 181
Parham, T., 266
Patitu, C. L., 224
Patterson, R. P., 256
Peck, M. S., 164
Pedagogy of Hope (Freire), 54

Pedagogy of the Oppressed (Freire),
  54
Pedersen, P., 32, 34, 41, 83, 115, 149
Peer debriefing to monitor for biases,
  158
Perry, W., 45
Person-centered counseling, 149
Personality theory, 85
Pew Internet & American Life Project,
  195
Piaget, J., 165
Polish immigrants and multicultural
  interaction project, 129–138
  acculturation model, use of,
    135–137
  appropriate counselor
    interventions, strategies, and
    techniques, 134–135
  interviewing (case study),
    129–135
Ponterotto, J. G., 41, 111
Pope-Davis, D. B., 208
Prayer, use of, 169
Preoccupation with cultural
  similarities/differences, 10
*Principles for Diversity—Competent
  Group Workers*, 142
Privacy issues
  cybercounseling, 196–197
  South Asian families, 99
Psychoeducation, usefulness of, 102
Psychosocial development of
  multicultural counselor
  students, 45

A Race Is a Nice Thing to Have
  (Helms), 222
Racial identity of White counselor
  trainees, 17–28
  development of, 19–20, 46–47
  domains for training
    applications, 20–26
  impact on effectiveness with
    clients, 17–18, 26

Racial identity of White counselor
  trainees (*continued*)
  multicultural competency and,
    20-21
  receptivity to training and, 18
  research on, 18
Racism
  Black gay men, 110-111
  University of Florida incident on
    campus, 212-213
  White counselor trainees, self-
    awareness of, 23-24
  White institutions of higher
    education and, 240
Rage of the Privileged (Cose), 24-25
Rainie, L., 195, 196
Ramirez, M., 84, 85, 86
Rapport with client
  African American women
    existential therapy, 158
    substance abuse therapy, 73, 76
  assessment procedures, 85, 88-89
  Black gay males, 113-114
  cybercounseling, 200
  Polish immigrant, 134-135
Reciprocal pedagogy in training of
  multicultural counselors, 52-60,
  129
Reciprocal supervision in training of
  multicultural counselors, 60-62
Religious beliefs, 135. *See also*
  Spirituality
  African American client (case
    study), 156
  cultural differences in practicing
    same religion, 168
  definition of, 162-163
Respect
  existential approach and, 152
  noninterference or mutual respect
    in group work, 145-146
Resume writing, 188-189
Retaining cultural identification, 6
Reynolds, A. L., 164
Richards, P. S., 162

Richardson, L. F., 120
Ridley, C. R., 81, 82, 85, 86, 87
Role-playing
  interview simulations to train
    counselors, 29-30, 57-58
  sexual identity counseling, 179
Roysircar, G., 18, 132
Roysircar-Sodowsky, G., 82

Safe places for multicultural
    exploration, 261, 262
Sagaria, M.A., 224
Sanchez, J., 20, 21, 232
Sandhu, D. S., 73
Santiago-Rivera, A. L., 83
Sauer, E., 18
School counseling of adolescents for
    sexual identity, 173-183
  African American boy (case study),
    174-175
  connecting to support group,
    180
  coping skills, 178
  decision making, 179-180
  identity development and self-
    acceptance, 177-178
  influence of self on society, 178
  interventions, 176-180
  literature review, 175-176
  multicultural competencies for,
    173-174
  recommendations, 181-182
  uncontrollable factors, dealing
    with, 178-179
Security level of online mental health
    providers, 197
Sedlecek, W. E., 82
Segregation in military, 256
Self-acceptance and sexual identity
    counseling, 177-178
Self-awareness
  Blueprint for Organizational
    Diversity and, 237-238
  cognitive complexity and, 93

cultural self-awareness of
counselor, 82, 111, 150
existentialism and culture-centered
counseling, 150
interviewing immigrant in course
project, 132-133
racial identity development of
White counselor trainees,
21-26
result of experiential training of
multicultural counselors, 8-9
sexual identity counselors in
schools, 181
simulation in multicultural training
to develop, 32-34
Self-disclosure by therapist
cybercounseling, 200
South Asian family counseling,
102
Self-esteem
Black gay males, 112, 113, 116
South Asians, 105
Self-hatred. See also Shame
Black gay men, 110
minority group members, 187
Native American youth, 123
Self-talk and cognitive restructuring
model, 116
Self-work of counselors, 114
Separation and acculturation, 136
Sevig, T. D., 163-164
Sexism. See Gender roles and
differences
Sexual aggression
cognitive interventions, 126
Native American youth, assessment
and treatment. See Native
Americans
Sexual identity
of Black gay males, 109-118. See
also African American gay men
counseling of school adolescents,
173-183. See also School
counseling of adolescents for
sexual identity

employment counseling case study
of Latina bisexual woman,
187-190
research on, 187
Shame of Black gay men, 110-111
deconstructing, 114-115
Simek-Morgan, L., 83
Simulations in multicultural training,
29-37, 47
Critical Incidents, 34-35
cybercounseling, 199
implications of and
recommendations based on, 36
role-play interview simulations,
29-30
Synthetic Culture Laboratory,
32-34
Triad Training Model, 30-32
Skin color and South Asians,
100-101
Skin Deep (video by Reid), 222, 225
Smith, E. J., 41
Social/political advocacy, 264-265
Sodowsky, G. R., 41, 42, 120, 131, 135,
136
South Asian family counseling,
97-107, 264
bibliography or psychoeducation,
usefulness of, 102, 103
case study, 102-104
cultural genogram, 101-102, 103,
264
educational and career issues, 101,
105
family relations and gender roles,
98-99, 104
implications for, 104-105
interventions, 101-104
intimacy and sexuality, 100-101,
104, 105
second-generation children, 99,
101, 103, 104, 105
self-disclosure by therapist, 102
stigma associated with counseling,
104

South Asian family counseling
(*continued*)
stories or narratives, usefulness of,
102, 103-104
Speight, S. L., 164
Spirituality
African American women and, 73,
76
definition of, 162-163
in multicultural counseling,
161-171
good practices, 168-169
identity development models,
163-165
purpose of including in
multicultural counseling,
163
Native Americans, 123, 124
Nguzo Saba and, 117
overcoming counselor biases,
161-162, 168, 169
prayer, use of, 169
referrals to programs or to clergy,
168-169
stages of faith or spiritual
development (Fowler's model),
165-168, 169
case studies using, 166-168
Sri Lanka. *See* South Asian family
counseling
Stadler, H., 20, 21, 232
State University of New York at
Albany, Department of
Educational and Counseling
Psychology, Diversity
Conference, 44
Steward, R. J., 18
Stories of client. *See* Learning from
stories of the client
Substance abuse of African American
women, 67-80. *See also* African
American women
Sue, D., 25
Sue, D. W., 20, 25, 41, 111, 129, 131,
132, 137, 220, 232

Suffering. *See* Pain
Suicide rate of Native Americans,
86-87
Support groups
African American gay men, 116
African American transsexual
adolescents, 180
minority employment counseling,
189
online chat rooms, 197
Suskind, R., 222, 225
Sutton, C., 42
Synthetic Culture Laboratory
(simulation in multicultural
training), 32-34
Systemic Model for therapy, 71

Taffe, R. C., 41
Talbot, D. M., 221
Taylor, M. J., 68
Terrell, M. C., 224
Testing of clients for multicultural
norming, 87, 94
Theus, L., 259
This Kind of War (Fehrenbach),
255
Thomasson, K., 122, 126
Thompson, B. J., 7
Tidwell, L. C., 200
Toporek, R. L., 20, 21, 208, 232
Torpy, E., 68
Toward Digital Inclusion (U.S.
Department of Commerce
report), 194-195
Training of multicultural counselors
authentic commitment to
multiculturalism, 262-263
challenging counselor's beliefs and
attitudes, 120, 127-128
classroom learning, 55-59. *See also*
Classroom learning of
multicultural counselors
for college counseling, 221-223
cultural considerations, 51-63

cybercounseling, 199
experiential training, 3–15, 263. *See also* Experiential training of multicultural counselors
immigrant project, 129–138. *See also* Polish immigrants
mentoring, 39–50, 264. *See also* Mentoring of counselor trainees
racial identity of White trainees, 17–28. *See also* Racial identity of White counselor trainees
reciprocal pedagogy, 52–60, 129
reciprocal supervision, 60–62
recruitment, 52
retention of students, 52–54
simulations, 29–37, 47. *See also* Simulations in multicultural training
spirituality not covered in, 161
theoretical foundations, 54–55
university or college training, 208–209, 221–223
Transgender, 175
Transsexuals, 175–176
Triad Training Model (simulation in multicultural training), 30–32
Truman, H., 256
Trust. *See* Rapport with client
Tutoring, 6

Umoja, 116
Understanding the client. *See also* Learning from stories of the client
classroom learning to develop listening skills, 55–56
experiential training of multicultural counselors, 4, 5
simulations in multicultural training (Triad Training Model), 30–32, 35
validation of client's belief system, 83

Universities. *See* Colleges and universities; *specific institution by name*
counseling on campus. *See* University counseling and multicultural counseling competencies (MCC)
historically Black. *See* Historically Black colleges and universities (HBCUs)
White institutions. *See* White institutions of higher education (WIHE)
University counseling and multicultural counseling competencies (MCC), 206–228. *See also* University of Florida counseling center
accreditation and, 222–223
adjustment difficulties of cultural minority students, 218–219
administrative support for MCC infusion, 210
consultation and program development, 223–225
counseling-mentoring approach, 219–221
hiring practices and diversification of staff, 209, 213, 214, 224
outreach activities, 211–212, 224–225, 264
outside consultant, use of, 209, 214
programming, 224–225
teaching students, 221–223
training of counselors at, 208–209, 221–223
University of Florida counseling center, 205–216
ASPIRE program for retention of African American students, 211
Brown Bag Diversity Lunch Series, 211, 262
current trends and recommendations, 213–214

283

University of Florida counseling
center (*continued*)
environmental modifications for
MCC, 210
hiring practices and diversification
of staff, 209, 213, 214
innovative MCC programs,
211–212
intern consultation services,
208–209
larger institutional system and,
212–213
mission statement, 207–208
Multicultural Services Committee,
208, 210
ongoing staff development, 209,
214
outreach activities, 211–212, 264
racist incident on campus,
212–213
safe places created for
multicultural exploration, 262
training of counselors at,
208–209
University of Maryland at College
Park, Counseling and Personnel
Services Department and
commitment to
multiculturalism, 223
University of Montana and minority
person on financial aid staff,
224
University of Nebraska-Lincoln,
Department of Educational
Psychology, Ethnic Minority
Affairs Committee, 220
U.S. Department of Commerce report
on digital divide(*Falling
Through the Net*), 194–195

Validation in group work, 145–146
Value biases, examination of
racial identity development of
White counselor trainees, 22–24

result of experiential training of
multicultural counselors, 9
Vazquez-Nutall, E., 41, 111
Vocabulary and generative words,
54–55
Vontress, C. E., 149

Walker, C., 250
Walther, J. B., 200
Web sites of counselors, 196. *See also*
Cybercounseling
Wehrly, B., 85
Wessel, T., 251
White counselor trainees, 17–28. *See
also* Racial identity of White
counselor trainees
White institutions of higher education
(WIHE), 229–242. *See also*
University of Florida counseling
center
Blueprint for Organizational
Diversity, 232, 233, 237–240
consultations requested on cultural
diversity, 229–230
cultural audit, 239–240
Dimensions of Personal Identity
Model applied to, 234–236
domains of MCC adapted to,
232
faculty of color at, 238, 239,
251
guidelines to encourage diversity,
251
learning principles for institution,
236–237
multicultural counseling
competencies (MCC), 232–234,
240
personal framework, 231–232
premises of consultant about
consultation, 236–240, 262
recruitment and retention issues
of minority students, 230,
238

review of institution practices, 231
Williams, E. N., 7
Wise, S. L., 41
Women. *See also* Gender roles and
  differences
  African American. *See* African
    American women
  drinking patterns, cultural
    comparisons, 68
  in military service, 256-258
  South Asian, 98-99, 104
www.metanoia.com, 197
Wyse, M., 122, 126

Yalom, I. D., 144
Youth
  counseling regarding sexual
    identity, 173-183. *See also*
    School counseling of
    adolescents for sexual identity
  Native American sexually reactive
    youth, assessment and
    treatment of, 119-128. *See also*
    Native Americans

Zane, N., 220